Praise for
Meeting Christ in the Book of Mormon

"President Ezra Taft Benson promised: 'The Book of Mormon will change your life.' For me, that promise has become a reality. I discovered the Book of Mormon my freshman year of college and, through it, also discovered a much deeper relationship with Christ. The Spirit I feel when I read that sacred text is undeniable. Each time I sup from its pages I am drawn to a deeper love for the Lord and a greater desire to live a life of holiness, compassion, and understanding. While everyone's journey is different—and there can be no singular recipe for gaining faith in Christ and His Church—nevertheless, the Book of Mormon necessarily must be one of the ingredients in any true and complete conversion. In *Meeting Christ in the Book of Mormon*, Ryan Sharp introduces us to more than a dozen 'recipes' for conversion—each different and all profound. He shares the stories of the Book of Mormon's most notable figures and offers his readers principles and patterns for conversion to Christ and His kingdom. Any who read this book with a contemplative heart will come away feeling they have met Christ anew. This wonderful contribution to the corpus of Latter-day Saint literature is a testament to the salvific and grace-filled work of the Lord in the lives of all those who seek Him."

—Alonzo L. Gaskill, associate professor of Church history and doctrine, Brigham Young University; author of *Sacred Symbols* and *The Truth about Eden*

"This engaging book highlights a valuable approach to finding Christ in the Book of Mormon. It is full of interesting examples, stories, and analogies. Ryan does a great job helping readers focus their attention on Christ and His marvelous presence. Audiences will enjoy the fresh insights into how the Book of Mormon helps us come to know Christ."

—John Hilton, assistant professor of ancient scripture, Brigham Young University

"Wow. Ryan Sharp has done something special here. His passion for the Book of Mormon radiates from these pages. I've been teaching the Book of Mormon for almost two decades, and he was giving me new insights throughout each and every chapter of this book. If you love the Book of Mormon, you'll love what Ryan Sharp has to teach you."

—Hank Smith, PhD; BYU religion instructor; popular LDS speaker and author

MEETING

Christ

in the
BOOK of
MORMON

MEETING *Christ*

in the

BOOK *of* MORMON

RYAN H. SHARP

FOREWORD BY
ROBERT L. MILLET

CFI
An Imprint of Cedar Fort, Inc.
Springville, Utah

ISBN 13: 978-1-4621-1753-6

Published by CFI, an imprint of Cedar Fort, Inc.
2373 W. 700 S., Springville, UT 84663
Distributed by Cedar Fort, Inc., www.cedarfort.com

LIBRARY OF CONGRESS CATALOGING-IN-PUBLICATION DATA

Sharp, Ryan, 1982- author.
Meeting Christ in the Book of Mormon / Ryan Sharp.
    pages cm
Includes bibliographical references and index.
ISBN 978-1-4621-1753-6 (alk. paper)
1. Book of Mormon--Criticism, interpretation, etc. 2. Church of Jesus Christ of Latter-day Saints--Doctrines. 3. Mormon Church--Doctrines. I. Title.
BX8627.S48 2015
289.3'22--dc23
                                2015024030

Cover design by Shawnda T. Craig
Cover design © 2015 Lyle Mortimer
Edited and typeset by Kevin Haws

Printed in the United States of America

10 9 8 7 6 5 4 3 2

Printed on acid-free paper

Dedication

To my stalwart wife, Jessica, and our five sons: Braxton, Logan, Caleb, Parker, and Talmage. May we always rely on the Book of Mormon in continually seeking the divine grace of the Lord Jesus Christ.

And to the late Dirk Smibert, whose inspired leadership and reliance on the Book of Mormon facilitated my own transformative experiences with the Divine.

Contents

Acknowledgments

First and foremost, I wish to acknowledge my wife, Jessica, for her patience and support. Her energy and excitement motivated me through this entire process. I acknowledge Aaron Coombs for offering the idea and encouragement to write this book. I would also like to acknowledge Jodi Reid for her tireless efforts and countless hours editing and helping to improve the manuscript. I wish to express gratitude to Robert L. Millet for his guidance and feedback on this book, as well as his continued mentoring.

I also wish to thank Shawnda Craig for producing such an engaging and attractive cover. And finally, I acknowledge Emily Chambers, Kevin Haws, and the editorial team at Cedar Fort for their wonderful work in preparing this manuscript for publication.

Foreword

During the last quarter of the twentieth century and the first two decades of the twenty-first, we have witnessed a veritable explosion of research and written work on the Book of Mormon. Areas of study as varied as Near Eastern history, anthropology, Meso-American origins, warfare, linguistics, intertextual analysis, authorship, Hebraisms, chiasmus, and geography have fanned the flames of faith among many Latter-day Saints—and even snared the attention of serious thinkers outside the faith. This is as it should be. During his tenure as prophet, President Ezra Taft Benson encouraged the members of the Church to study every conceivable facet of the Book of Mormon. The Book is true and from God, a divine record and revelation kept and preserved for the people of the last days. It is both worthy of serious study and rigorous enough to withstand penetrating scrutiny and analysis.

As the recipients of this sacred treasure, we rejoice in the expanding interest and broadening influence of the Nephite-Jaredite record and are confident that God will, in His own time and in His own way, provide proofs, both external and internal, of its truthfulness. And yet, as Elder Neal A. Maxwell pointed out, "all the scriptures, including the Book of Mormon, will remain in the realm of faith. Science will not be able to prove or disprove holy writ. However, enough plausible evidence will come forth to prevent scoffers from having a field day, but not enough to remove the requirement of faith. Believers must be patient during such unfolding" (*Plain and Precious Things* [Salt Lake City: Deseret Book, 1983], 4).

While it is thrilling to witness the angles of inquiry employed by serious investigators of the book, one avenue of study is supreme and paramount; indeed, it towers in importance above all others. Elder Russell M. Nelson observed,

> I have read [the Book of Mormon] many times. I have also read much that has been written about it. Some authors have focused upon its stories, its people, or its vignettes of history. Others have been intrigued by its language structure or its records of weapons, geography, animal life, techniques of building, or systems of weights and measures. Interesting as these matters may be, *study of the Book of Mormon is most rewarding when one focuses on its primary purpose—to testify of Jesus Christ. By comparison, all other issues are incidental.* . . . When Mormon abridged these records, he noted that he could not write a "hundredth part" of their proceedings. Thus, *historical* aspects of the book assume *secondary* significance. (In Conference Report, October 1999, 69; emphasis added)

The testimony of Jesus, which John the Beloved identified as the spirit of prophecy (Revelation 19:10), fills the pages of the Book of Mormon. The Redeemer is both subject and object of this record, of whom all the ancient prophets spoke and toward whom all true seekers press. This is why the book you are now holding in your hands (or the one you are now reading on your electronic device) is such a significant contribution to Latter-day Saint literature. Ryan Sharp, an excellent and insightful gospel teacher, has focused his writing on the Message of messages, the Doctrine of doctrines—that Jesus is the Christ, the Promised Messiah, and that one's encounter with Him is primary and preeminent. What did Nephi learn and experience when he "met" the Holy One of Israel some six hundred years before that same One would tabernacle the flesh as Jesus of Nazareth? How did that divine encounter influence the rest of his life? How did such encounters transform, orient, and reorient Jacob, Benjamin, Abinadi, Alma, and Moroni? And what invaluable lessons from their unspeakable encounters do you and I learn as we follow their direction and "liken [the] scriptures" (1 Nephi 19:23) unto ourselves?

No man or woman is ever the same who encounters the Lord of Life, the God of Creation. Simply stated, to come unto Christ is to invite spiritual change, to open oneself to a grand metamorphosis. And what a delightful change it is! This is the essence of the striking service Brother Sharp has rendered to you and me in this book. Through a careful study of the scriptural text itself, coupled with a wonderful immersion in that prophetic commentary offered by the Savior's latter-day anointed servants, we become aware of "new writing" (see 1 Nephi 16:29) that begins to show up on the pages of our copy of the Book of Mormon. That is, we begin to see things we hadn't seen before, to feel things we hadn't felt, to sense just how profound those simple pronouncements really are. We begin to want what Nephi had, to covet what Enos experienced, to know what Benjamin knew. "What must we do today and always?" President Benson asked. "Why, we must do the same as the wise men of old. They sought out the Christ and found Him. And so must we. Those who are wise still seek Him today" (*A Witness and a Warning* [Salt Lake City: Deseret Book, 1988], 50). That your supernal quest to encounter and be transformed by the Master will be sweet, sustained, and soul-satisfying is my hope and prayer.

—Robert L. Millet, professor emeritus of
ancient scripture, Brigham Young University

Introduction

The Keystone of Our Experience with Christ

While recently teaching a summer seminary class, I asked the group what they were looking forward to most about the coming year of studying the Book of Mormon. The answers were inspiring as they talked about gaining a testimony of the Church, deepening their understanding of the doctrine, and learning more about the Atonement of Jesus Christ. One senior excitedly and emotionally proclaimed, "I don't know about the rest of you, but I have been waiting for this for three years! I love the Book of Mormon!" If my experience as a reader and teacher of the Book of Mormon is any indication, one of the primary reasons its influence is so profound lies in its powerful witness of Christ and the purity of His doctrine.

However, while the Christ-centered doctrinal focus of the book is paramount, perhaps the stories and life-altering divine encounters illustrated are a major part of its underlying catalyst to conversion. Indeed, while this sacred record has been referred to as "the keystone in our *witness* of Christ,"[1] it might also appropriately be called the keystone of our *experience* with Christ. Consequently, in this book, I hope to illustrate and highlight one of the most important themes in the Book of Mormon—when individuals have personal and direct encounters with the divine, their lives are forever changed. As we study and analyze the Book of Mormon through this lens, we can sense the sanctity and solemnity of the personal divine encounters of each of its prophetic characters.

Elder Jeffrey R. Holland recently shared a story and taught a profound lesson that has deeply resonated with me and left an indelible imprint in my heart. You will recall that he told the story of Peter and the poignant and tender feelings that must have been experienced by the early Apostles after the death and Resurrection of the Master. He told of the exchange between Christ and Peter, specifically highlighting the Savior's invitation for Peter to demonstrate his love by his loyalty and commitment in building the kingdom and feeding the flock. After masterfully laying the foundation for this monumental truth, Elder Holland made his point: "We have a life of devoted discipleship to give in demonstrating our love of the Lord. We can't quit and we can't go back. *After an encounter with the living Son of the living God, nothing is ever again to be as it was before.*"[2]

Everything changes! When individuals have continual firsthand personal experience with the Atonement of Jesus Christ, their lives are forever changed. The music they listen to, the movies they watch, the language they use, the desires of their hearts, the way they treat others—it all changes. "Enter their homes, and the pictures on their walls, the books on their shelves, the music in the air, their words and acts reveal them as Christians. They stand as witnesses of God at all times, and in all things, and in all places. They have Christ on their minds, as they look unto Him in every thought. They have Christ in their hearts as their affections are placed on Him forever."[3] In short, they have "no more disposition to do evil, but to do good continually" (Mosiah 5:2). The self-stated purpose of the Book of Mormon is to lead to such a divine change!

The Book of Mormon Was Written and Preserved to Bring Us Nearer to God

In the Introduction of the Book of Mormon, Joseph Smith said, "I told the brethren that the Book of Mormon was the most correct of any book on earth, and the keystone of our religion, and a man would get nearer to God by abiding by its precepts, than by any other book."[4] Perhaps this now prominent statement was inspiringly placed in the Introduction of the Book of Mormon to prime the hearts and minds of readers. It may have been placed there to help them recognize, from the outset, that these words are pure and holy, and that they, the readers, must "beware how [they] hold them" (D&C 41:12) because they carry with them the challenge of change. This record was foreordained to be sent "forth out of the earth, to bear testimony of [Jesus Christ]" and of "his resurrection from the dead" (Moses 7:62). Its central purpose is to testify that the resurrected Christ stands, with hands outstretched, inviting and promising that His "arm is lengthened out all the day long" (2 Nephi 28:32) and that because His "arm of mercy hath atoned for [our] sins" (D&C 29:1), those who come unto Him can be "encircled about eternally in the arms of his love" (2 Nephi 1:15). The ultimate purpose of this book is to be a guide, leading its reader in drawing "nearer to God" and eventually into His divine embrace.

Elder Russell M. Nelson shared a story that underscores the converting power of the Book of Mormon. He described having two colleagues—a nurse and her husband doctor—who asked him why he chose to live the way he lived. He insightfully responded, "Because I know the Book of Mormon is true." He then loaned them a copy of it, with an invitation to read it for themselves. About a week later, this lovely couple approached him, returned the book, and politely said, "Thanks a lot." Humorously, and inspiringly, Elder Nelson responded, "What do you mean, thanks a lot? That's a totally inappropriate response for one who has read this book. You didn't read it, did you! Please take it back and read it; then I would like my book back."

Elder Nelson continued, "Admitting that they had only turned its pages, they accepted my invitation. When they returned, they said tearfully, 'We have read the Book of Mormon. We know it is true! We want to know more.' They learned more, and it was my privilege to baptize both of them."[5]

The Book of Mormon is written, designed, and blessed to touch the human heart and to bring its reader closer to the Lord. Elder Nelson knew this and, perhaps even more important, he trusted that if this couple read with a sincere heart, they would feel the influence of the Holy Ghost drawing their hearts closer to God. We must likewise have that same degree of confidence and trust in the converting power of the Book of Mormon. To this point, our beloved President Thomas S. Monson promised, "It will change your heart and change your life."[6]

This couple's experience is insightful. Could you imagine if Elder Nelson had sheepishly taken the book back and somewhat awkwardly tried to change the subject of the conversation? The story would most likely have ended with the couple still admiring Elder Nelson as a person, but without any further knowledge or experience with the personal impact of the Book of Mormon and the divine power found therein. Elder Nelson modeled what Elder Holland once counseled when he said, "The first thing you will do when an investigator tells you he or she had not read and prayed about the Book of Mormon is be devastated! . . . Much of the time we are just too casual about all of this. This is eternal life. This is the salvation of the children of God. Eternity hangs in the balance. . . . It is the most important path this investigator will ever walk. But if he or she doesn't know that, at least you do! . . . So take control of this situation."[7]

The message and warning of these two Apostles reminds us that in order to experience the divine promises of this consecrated record, we cannot treat "lightly the things [we] have received" (D&C 84:54). We must realize that if we are willing to pay a price to unlock the converting power of the Book of Mormon, we will come to see and experience the familiar warmth of God's eternal love, which "will awaken in us individually the life of discipleship as never before."[8]

How the Book of Mormon Brings Us Nearer to God

There are many ways in which the Book of Mormon is a critical catalyst for conversion. For example, it deepens our understanding and testimony of the Bible and of the Lord's mortal ministry. As the keystone of our religion, it also verifies the truthfulness of the message of the Restoration, thus leading us to make covenants with the Lord. Additionally, as we lay hold upon the word of God, we are touched, directed, and protected by the Holy Spirit. President Ezra Taft Benson taught that "it tells in a plain manner of Christ and His gospel. It testifies of His divinity and of the necessity for a Redeemer and the need of our putting trust in Him. It bears witness of the Fall and the Atonement and the first principles of the gospel, including our need of a broken heart and a contrite spirit and a spiritual rebirth."[9] In other words, its primary focus is on the "plain and most precious" (1 Nephi 13:26) doctrines of Christ. While each of these ideas deserves further consideration, I will focus on the converting power of the doctrine of Christ.

We are taught that "true doctrine, understood, changes attitudes and behavior" and that "the study of the doctrines of the gospel will improve behavior quicker than a study of behavior will improve behavior."[10] Furthermore, while the Book of Mormon restores many different plain and precious doctrines that had been previously lost, it is clear that there is no democracy when it comes to doctrine. In other words, not all doctrines are of equal importance. The Prophet Joseph emphasized this concept when he said, "The fundamental principles of our religion are the testimony of the Apostles and Prophets, concerning Jesus Christ, that He died, was buried, and rose again the third day, and ascended into heaven; and *all other things which pertain to our religion are only appendages to it.*"[11] Taking the liberty to join these two prophetic statements, we might appropriately conclude that an understanding of the doctrine of the Atonement of Jesus Christ will change behavior quicker than a study of any other doctrine of the gospel.

Given the centrality of the doctrine of the Atonement, it is somewhat disheartening that when we bring up "the plan of salvation" (Jarom 1:2; Alma 24:14; Moses 6:62) in a classroom setting, almost immediately our students myopically envision a large bubble chart stretching across the whiteboards of their minds. While this bubble chart effectively provides what might be called the "geography" of the plan, the plan is *really* summarized in one verse of scripture: "For God so loved the world, that he gave his only begotten Son, that whosoever believeth in him should not perish, but have everlasting life" (John 3:16).

This centrality of the doctrine of the Atonement of Jesus Christ is manifest on virtually every page of the Book of Mormon, as it makes reference to Jesus Christ by one of His names or titles about once every 1.7 verses![12] From the first chapter to the last, the prophetic invitation of the Book of Mormon is to "come unto Christ" (Moroni 10:32; see 1 Nephi

1:14), to have "faith in Christ" (Moroni 10:4), to "have hope through
the atonement of Christ" (Moroni 7:41), to be "sanctified in Christ"
(Moroni 10:33), to be filled with "the pure love of Christ" (Moroni
7:47), to be made "alive in Christ" (Moroni 8:22), and to "press forward
with a steadfastness in Christ" (2 Nephi 31:20) so that we may one day
become "perfect in Christ" (Moroni 10:33). Consequently, the Book
of Mormon profoundly and definitively answers "the great question"
(Alma 34:5) about salvation through Christ and His Atonement as it
boldly declares that "there is no other way nor means whereby man can
be saved, *only* through the atoning blood of Jesus Christ" (Helaman 5:9;
emphasis added; see also Acts 4:10–12; 2 Nephi 9:41; 25:20; 31:20–21;
Mosiah 3:17; 4:6–8; 5:7–8; Alma 38:9; D&C 18:23–25).

A Fresh Approach to the Book of Mormon

Underscoring this truth, Elder Holland suggested that "one way
of reading and remembering this sacred record is to move, in effect,
from one teaching about the Savior to the next. Those discourses
come with such regularity, like a series of mountaintop sightings to a
needy traveler, that they elevatingly lead the reader through the Book
of Mormon from beginning to end."[13] This is a powerful approach
to reading the Book of Mormon and will lead the reader to a greater
understanding and witness of Christ and of His atoning sacrifice.
Moreover, the Book of Mormon is deep and not only contains the
pure doctrine of Christ and His Atonement but also a *witness* to the
truthfulness of that doctrine.

Consequently, the foundational premise of this book is that
these powerful prophets follow the wisdom shared by Elder Bruce
R. McConkie when he said, "The crowning, convincing, converting
power of gospel teaching is manifest when an inspired teacher says,
'I know by the power of the Holy Ghost, by the revelations of the
Holy Spirit to my soul, that the doctrines I have taught are true.'"[14]
In other words, while these gospel teachers taught the doctrine of
Christ in its purity, they also recorded their own personal experience
with the Savior's Atonement and the subsequent changes wrought in
their hearts.

Similarly, Dr. Richard Bushman said, "The entire Book of Mormon
is an elaborate framed tale of Mormon telling about a succession of

prophets telling about their encounters with God."[15] Rather than highlighting the powerful Christ-centered *teachings* from the Book of Mormon, I will attempt to walk readers through the book sequentially, focusing on the life-altering *personal experiences* these people had with the grace of Christ. In each chapter, the introductory heading provides a summary statement, illustrating how each experience reveals a truth about the depth and breadth of the life-changing power of the Atonement in the lives of those who have had an "encounter with the living Son of the living God."[16]

Chapter 1: Lehi

Lehi's story provides a powerful lesson to those who are experiencing the heartache that comes when a loved one strays. His account underscores the truth that, because of the character of Christ, "[those] who are so forgetful and even rebellious are never forgotten by Him! [They] *are* His 'work' and His 'glory,' and He is *never* distracted!"[17]

A New Lens

A good friend of mine recently shared a story with me that teaches a profound principle. This friend is the father of four little boys, the oldest of which was nine years old at the time of the experience. In connection with the beginning of the school year, he and his wife had taken their boys in for their annual back-to-school eye exam. This nine-year-old boy had never complained about his eyesight, nor had his pediatrician ever discovered anything amiss in his exams. However, after this particular examination with an optometrist, the doctor met with the parents and explained that their son had failed the exam and that he would need to be fitted with glasses. While this came as a surprise to both my friend and his boy, they were grateful for the discovery and acquired the needed glasses. When the glasses were ready, this young boy put them on, looked up at the lights, and excitedly proclaimed, "Wow! Is that what lights *really* look like?!"

Prior to this experience, his understanding had been that what we refer to as "lights" meant something bright that looks a little fuzzy or blurry. This same excitement continued as he looked at trees, road signs, and even labels in the grocery store. His parents observed that, after putting on these glasses, their son began to see things in a new way, a more clear and focused way.

Speaking to a group of BYU students in a campus devotional, Elder Dallin H. Oaks taught, "The most significant academic talks I heard during my service at BYU had one common characteristic. Instead of providing new facts or advocating a particular position, as many lectures do, the most significant talks changed the listeners' way of thinking about an important subject."[18] In other words, these talks provided a new, clearer lens through which the listeners viewed the subject being discussed.

So while the first prophet in the Book of Mormon is Lehi, we actually see him through the lens of Nephi, his son. As in the story above, I believe that Nephi serves as something of a literary or even theological optometrist, as his opening lines provide a clear lens, perhaps even a new lens, through which Lehi's experience and the rest of the book can be viewed. We will get to Lehi's experience shortly, but we will allow Nephi to provide the context and set the stage.

"I, Nephi, having been born of goodly parents . . ." (1 Nephi 1:1). How many times have we read this particular passage of scripture? Because this verse is so familiar to most of us, we run the risk of being literarily lazy in just passing it over with the thought that we already know what it says, and thus we can just skim read it. Contrary to that line of thinking, I would suggest that, in addition to this being perhaps the most oft-read verse in the Book of Mormon, it might well be that it is among the most important.

For instance, in this opening verse, Nephi introduces a theme—which I believe is intentionally placed right in the beginning of the book—to focus the reader's attention and to provide a lens through which they can study the subsequent pages of the book. (Perhaps having seen our day, Nephi knew of our fallen and fickle natures and that we would read this verse more than any other. Just a thought.) After saying that he has "seen many afflictions in the course of [his] days" (1 Nephi 1:1), Nephi testifies that these challenges and struggles have led him to be highly favored of the Lord. Being highly favored of the Lord suggests that the Lord knows him, is aware of him, and is watching over and ministering unto him. Nephi continues this idea by saying that he has "a great knowledge of the goodness and the mysteries of God" (1 Nephi 1:1). As will be demonstrated later in this book, Nephi's knowledge of the goodness of God came as a direct result of having firsthand experiences with the Lord, thus *experiencing* His grace and goodness. Furthermore, since the mysteries of God are those things that can only be known through revelation,[19] Nephi's understanding the mysteries once again implies that he had direct contact with deity. I believe that this premise, and its placement in the first verse of the Book of Mormon, is divinely inspired and opens up the mind of the reader to look for the life-altering impact of personal experiences with the Lord.

Lehi's Divine Encounter

In accordance with this theme, the reader is immediately introduced to the first prophet of the Book of Mormon, Lehi. You may recall that in 1 Nephi 1, Lehi was pouring out his heart to the Lord in behalf of his people. As he prayed, he experienced a divine manifestation as "there came a pillar of fire and dwelt upon a rock before him" (1 Nephi 1:6). The vision continued as the heavens opened and he saw God sitting upon His throne, angels singing and praising God, and Christ descending out of the midst of heaven, with twelve others following Him. As the vision continued, Lehi was given a book, and as he read the book, he was "filled with the Spirit of the Lord" (1 Nephi 1:12). This book, we are told, "manifested plainly of the coming of a Messiah, and also the redemption of the world" (1 Nephi 1:19).

As Lehi read the words and promises written in the book, he exclaimed many things unto the Lord. Included in this divine praise was his gratitude that, because God is merciful, He will not suffer those who come unto Him that they shall perish (see 1 Nephi 1:14). And so we see that this *first* story in the *first* chapter of the *first* book in the Book of Mormon contains the clear invitation and promise that, because of His mercy and grace, those who come unto Christ and seek His divine hand will be protected and watched over. I do not believe it is happenstance that the concluding invitation in the *last* chapter of the *last* book in the Book of Mormon is the heartfelt plea, "Come unto Christ, and be perfected in him" (Moroni 10:32). These two invitations to come unto Christ serve as scriptural bookends, as they underscore the Book of Mormon's overarching message and invitation to experience firsthand the majesty of the Savior's grace.

Consider the theme of Christ's invitation to come and experience His grace as you read the following phrases from Lehi's narrative: "Lehi, as he went forth prayed unto the Lord" (1 Nephi 1:5); "as he prayed unto the Lord, there came a pillar of fire" (1 Nephi 1:6); "he saw One descending out of the midst of heaven" (1 Nephi 1:9); "great and marvelous are thy works, O Lord God Almighty" (1 Nephi 1:14); "the Lord had shown so many marvelous things unto my father" (1 Nephi 1:18); "the tender mercies of the Lord are over all those whom he hath chosen" (1 Nephi 1:20); "the Lord spake unto my father, yea, even in a dream" (1 Nephi 2:1); "the Lord commanded my father" (1 Nephi 2:2); "he was obedient unto the word of the Lord" (1 Nephi 2:3); and they "made an offering unto the Lord, and gave thanks unto the Lord" (1 Nephi 2:7). We are scarcely even on the fourth page of the book, and yet it is already completely clear that this book contains an account of a God who is intimately involved in the lives of His people. Thus, even "while we gaze in awe at His majesty, He does not ask us to stay our distance but bids us to come unto Him."[20]

The Effects of Lehi's Divine Encounter

Now, with that foundation securely established, let's return again to the narrative of Lehi and his revelatory experiences. Or, perhaps more appropriately stated in the spirit of the previous paragraphs, let's return again to the narrative of the Lord and His divine manifestations to His servant Lehi. Nephi records that "after the Lord had shown so many marvelous things unto my father, Lehi . . . he went forth among the people, and began to prophesy" (1 Nephi 1:18). We see that, from the first story in this inspired record, we are learning that experiences with divinity should bring forth action, change, and a desire to reach out to others. Furthermore, Lehi's account will demonstrate that even with our best efforts to rescue others, some

continue to choose disobedience and rebellion. We will see, however, that "though some of the sheep may wander, the eye of the Shepherd is upon them, and sooner or later they will feel the tentacles of Divine Providence reaching out after them and drawing them back to the fold."[21] Indeed, we will see Lehi demonstrate how we can effectively minister to these precious sheep while putting our ultimate trust in our Divine Shepherd.

After Lehi obediently went forth preaching, prophesying, and warning, the people responded by mocking, threatening, and seeking to take away his life. This precarious situation brought forth further revelation, this time in a dream. Lehi was instructed of the Lord to "take his family and depart into the wilderness" (1 Nephi 2:2). Take his family into the wilderness? How would this loving father choose to break such news to his family? How would he choose to tell them that they are supposed to leave their comfortable circumstances, forsake their home and riches, and move into the uncomfortable bleakness of the barren wilderness? While we are not told the details of his presentation, I like to think that Lehi gathered his family together in something of a family council. Imagine what that might have been like!

While we are not told the details of this "council," we *are* told the outcome. Surely speaking "with all the feeling of a tender parent" (1 Nephi 8:37), Lehi's mentoring words led his family to depart, leaving behind their home, land, gold, silver, and precious things, taking with them only their tents and some basic provisions. Lehi's experience with the Lord gave him the motivation, strength, and determination to follow through with this challenging divine direction. This same trust in the Lord also led to the subsequent trips to Jerusalem for the plates and Ishmael's family.

Upon receiving this direction, we read that "he was obedient unto the word of the Lord, *wherefore* he did as the Lord commanded him" (1 Nephi 2:3; emphasis added). I believe there is a profound lesson in that phrase that may often be overlooked. If the purpose of the phrase was to simply illustrate that Lehi obeyed this commandment, it might have read something like this: "and he hearkened unto the word of the Lord and was obedient to his command." However, it does *not* say that. It seems to me that this phrase could be providing a glimpse into Lehi's character, which had been forged by personal experiences with the Lord. It seems to be saying that because Lehi's character had been changed and shaped by the grace of God, his nature was submissive and obedient. Thus, another way of reading this verse could be: "through personal experiences with divinity, Lehi had a submissive, humble, and trusting character; *wherefore* he did as the Lord commanded him."

In that same spirit, Lehi's experiences continually demonstrate how the Lord's personal involvement in the lives of His people is the greatest determining influence on virtually everything they do. For example, Lehi began preaching and prophesying because he had a personal experience with the Lord. He moved his family from the comfort of their riches into the wilderness because he had a personal divine encounter. He sent his boys back to retrieve the plates, trusting that God would preserve both them and the records, because he had a personal divine encounter. Nephi gave his now famous "I will go and do" response only after *he* had a personal divine encounter (1 Nephi 2:16). Nephi had the courage to follow through with slaying Laban *after* he had another divine encounter. He had the tenacity to finish the ship in spite of familial opposition because he had personal revelatory experiences with the Lord on the mountain. And on and on and on. Thus, the storyline alone illustrates what Nephi would later articulate, which is that the central focus of these inspired writers is to "persuade men to come unto the God of Abraham, and the God of Isaac, and the God of Jacob, and be saved" (1 Nephi 6:4). This statement and theme prepares the minds of readers to look for the Messianic imagery presented a couple of chapters later in Lehi's vision of the tree of life (see 1 Nephi 8).

The Fruit of Partaking of the Atonement

Now, let's return to the story. As they returned to the wilderness, we are told that they returned to the tent of Lehi and gave thanks by offering a sacrifice unto the Lord. It is at this point, while tarrying in the wilderness, that Lehi experienced the famed vision of the tree of life. As its title signifies, the central focus of the vision of the tree of life is, of course, the tree. Including the chapter heading, the word *tree* is mentioned ten times in the vision, *fruit* is mentioned

twenty-one times, and the various forms of the word *partake* are mentioned fourteen times. Elder Neal A. Maxwell taught, "The tree of life . . . is the love of God (see 1 Nephi 11:25). The love of God for His children is most profoundly expressed in His gift of Jesus as our Redeemer: 'God so loved the world, that he gave his only begotten Son' (John 3:16). *To partake of the love of God is to partake of Jesus' Atonement and the emancipations and joys which it can bring.*"[22] This vision provided a powerful witness of the importance and influence of partaking of the Atonement and the joy and fulfillment found when we humbly fall down at the feet of Christ (see 1 Nephi 8:30). In his account, however, Lehi not only testified of the joy that comes from the Atonement of Jesus Christ, but also of his efforts to rescue his loved ones who were wandering into forbidden paths, which is both instructive and inspiring.

The emphasis of this vision on partaking of the fruits of the Atonement is magnified as we consider the words used to describe the tree and the fruit: sweet, white, desirable, beauty, precious, joyous, and pure. Remembering that partaking of the fruit represents partaking of "Jesus' Atonement and the emancipations and joys which it can bring." It is interesting that each descriptor outlined is used in a superlative sense; in other words, they are used to express the degree to which each illustrative word is greater than anything else. Some examples are when Lehi told us about the tree and the fruit. He began by saying that it was sweet. However, he didn't just say that it was sweet. What he actually said is, "I beheld that it was *most* sweet, *above all* that I *ever before* tasted (1 Nephi 8:11; emphasis added; see also Alma 32:42). He continued by describing it as white. Once again, though, he did not just leave it at that. He said, "I beheld that the fruit thereof was white, to exceed all the whiteness that I had ever seen" (1 Nephi 8:11). In fact, Nephi was even more specific in explaining that "the whiteness thereof did exceed the whiteness of the driven snow" (1 Nephi 11:8). These superlatives continued (emphasis added):

- Desirable: "I knew that it was desirable *above all* other fruit (1 Nephi 8:12, 15); *most* desirable above *all things*" (1 Nephi 11:22)
- Beautiful: "The beauty thereof was *far beyond, yea, exceeding of all* beauty" (1 Nephi 11:8)

- Precious: "Thou hast shown unto me the tree which is precious *above all* (1 Nephi 11:9); *most* precious and *most* desirable *above all other* fruits; yea, and it is the *greatest of all* the gifts of God" (1 Nephi 15:36)
- Joyous: "Yea, and *the most* joyous to the soul" (1 Nephi 11:23)
- Pure: "Pure *above all* that is pure" (Alma 32:42)

There is an important principle to be learned as we consider these descriptions of partaking of the fruit of the tree of life. When you experience firsthand the divine touch of the Savior's Atonement, you learn that nothing in this world can compare to it! Think about that for a second. If you have borne the burden or stain of sin and been rescued and cleansed through the blood of Christ, you know the difficulty of trying to articulate what those feelings are like. Interestingly, when we do try to describe it, we also use words like *sweet, white* (or *clean*), *beautiful, precious, joyful,* and *pure.* And then as we share these words, we realize that they don't quite capture the majesty of the experience, and so we also use superlatives in saying something like, "It was *the most* beautiful experience I have ever had!" Or, "I had *the most* overwhelming and precious experience as I felt the love of God fill my heart and lift my soul." Indeed, at some point, we are left to humbly and meekly say, with Ammon, "I cannot say the smallest part which I feel" (Alma 26:16). Such is the divine experience of partaking of the fruit of God's love, even the Atonement of Jesus Christ.

Helping Others Partake of the Fruit

But what do we do when *we* have tasted of the fruit but are struggling to persuade others to do likewise? Anyone who has read this vision through the eyes of a parent has felt something of the pain that is manifest therein. After this faithful father partook and experienced the sweetness and joy of the fruit, we are told that he "began to be desirous that [his] family should partake of it also" (1 Nephi 8:12). Commenting on this passage, Elder David A. Bednar recently said, "As he turned to Christ, he also turned outward in love and service."[23] Hasn't that been your experience also? As we experience the rescuing power of the Atonement and the happiness that comes through it, it seems like we almost innately and immediately think of those we love and desire the same experiences for them. Already knowing of their challenges, heartaches, and trials, we pray for them, weep with them, and some-times even mourn for them. As we realize that the Atonement of Jesus Christ can heal even the deepest wounds and the most hardened hearts, we reach out with faith and hope for those who are struggling.

In his vision, Lehi painfully saw that two of his own sons were among those who fell "away into forbidden paths" and "wandered off and were lost" (1 Nephi 8:23, 28). As he saw this, his heart ached and he began to fear. The record says that "he feared lest they should be cast off from the presence of the Lord" (1 Nephi 8:36). The next statement provides a glimpse into Lehi's soul: "He did exhort them then with all the feeling of a tender parent" (1 Nephi 8:37). Here is a deeply committed and caring father pouring out his soul, perhaps even begging his boys to partake of the fruit that has provided him so much happiness. After *his* soul was touched and changed by the Savior, his greatest desire was to reach out to those he loved, particu-larly those who were struggling and wandering.

Perhaps a modern example will help illustrate this pattern. One of my greatest joys as a seminary teacher is being able to watch this change happen in the lives of the youth. I remember one such experience that was particularly poignant. We were studying the New Testament, and I had challenged the youth to read the entire work by the end of the semester. While a few scoffed at the challenge, many of these amazing young people took it seriously. I will never forget the experience of one young lady who was just entering her senior year. She was mature for her age, and it was clear that she had experienced some challenging things in her young life. I recall that, at the beginning of the semester, she seemed quite distant from me and seemingly disinterested in the class. However, she was one who had taken the challenge to study the New Testament and quickly became immersed in the four Gospels. She said that as she began studying, she felt something different. She commented that only spending ten minutes in the scriptures did not provide her enough time to really process what she was learning and have the experience she felt she needed.

This young lady truly began to experiment and "try the virtue of the word of God" (Alma 31:5) as she spent more time pouring over the scriptures. After a couple of weeks, she was spending at least an hour in the scriptures every night. In fact, she sometimes spent two or more hours in the word! She wrote a letter, in the which she bore this powerful testimony:

> If given the time and read properly, I know the scriptures can truly change any person's life. . . . With any problem anyone ever has, whether it's school, work, friends, family, etc., if they turn to the scriptures for answers, it can be solved easily and with God's advice. The scriptures are the most heavenly things we have personal access to in our homes, and yet we take them for granted so much. I know that by living the principles of the word of God, your life can change. I'm so thankful for the scriptures in my life. I have truly actually felt the "scales of darkness" (Mosiah 4) slowly fall from my eyes and reveal God's way personally to me.[24]

It was an absolute delight to watch this young lady partake of the fruit of the tree, even the Atonement of Jesus Christ, and then watch the transformation that took place in her life. While this experience was extremely rewarding, one of the greatest highlights came a few months later. She had previously told me of her less-active father and how she desperately wanted him to feel what she felt. As we spoke, we talked about the need to share our testimonies and then to trust in the Lord's will—and also His timing. She then shared an experience she had, in which her father asked her what she would like for her birthday. She was turning eighteen, and both she and her father realized that this would be a significant milestone in her life. Accordingly, he determined to let her decide what gift she wanted for this special celebration. How I wish I could have been there to witness the sweet exchange that took place as this young woman looked up at her father, hugged him, and said, "Dad, to be honest, the thing that I want most is for you to take me to the temple to perform baptisms for the dead."

Now remember, this father had not been active in the Church for years at this point. In other words, this young lady was not just asking for a nice afternoon at the temple with her father; she was actually asking him to partake of the fruit of the tree and to once again become a worthy priesthood leader in their home. I can only imagine the feelings that accompanied this conversation. I am inspired every time I am reminded of the faith of this seventeen-year-old. As is often the case, as she tasted and experienced the Lord's power to change the human heart, she wanted a beloved family member to

experience the same thing. I am happy to report that both she and her father, having put their faith and their trust in the Lord, were able to go on this father-daughter date to the house of the Lord about six months later.

And Thus We See

In conclusion, let us turn our attention again to Lehi. Having poured out his soul to his rebellious sons and counseled them with tenderness and love, Lehi demonstrated an important principle. The record states that "*after* he had preached unto them, and also prophesied unto them of many things, he bade them to keep the commandments of the Lord; and *he did cease speaking unto them*" (1 Nephi 8:38; emphasis added). Note that Lehi continued to preach, prophesy, and invite, but when he had done all in his power to reach out to his eldest sons, he applied the Lord's counsel to "be still and know that I am God" (D&C 101:16).

Sometimes our anxious feelings for a struggling loved one cause us to overcompensate. Such overcompensation often manifests itself in over-lecturization, which almost inevitably closes communication channels, leaving the individual in a more difficult state than when we began. Thus *after* having taught, warned, and invited, it is often essential to provide these struggling loved ones with some sacred space. I say *sacred space* because it is often during these times when the Lord "will supply [His] own 'evidence of things not seen' (Hebrews 11:1)."[25]

Remember, the Lord is "able to do [His] own work" (2 Nephi 27:21). He knew and loved these struggling individuals even before you did; indeed, He knows and loves them even *more* than you do! The wounds engraved "upon the palms of [His] hands" (1 Nephi 21:16) are everlasting evidence that He will remember you and that He will remember those you care for.[26] Surely Lehi's personal experiences with the Savior shaped his understanding and trust in the Lord's power and in His divine love. *His* grace is sufficient, *His* hands are outstretched, and *His* commitment is unmatched. When it comes to ministering to those loved ones who have wandered, we can, like Lehi, be still and know that He is God!

Chapter 2: Nephi

Nephi's life was a model of obedience and faith. Through his testimony and ministry, we can gain a much greater understanding of the Savior's enabling and eternal grace. While we all experience feelings of divine discontent, the Atonement of Jesus Christ has the power to strengthen us during the growing pains of discipleship.

Lessons Learned from Last Words

During my undergraduate studies, I had the treasured opportunity to study the lives of some of the most innovative and influential American leaders, writers, and thinkers. While studying these individuals, I was particularly impressed by some of the things they said and did toward the ends of their lives. I believe that hearing or reading the final words of an individual can be really instructive as to what they felt was most important. One of the most interesting examples I read comes from the life of Thomas Jefferson. As the principal author of the Declaration of Independence, Jefferson is distinguished for his commitment to democratic principles and his eloquence in stirring the hearts of the people through pen and speech. For Jefferson—and for so many of us since—the mere mention of July 4, 1776, immediately stirs something in our souls.

There is a story in the annals of American history that has Jefferson on his deathbed with a handful of others in the room. While there is a slight discrepancy in the accounts regarding the actual phrasing used by Jefferson, the primary idea is the same. According to one of the accounts, Jefferson had slept for most of the day on July 3, and then woke up later that evening, thinking he had slept through the night and it was now morning. As Jefferson awoke, he asked a simple yet telling question: "Is this the fourth?" One of those in attendance calmly assured him, "It soon will be." According to this account, these were the last words Jefferson spoke before passing away at four a.m. on July 4, 1826, fifty years to the day of the signing of the Declaration of Independence.[27] Clearly, his final words encapsulated his greatest passion and focus.

While we read of these types of stories throughout history, many of the most poignant examples come from the history of the Church and from our own scriptures. Brigham Young once explained that he "was as well acquainted with [Joseph Smith], as any man. I do not believe that his father and mother knew him any better than I did. I do not think that a man lives on the earth that knew him any better than I did; and I am bold to say that, Jesus Christ excepted, no better man ever lived or does live upon this earth. I am his witness."[28] President Young loved the Prophet Joseph and has been quoted saying,

> I never did let an opportunity pass of getting with the Prophet Joseph and of hearing him speak in public or in private, so that I might draw understanding from the fountain from which he spoke, that I might have it and bring it forth when it was needed. . . . Such moments were more precious to me than all the wealth of the world. No matter how great my poverty—if I had to borrow meal to feed my wife and children, I never let an opportunity pass of learning what the Prophet had to impart.[29]

No wonder Brigham said, "I feel like shouting Hallelujah, all the time, when I think that I ever knew Joseph Smith, the Prophet."[30]

During his final hours, Brigham Young was suffering and had become restless. He was given some opiates to help relieve the pain, and his nephew Seymore B. Young suggested they place him in the bed near the open window so that he could get fresh air, and also so that his family members could be close to him. Brigham's daughter

Zina recorded that when they moved him to the bed, he seemed to revive a bit. She then said that Brigham opened his eyes, gazed heavenward, and exclaimed, "'Joseph! Joseph! Joseph!' and the divine look in his face seemed to indicate that he was communicating with his beloved friend, Joseph Smith, the Prophet. This name was the last word he uttered."[31] What a profound and dramatic reunion that must have been for them, and what an important experience for all of us to remember as we consider the lives and sacrifices of these two great men.

It is against this backdrop that I want to introduce the experience of Nephi. When you think of Nephi, what are some of the first thoughts that come into your mind? I would venture to say that as you thought of him, many of you likely heard this familiar chorus in your mind: "I will go; I will do the thing the Lord commands. I know the Lord provides a way; he wants me to obey."[32] When we think of Nephi, we likely think of words like *obedience, commitment,* and *leadership.* While we do not know what Nephi's final spoken words were, we do have the final words he chose to record on the plates.

We are indebted to Jacob for the few things we know about Nephi's final moments. We know that Nephi saw that he must soon die and, being "a great protector for them" (Jacob 1:10), he anointed a king and a ruler over the people. Jacob also went on to explain that the people loved Nephi so deeply that they "were desirous to retain in remembrance his name" (Jacob 1:11) and would call Nephi's successors second Nephi, third Nephi, and so on. Following this, Jacob somewhat abruptly recorded, "And it came to pass that Nephi died" (Jacob 1:12). For those who read of Nephi's experiences and felt connected with him, that statement stirs some interesting emotions, and we sometimes wish Jacob would have broken it to us a little easier than that! Thus, as I reread these passages, I will sometimes return to the final words Nephi chose to record, which are found in the concluding chapters of 2 Nephi.

As Nephi drew toward a conclusion, he explained that "the things which I have written sufficeth me, save it be a few words which I must speak concerning the doctrine of Christ" (2 Nephi 31:2). He proceeded to provide a profound treatise on the doctrine of Christ and on our need to rely on Him. Nephi closed his record with a warning, declaring, "What I seal on earth, shall be brought against you at the judgment bar" (2 Nephi 33:15). He then provided this final gem: "For thus hath the Lord commanded me, and *I must obey*" (2 Nephi 33:15; emphasis added). I remember reading this verse one day and thinking to myself, *Of course this is how Nephi would conclude his record! What else would we expect Nephi to say?!* Because his days were devoted to obedience and trust in the Lord, this consecrated life is both an object lesson and the catalyst through which this message of obedience is carried into the hearts and minds of the readers. This idea begs the question of *how* Nephi became so obedient. Sometimes we assume he just always was. Fortunately, the Book of Mormon sheds some light on the matter.

How Nephi Became *Nephi*

After Lehi and family had settled into the valley of Lemuel, Nephi's older brothers began to murmur. We are typically pretty quick to criticize Laman and Lemuel, and even mock them because of their constant murmuring and spiritual inconsistency. However, Elder Dallin H. Oaks gave the following insight, which helps us better understand the contrasting responses we so often see from Nephi and his brothers. He said,

> We live in a world where many advocate and practice things that are contrary to "the things that be of God"—His plan of salvation. This produces much of the misunderstanding and opposition our young people face from friends and associates. . . .
>
> I suggest that it may be preferable for our young people to refrain from arguing with their associates about such assertions or proposals. They will often be better off to respond by identifying the worldly premises or assumptions in the assertions they face, and then by identifying the different assumptions or premises that guide the thinking of Latter-day Saints. This won't elicit agreement from persons who don't share our faith, but it can move the discussion away from arguing over conclusions to identifying the real source of disagreement.[33]

In other words, if we want to understand Laman and Lemuel, we need to look at their underlying assumptions rather than simply critique their behavior. In 1 Nephi 2, we read of these two brothers calling Lehi a "visionary man" and suggesting that they would have been better off staying with their luxuries in Jerusalem rather than wandering around in the wilderness. Perhaps in an effort to help us better understand Laman and Lemuel, Nephi demonstrated the approach suggested by Elder Oaks.

In 1 Nephi 2:12, Nephi taught, "And thus Laman and Lemuel, being the eldest, did murmur against their father." (There is the behavior.) "And they did murmur because they knew not the dealings of that God who had created them." (There is the underlying assumption.) Because they did not understand the nature of God and how He works with His children, they were not able to understand the visions of their father. As further evidence of this, Nephi explained that Laman and Lemuel did not "believe that Jerusalem, that great city, *could* be destroyed" (1 Nephi 2:13; emphasis added). Interestingly, it seems as if the issue wasn't whether or not God *would* destroy the city; it was whether or not God *could* destroy it. Clearly, Laman and Lemuel's underlying assumptions about God were significantly skewed.

You may be wondering why I'm spending so much time belaboring this point. I believe that the experiences and responses of Laman and Lemuel provide an invaluable literary foil in helping us better understand Nephi and his responses to the same commandments. Take, for example, the commandment to return to Jerusalem to obtain the plates of brass. Because Laman and Lemuel did not understand the dealings of God, they thought their father had asked them to do something that did not make sense, and was thus a "hard thing" (1 Nephi 3:5).

Contrast this with Nephi's immortal response, "I will go and do the things which the Lord hath commanded, for I know that the Lord giveth no commandments unto the children of men, save he shall prepare a way for them that they may accomplish the thing which he commandeth them" (1 Nephi 3:7). In light of this contrast, I want to suggest that one way of reading this verse might simply be: "I will go and do the things which the Lord hath commanded, for I know [the Lord]." Nephi responded the way he did because he had, through personal experience, come to know the Lord.

So how did Nephi come to know the Lord? What led to these firsthand experiences? The journey seems to begin (or at least the *recorded* journey seems to begin) directly after the account of Laman and Lemuel's murmuring. In response to their murmuring, Lehi spoke "with power, being filled with the Spirit, until their frames did shake before him" (1 Nephi 2:14). It is immediately after this powerful experience—and perhaps even *because* of this experience—that Nephi turned autobiographical in explaining that he had "great desires to know of the mysteries of God" (1 Nephi 2:16).

We learn that this desire led Nephi to cry unto the Lord, and this prayer was answered in a miraculous manner as the Lord visited him, softened his heart, and thus led him to believe. This experience with the Lord not only showed Nephi of the Lord's intimate love and involvement in his life, but it also produced a determination to grow in obedience and faithfulness. Surely this was a fundamental factor in Nephi's willingness to return to Jerusalem.

Nephi's personal experiences with the Lord continue as he was led by the Spirit in acquiring the plates, assisted in convincing Ishmael to bring his family into the wilderness, and, perhaps most profoundly, literally guided by an angel to understand Lehi's vision of the tree of life—and the additional divine instruction that would follow. Furthermore, we know a divine hand guided him in dealing with his broken bow, building and captaining a ship, and helping his father settle a new land. An entire book could be dedicated to recounting Nephi's experiences with the Lord. In fact, an entire book *has* been dedicated to it—it is called the First Book of Nephi!

Nephi's Psalm as a Pattern for Experiencing the Enabling Power of the Atonement

You will recall that this chapter began with the idea that we can gain valuable insight by paying attention to an individual's final words. Remember Nephi's final statement: "For thus hath the Lord commanded me, and I must obey" (2 Nephi 33:15). I hope that it has been plain to see that one of the primary reasons Nephi was able to submit to the Lord so *willingly* was that he knew Him so *personally*. Nephi had experienced firsthand the majesty of God's love and had come to possess a deep trust in His divine will.

Unfortunately, some readers of the Book of Mormon have a little difficulty relating to Nephi because of this unfailing faithfulness. To some, he almost seems infallible, without personal weakness. Perhaps it is for this reason that 2 Nephi 4 resonates so deeply in the hearts of so many. In what has sometimes been called "Nephi's psalm," we are invited to glimpse into the soul of this amazing man.

In approaching Nephi's psalm, it is important to understand that the context here underscores the content. Nephi just lost his father, who was his prophet and most influential mortal mentor. Furthermore, the passing of Lehi put the prophetic mantle and responsibilities of leadership squarely upon Nephi's shoulders. On top of all of that, his brothers and some of the sons of Ishmael became angry because of the counsel given them and thought to take it out on Nephi—again. You can almost hear the exhaustion in Nephi's voice as he explained that he "was *constrained* to speak unto them, according to his word" (2 Nephi 4:14; emphasis added). As he speaks of being "constrained," you can feel his frustration and heartache over this difficult situation. It is in this context that we get an intimate glimpse into Nephi's soul (see 2 Nephi 4:15–35) and an opportunity to connect with some of the emotions and insecurities he felt.

As this psalm begins, we read some of the most tender verses in all of scripture. Nephi seems to personify what Elder Neal A. Maxwell once called "divine discontent." In speaking of this divine discontent, Elder Maxwell said, "We can distinguish more clearly between divine discontent and the devil's dissonance, between dissatisfaction with self and disdain for self. We need the first and must shun the second, remembering that when conscience calls to us from the next ridge, it is not solely to scold but also to beckon."[34] These moments of divine discontent represent one way in which our loving Father invites us to become a little more like Him. Consider, for example, this heartfelt plea from Nephi: "Notwithstanding the great goodness of the Lord, in showing me his great and marvelous works, my heart exclaimeth: O wretched man that I am! Yea, my heart sorroweth because of my flesh; my soul grieveth because of mine iniquities. I am encompassed about, because of the temptations and the sins which do so easily beset me. And when I desire to rejoice, my heart groaneth because of my sins" (2 Nephi 4:17–19).

How many have felt such stirrings? How many have felt to cry out, "Why, when I know the things I know, do I do the things I do?" All earnest seekers of truth have likely felt these emotions tugging at their heartstrings. As Nephi continued this prayer, it is almost as if the Lord intervened and lifted his soul in the middle of the experience as he cried, "*Nevertheless, I know in whom I have trusted. My God hath been my support*" (2 Nephi 4:19–20; emphasis added).

When considering the influence of the Savior's grace, it is essential to remember that His Atonement not only enables us to be cleansed from sin, but that it also enables us to find strength during such moments of internal struggle. Nephi's experience shows us a powerful pattern in how we can access and experience this divine strength. The pattern is we experience divine discontent; this feeling often leads to a recognition of the blessings provided by the hand of the Lord; this remembrance elicits a resolve to improve; and the experience culminates in a recognition that, as imperfect mortal beings, we are inescapably reliant on the Lord and therefore must trust in His grace.

With this pattern in mind, consider Nephi's experience following his moments of divine discontent. He reflected on the many experiences he'd had wherein he had seen and felt the hand of God directly guiding him in his life. He recognized these blessings by saying "God hath" or "he hath," and then proceeded to describe the way in which the Lord was with him.

For example, he began this section of the psalm with this testimony: "My *God hath* been my support; *he hath* led me through mine afflictions in the wilderness; and *he hath* preserved me upon the waters of the great deep" (2 Nephi 4:20; emphasis added). He also said (emphasis added), "*He hath* filled me with his love" (21), "*he hath* confounded mine enemies" (22), and "*he hath* heard my cry by day, and *he hath* given me knowledge by visions in the night-time" (23). Nephi concluded this section of the psalm by testifying how the Lord strengthened him as He sent angels to minister to him and as he was carried "upon the wings of his Spirit" (2 Nephi 4:25), being taken to exceedingly high mountains where he learned and experienced things too great and too precious to even record. During these moments when we feel this stirring of the soul to do and be better, it is wise to take an opportunity to reflect on and remember how merciful the Lord has been in our lives,

and how we have felt His divine grace enable and ennoble us. This reflecting and remembering will often produce greater faith and deeper trust in the Lord and His holy purposes.

Nephi's recognition of blessings led to what may be considered the climax of the psalm when he cried out, "Awake, my soul! No longer droop in sin. Rejoice, O my heart, and give place no more for the enemy of my soul" (2 Nephi 4:28). Thus, Nephi's recognition of the hand of God in his life led to this powerful resolve to improve. Similarly, in our lives, it is often these moments when we come up short that we say to ourselves, "Why should *I* yield to sin?" (2 Nephi 4:27; emphasis added). This determination helps us understand that if permanent change is going to happen along this path of discipleship, it will only come "through the merits, and mercy, and grace of the Holy Messiah" (2 Nephi 2:8). After offering poignant and moving strains of praise, Nephi concluded with his assurance that, as we put our trust in Christ, "the rock of [our] righteousness" (2 Nephi 4:35), He will continue to deliver, redeem, and strengthen us. What a powerful message to those who are "imperfect but still striving in the household of faith."[35]

Amazing Grace

In an effort to liken Nephi's experience and counsel to a more modern context, consider the following story. Most Christians— and likely most everyone else—are at least familiar with the popular hymn "Amazing Grace." Less familiar is the story behind the hymn. An eighteenth-century preacher named John Newton penned the words of this inspiring hymn. Newton's father was a shipmaster who showed his young eleven-year-old son the particulars of the trade.

These experiences prepared Newton for a career at sea in which, by his own admission, he was enveloped in the most blasphemous, immoral, and repugnant behavior while also seducing others to indulge with him. This life of sin and rebellion culminated as he eventually became the captain of a slave ship. He had a life-altering experience, however, on one of his voyages as his ship was nearly wrecked in an intense storm. This experience led him to his knees, seeking the grace of God and experiencing His divine forgiveness and love. This experience inspired the now immortal lines:

> Amazing grace! (how sweet the sound)
> That sav'd a wretch like me!
> I once was lost, but now am found,
> Was blind, but now I see.[36]

One day, after listening to this inspiring song, I found myself singing it out loud as I was trying to get one of my little boys into bed. He looked up at me and, with all the sincerity of a three year old, said, "Daddy, what means *wretch*?" I looked back at him and said, "Buddy, a wretch is a bad person."

I then caught myself and quickly corrected my answer, saying, "Actually, a wretch is somebody who sometimes makes a bad choice and needs Jesus to help him." He then sweetly muttered, "Daddy, I hate making bad choices." I told him that I did too, but I then took this tender opportunity to teach him about the mercy and grace of Christ. I let him know that Jesus can help us be forgiven for bad choices and to find the strength to make good ones.

And a Thus We See

As we imperfectly make our way on this journey of discipleship, we, like Nephi, will have experiences that remind us we are not yet what we ought to be, or even what we want to be. However, as we ponder the Savior's enabling grace, we can humbly acknowledge, "Though I am not what I ought to be, what I wish to be, and what I hope to be—yet I can truly say, I am not what I once was . . . and by the grace of God I am what I am."[37]

On this mortal journey, it is essential that we humbly acknowledge our weaknesses and inadequacies. However, in that same moment, we must also humbly acknowledge the greatness of the grace of God and His enabling power, remembering that it was in and through this grace that Nephi became an obedient and powerful leader.

It is with this trust and reliance on the merciful hand of the patient Redeemer that we move forward with the hopeful plea to the Lord, "Wilt thou encircle *me* around in the robe of *thy* righteousness!" (2 Nephi 4:33; emphasis added). In that day, we too can stand with Nephi as we are given these perfect and divine celestial white robes that, as Nephi was taught, were only "made white in the blood of the Lamb" (1 Nephi 12:11). The Savior's Atonement enables and ensures that we are encircled in the robes of His righteousness so that we can eventually be "encircled about eternally in the arms of his love" (2 Nephi 1:15).

Chapter 3: Isaiah

Some of the sweetest and most profound experiences of
mortality are being able to feel the cleansing and sanctifying
effects of the Atonement. Isaiah's account teaches us that
these divine experiences are instrumental in the develop-
ment of a submissive and consecrated heart.

What's in a Name?

Virtually every parent has experienced numerous emotions while
awaiting the arrival of a new child. Discussions and predictions
begin almost immediately as to whether the baby will be a boy or
a girl (though in my house of five little boys, we have determined
that we are only capable of having boys), who the baby will look like,
who they will act like, and so on. As these conversations continue,
one of the inevitable discussions that seems to be the most pressing is, "What should we name this little one?" Each couple likely
has their own way of approaching this awesome responsibility. Some
begin this discussion by immediately writing a list of names they
like, which are gender specific. Some choose names they feel strongly
about that might be considered unisexual. Some choose to wait until
the baby is born before making this decision, while others, particularly mothers, may have decided on names shortly after graduating
from Primary and becoming Beehives! No matter how parents decide

to approach this, almost all of them feel something of the weight and importance of the task.

The scriptures contain numerous examples of the significance of a child's name. In the scriptures, some names were given to provide instruction. For example, Isaiah named a son Shear-jashub, which means "the remnant shall return." Other times, names were given to provide warning. Isaiah named another son Maher-shalal-hash-baz, which translates into "destruction is imminent"—I have considered several times changing the name of my two-year-old son from Parker to Maher-shalal-hash-baz. While scriptural names are sometimes given to individuals to provide instruction and warning, it seems that the most common scriptural consideration in naming a child is the underscoring of a certain mission. Consider the following names, as taken from the Bible Dictionary: Eve (the mother of all living); Ephraim (fruitful); Gideon (hewer down of men, or warrior); or the ultimate example, Jesus (God is help, or Savior). It should also be noted that the Lord often changed a person's name to symbolize a covenant made or a mission to perform (Abraham, Jacob, Peter, and so on).

Jehovah Saves

While I have mentioned Isaiah naming his children, it is perhaps more instructive to consider the prophet Isaiah himself. Isaiah's name literally means "the Lord is salvation" or "Jehovah saves."[38] Perhaps when we read Isaiah, we can remember that this represents his overarching message. His mission was to help others know and experience the redeeming and saving power and character of Christ. I would suggest that one useful way of reading Isaiah's words is to look for and highlight his witness of the Lord's divine mission and of His power to save. To better illustrate, please consider the theme in the following phrases:

- "Though your sins be as scarlet, they shall be as white as snow" (Isaiah 1:18)
- "God is my salvation; I will trust, and not be afraid: for the Lord Jehovah is my strength and my song; he also is become my salvation" (Isaiah 12:2)
- "With joy shall ye draw water out of the wells of salvation" (Isaiah 12:3)

- "The Lord will have mercy on Jacob, and will yet choose Israel" (Isaiah 14:1)
- "Thou hast forgotten the God of thy salvation, and hast not been mindful of the rock of thy strength" (Isaiah 17:10)
- His rest is "like a cloud of dew in the heat of harvest" (Isaiah 18:4)
- "Thou hast been a strength to the poor, a strength to the needy in his distress, a refuge from the storm, a shadow from the heat" (Isaiah 25:4)
- "The Lord God will wipe away tears from off all faces" (Isaiah 25:8)
- The Lord is "a foundation . . . stone, a tried stone, a precious corner stone, a sure foundation" (Isaiah 28:16)
- "The grass withereth, the flower fadeth: but the word of our God shall stand for ever" (Isaiah 40:8)
- "He shall feed his flock like a shepherd: he shall gather the lambs with his arm, and carry them in his bosom" (Isaiah 40:11)
- "They that wait upon the Lord shall renew their strength; they shall mount up with wings as eagles; they shall run, and not be weary; and they shall walk, and not faint" (Isaiah 40:31)
- "Fear thou not; for I am with thee: be not dismayed; for I am thy God: I will strengthen thee; yea, I will help thee; yea, I will uphold thee with the right hand of my righteousness" (Isaiah 41:10)
- "Fear not: for I have redeemed thee, I have called thee by thy name; thou art mine" (Isaiah 43:1)
- "I, even I, am he that blotteth out thy transgressions for mine own sake, and will not remember thy sins" (Isaiah 43:25)
- "I have blotted out, as a thick cloud, thy transgressions, and, as a cloud, thy sins: return unto me; for I have redeemed thee" (Isaiah 44:22)
- "Look unto me, and be ye saved, all the ends of the earth" (Isaiah 45:22)
- "I have chosen thee in the furnace of affliction" (Isaiah 48:10)
- "I have graven thee upon the palms of my hands; thy walls are continually before me" (Isaiah 49:16)

- "Surely he hath borne our griefs, and carried our sorrows" (Isaiah 53:4)
- "He was wounded for our transgressions, he was bruised for our iniquities: the chastisement of our peace was upon him; and with his stripes we are healed" (Isaiah 53:5)
- "For a small moment have I forsaken thee; but with great mercies will I gather thee" (Isaiah 54:7)
- "With everlasting kindness will I have mercy on thee" (Isaiah 54:8)
- "He hath sent me to bind up the brokenhearted, to proclaim liberty to the captives . . . to give unto them beauty for ashes" (Isaiah 61:1, 3)
- "For since the beginning of the world men have not heard, nor perceived by the ear, neither hath the eye seen, O God, beside thee, what he hath prepared for him that waiteth for him" (Isaiah 64:4)
- "As one whom his mother comforteth, so will I comfort you" (Isaiah 66:13)

Against the backdrop of these powerful phrases, is it any wonder that when Nephi wanted to "more fully persuade [his people] to believe in the Lord their Redeemer" (1 Nephi 19:23), he read to them from the pages of Isaiah? Studying Isaiah's poignant, poetic language begs the question of how he came to feel and know the things of which he testified and wrote. Mercifully, Isaiah left us with a little glimpse into his own firsthand experience with the Master. His tender, firsthand account both demonstrates and illuminates the Lord's ability to cleanse, heal, and empower His humble followers.

In Nephi's preface to what have become known as "the Isaiah chapters," he effectively demonstrated how a teacher should prepare the hearts and minds of the students to ensure that they focused on the main idea being presented. Nephi explained that his "soul delighteth in [Isaiah's] words." Then, in a moment that surely must have evoked the deepest emotion of his soul, Nephi affectionately testified that one of the reasons why he delighted in the words of Isaiah was that "he verily saw my Redeemer, even as I have seen him" (2 Nephi 11:2).

I wish to pause, parenthetically, and make one little observation that could potentially add a deeper context to Isaiah's experience. Nephi's personal connection with Christ never fails to touch my heart. When commenting on Isaiah and his experience, Nephi instructively said that Isaiah saw "*my* Redeemer" (2 Nephi 11:2; emphasis added). Note that he did not just say Isaiah saw "*the* Redeemer." Would it be appropriate for Nephi to have referred to Jesus as "the Redeemer"? Of course. But it seems to me that he wanted the reader to understand that his relationship with the Lord was not a casual acquaintance. In fact, as part of his concluding testimony Nephi declared, "I glory in plainness; I glory in truth; I glory in *my* Jesus, for he hath redeemed *my* soul from hell" (2 Nephi 33:6; emphasis added). While Jesus is the Savior of the world, Nephi reminds us that He is also our personal Savior. While His Atonement is *infinite* in its scope, it is also *intimate* in its influence.

Now, let's tie this back to Isaiah and his experience. We know that Nephi delighted in Isaiah's words. We know that he demonstratively referred to him simply as "the prophet" (much like we do with the Prophet Joseph, or the current prophet). But 2 Nephi 11:2 demonstrates a love and brotherhood much deeper and holier than even one of personal admiration. Nephi seemed to be trying to prepare the hearts of the readers to understand that Isaiah is a literal witness of Jehovah. He has seen Him! It is almost as if Nephi were saying to anyone who would read his words, "I do not delight in Isaiah's words simply because they are poetically powerful, though they certainly are. I do not delight in his words just because he *talks about* the Redeemer, though he certainly does. I delight in his words because he *has seen* the Redeemer. I delight in the words of Isaiah because we share the same witness and consecrated commitment to serve the Lord, whose divine grace we have both felt." What a powerful introduction to focus the reader's attention on Isaiah's message and his ministry!

Isaiah's "First" Vision

Isaiah's recorded ministry actually begins in Isaiah 6—or 2 Nephi 16, for our purposes. While Isaiah 6 is obviously not the first chapter in his book, it *is* generally considered to be his first revelation.[39] In fact, in Latter-day Saint vernacular, this chapter might easily be referred to as Isaiah's First Vision, as it contains Isaiah's account of his vision of the Lord and his subsequent call to the ministry.

In the first verse of this chapter, Isaiah testifies that "in the year that King Uzziah died [740 BC], I saw also the Lord sitting upon a throne." Oh, how I wish we had a poetic description of what that must have been like! Perhaps Isaiah would use language similar to the prophet Joseph and talk about "the transcendent beauty" of it, or refer to "the blazing throne of God" (D&C 137:2–3). Or maybe he would use imagery, like Ezekiel did, and describe the throne as "a sapphire stone" and the Lord's glory like "the appearance of fire" (Ezekiel 1:26–27). Regardless of the description he might have used, the point is that this man, this prophet, had an experience wherein he saw the Lord! That fact in and of itself should be enough to pique the interest of every person professing to love the Lord. But Isaiah does not just leave us alone to contemplate the vision he saw. No, Isaiah didn't want to just talk about Jehovah Himself; he wanted to ensure that the reader understood the Lord's power to heal and save. Thus, in 2 Nephi 16, Isaiah deepens our understanding of the influence of the Atonement by providing an autobiographical object lesson that demonstrates the sanctifying and enabling grace of Christ.

Isaiah explained that as he saw the Lord sitting upon a throne, He was surrounded by holy angels (see 2 Nephi 16:1–2). As the glory of the Lord illuminated the room, Isaiah recorded his own feelings of divine discontent as he said, "Wo is unto me! For I am undone [overwhelmed]; because I am a man of unclean [imperfect] lips; and I dwell in the midst of a people of unclean lips; for mine eyes have seen the King, the Lord of Hosts" (2 Nephi 16:5). This experience seems to be similar to that of Moses when, after experiencing the glory of God, he cried out, "Now, for this cause I know that man is nothing, which thing I never had supposed" (Moses 1:10). It is also reminiscent of Peter after he saw the Lord's miraculous hand in providing scores of fish immediately following the disappointed fishermen's unsuccessful day on the lake (see Luke 5:5–11). Remember that the record says that "when Simon Peter saw it, he fell down at Jesus' knees, saying, Depart from me; for I am a sinful man, O Lord" (Luke 5:8). While Isaiah's feelings were deeply sincere and heartfelt, they were certainly not unique.

Being thus humbled and filled with contrition, Isaiah reported that an angel came and, with a live coal, touched his lips with the promise that "thine iniquity is taken away, and thy sin purged" (2 Nephi 16:7). More than likely, this coal would have come from the altar of sacrifice (see Leviticus 16:12). We are told that, on this altar, Aaron was to sacrifice "the goat of the sin offering, . . . [which] shall make an Atonement for the holy place, because of the uncleanness of the children of Israel, and because of their transgressions in all their sins" (Leviticus 16:15–16). This coal likely became a powerful object lesson for Isaiah, reminding him that the main purpose of sacrifices being offered was to reconcile the imperfect, weak Israel with its perfect, mighty God. This coal was a symbol of cleansing (Isaiah 6:6, footnote 6a), pointing to Isaiah being "sanctified by the reception of the Holy Ghost" (3 Nephi 27:20). Thus, having received a "remission of [his] sins by fire and by the Holy Ghost" (2 Nephi 31:17), Isaiah's broken and contrite heart became pure and submissive, having yielded it unto God (see Helaman 3:35).

The Making of a Submissive and Consecrated Heart

One of the most important fruits of the sanctifying influence of the Atonement of Jesus Christ is the subsequent submission of one's will. Such submission often leads to a life of consecrated service in the kingdom. Consider, for example, the rest of Isaiah's experience. After having been told that his iniquity was taken away and his sin purged, he heard the divine query, "Whom shall I send, and who will go for *us*?" (2 Nephi 61:8; emphasis added). I love the way the Lord asked this question. He asked who would go *for us*. The word *for* denotes the idea that whoever is sent will be on an errand from the Lord, not his or her own. Perhaps the word *us* signifies the unity of the Godhead, and that when we are on the Lord's errand, we are entitled to the help of all three members of the Godhead. Or, because Isaiah's life was at such a transcendent point and his will was so identical to the Lord's, perhaps the word *us* could actually also include himself.

With a newly secured trust and confidence, and with a clear and obvious Messianic echo, Isaiah's humble reply to the Lord's inviting question was a submissive, "Here am I; send me" (2 Nephi 16:8; see also Abraham 3:27). This personal encounter with the Savior's grace not only provided the assurance that Isaiah was clean and worthy to serve, but it also helped him realize the divinity of his calling and the enabling promise of Christ's continued influence.

Isaiah's experience provides significant insight into the making of a consecrated heart. Sometimes we misunderstand our responsibility to render consecrated service. Many feel that the only way to offer consecrated service is to log countless hours in meetings, make continual personal visits, and study Church material for hours on end. While such behaviors *could* certainly be evidence of a consecrated heart, Elder Maxwell insightfully observed, "Increased consecration is not so much a demand for more hours of Church work as it is for more awareness of Whose work this really is!"[40] Truly, Isaiah learned firsthand Whose work he was engaging in, and this realization led him to willingly submit to serve when, where, and how the Lord asked.

Nephi spoke of the importance of likening Isaiah's words unto us so that we can profit and learn from them (see 1 Nephi 19:23). While this is important, I think that Nephi would be all right with me adding that it is equally important to liken Isaiah's personal experience unto ourselves. One of the most important principles we can learn from Isaiah is that a willingness to render consecrated service in the kingdom comes as one of the sweet fruits of experiencing the Savior's grace. Speaking of such consecration, Elder Maxwell boldly promised, "It would change the entire Church if in every ward, we could have just three or four more families who became truly consecrated disciples of Jesus Christ instead of just being active in the Church."[41] This kind of discipleship and consecration comes only as we put off the natural man, experience the redeeming power of the Messiah, and become the submissive, meek, humble, patient, and full of love Saints that Heavenly Father invites us to become (see Mosiah 3:19).

And *Thus We See*

In premortal spheres, Christ stepped forward and meekly accepted His singular mission, saying, "Here am I, send me" (Abraham 3:27). In ancient Israel, Isaiah likewise stepped forward and accepted *his* important mission with the response, "Here am I; send me" (2 Nephi 16:8).

In modern Israel—in various ways and by various means—the Lord provides commandments and invitations for us to fulfill *our* missions. In essence, He asks, "Whom shall I send, and who will go for us?" (2 Nephi 16:8). In our own ways and with our own missions, we can likewise submissively proclaim, "Here am I; send me." Now, consider the following responses to contemporary invitations we are given:

- "Father, if you need someone to stand by the Prophet Joseph Smith and keep his name safe in the midst of slanderous attacks and accusations, 'Here am I; send me.'"
- "If you need someone who is not just content but is *anxious* to serve with all his (or her) heart in an essential but less visible calling, 'Here am I; send me.'"
- "If you need someone to follow the prophet's constant plea to reach out and rescue those members of the Church who have fallen away, 'Here am I; send me.'"
- "If you need a father who will take an active and presiding role in raising his children unto thee, 'Here am I; send me.'"
- "If you need a woman who understands the sanctity of the home and the divine calling of motherhood, 'Here am I; send me.'"
- "If you need a disciple who experiences firsthand the sanctifying and cleansing power of the Atonement of thy Son, 'Here am I; send me.'"
- "If you are looking for a priesthood holder who will willingly and gratefully accept an invitation to provide a priesthood blessing during an inconvenient time or an inopportune circumstance, 'Here am I; send me.'"
- "If you need someone to trust in and rely wholly on Thy merciful hand during the difficult trials and heartaches of mortality, 'Here am I; send me.'"
- "If you are looking for a daughter who will look to Thy holy scriptures rather than the world's counterfeit solutions when seeking comfort, direction, or healing, 'Here am I; send me.'"
- "If you need a son who can keep the affections of his heart continually upon thee by avoiding the distracting tugs and pulls of the professional world, 'Here am I; send me.'"

- "If you need someone who is available at any time, in any place, under any circumstances to run an errand for thee, please dear Father, 'Here am I, send me.'"

As with the prophet Isaiah, our experiences with the Lord's Atonement and divine love will often lead to a softened and submissive heart. When these experiences happen, we are no longer content with blessing our families alone, but will range "throughout the whole world, anxious to bless the whole human race."[42] Indeed, our deepest and most heartfelt plea will be "more fit for the kingdom," and to be "more used" in this great and holy latter-day work.[43] In all of this, and throughout a lifetime of consecrated service, we will find that "some of the most rewarding times of our lives are those 'extra mile' hours given in service when the body says it wants to relax, but our better self emerges and says, 'Here am I; send me.'"[44]

Chapter 4: Enos

The scriptures describe prayer as an action, as they speak of wrestling, supplicating, and pouring out our hearts unto the Lord. Indeed, we believe that "prayer is a form of work,"[45] indicating a precious price to be paid by those seeking a divine blessing. Enos placed such a price upon heaven's approval and in so doing showed each of us the investment to be made to obtain the riches of eternity.

Paying the Proper Price

Some time ago, my wife and I had an opportunity that allowed us to try to teach one of our boys the value of money. Because we both feel the heavy responsibility of teaching our boys how to work, we have spent a lot of time counseling together, trying to determine how to best instill these values and habits in their hearts. Among other things, we decided that there would be some household chores that would be expected of them (like making their beds, cleaning their rooms, and so on).

We also determined that once the boys had completed their expected chores, they could choose, if they desired, to do additional chores, which would each be attached to a certain monetary value. Simply put, if they completed an extra chore, they earned the amount of money attached to that chore.

As was anticipated, the boys were excited about this prospect and immediately got to work on their regular list of chores. They burned through these faster than we thought possible and were anxious to move onto the more lucrative chores. Again, they approached these with great vigor and were thus able to earn a little money. A short time later, one of them asked us if we could go to the store. Curious as to what would elicit this question from a six-year-old boy, we asked why he wanted to go to the store. With a giddy grin on his face and a small wad of cash in his hand, he proudly proclaimed, "I have been saving my money and want to go buy an iPad."

Now, when I say a *small* wad of cash, you need to know that we are talking about a crinkled-up dollar bill and some sticky coinage, probably something to the tune of $1.45 or so! Trying to be careful to not dash his young hopes and aspirations, we tried to teach him the value of money and how things of significant value almost always require a significant price be paid. We congratulated him on his desire to save for something he wanted rather than just wasting his money on the first toy or treat he saw, and then we sent him on his way. He left somewhat disappointed, but with a better idea of the necessary price to be paid if he really wanted an iPad.

Thomas Paine, an influential author during the American Revolution, wrote, "What we obtain too cheap, we esteem too lightly: it is dearness only that gives every thing its value. Heaven knows how to put a proper price upon its goods."[46] The life of the prophet Enos movingly demonstrates both the value of forgiveness and the price to be paid in seeking such a divine miracle. Indeed, "Enos placed a proper price upon the blessings of heaven; yet he did so in such a way as to encourage those who in like manner seek the light and mercy of heaven. Having tasted of such things, he sealed his book in the spirit of rejoicing in Christ."[47]

The "Wrestle" of the Prophet Enos

Enos was the son of the prophet Jacob. From the Book of Mormon, we learn that Jacob, Nephi's younger brother, saw Christ and learned firsthand of "the greatness of God," and that "in the fulness of time he cometh to bring salvation unto men" (2 Nephi 2:2–3; see also 2 Nephi 11:3). While Jacob's writings are clear evidence that

his personal divine encounters led to a deep and "unshaken" faith in the Savior (see, for example, Jacob 7), the actual narrative is relatively sparse. Consequently, while there is much to be learned from the Christ-centered *teachings* of Jacob, we will spend our time focusing on the *experience* of his son Enos.

Unfortunately, we do not know a lot about Enos's early life, and any speculation as to what sins were committed that led to his miraculous divine encounter is scripturally unfounded. We know that his father taught him, and that he blessed the name of God for having a father who would willingly teach him in the nurture and admonition of the Lord (Enos 1:1). We know that he was journeying through the forest in search of beasts when something led him to turn his search inward and identify the beast inside of himself, even the natural man. Enos said that this shift of focus came as "the words which [he] had often heard [his] father speak concerning eternal life, and the joy of the saints, sunk deep into [his] heart" (Enos 1:3).

As Enos thought upon these words, his "memory was both cruel and kind. The pictures his father had painted in sermon and admonition now stirred his soul. He was warmed and inspired. He hungered for the good. Then memory opened the doors to his ugly past. His soul revolted at the reliving of the baser things but yearned now for the better. A rebirth was in process. It was painful but rewarding."[48] But what was it about these words that had such a deep impact on Enos?

Jacob might be one of the most underappreciated doctrinal voices we have in the Book of Mormon. He may also be one of the most underappreciated exemplary parents in all of scripture. For example, most parents have felt at least once or twice in their lives as though their counsel or even testimonies that are shared with their children have fallen on deaf ears. Did Jacob ever feel such disappointments? Probably. But Enos's account provides insight into Jacob's tenacity as he referenced "the words which [he] had *often* heard [his] father speak concerning eternal life, and the joy of the saints" (Enos 1:3; emphasis added). Jacob was consistent in the substance of his teaching, as he seems to have continually focused on the doctrines of eternity. These words from a loving parent played an important role in leading Enos to this remarkable experience with the Lord. David R.

Seely, a professor of ancient scripture at Brigham Young University, provided great insight into these impactful words:

> Jacob received the words he spoke from his father, from the scriptures, from the Lord through his voice or in vision, through messengers, and through the Holy Ghost. While the phrases "words . . . concerning eternal life" and "joy of the saints" do not occur in any of Jacob's sermons, all of the components of these phrases occur enough times separately to give us a sense of what they may have meant to Jacob and thus to Enos.
>
> Jacob mentions "word" 27 times and "words" 39 times. Of note are the occurrences of the phrases: "I have spoken the words of your Maker. I know that the words of truth are hard against all uncleanness; but the righteous fear them not" (2 Nephi 9:40) and, "Remember the words of your God; pray unto him continually by day, and give thanks unto his holy name by night" (2 Nephi 9:52). Both of these passages may be related to the phrase used by Enos because Enos was concerned about repentance and was moved by the weight of the words in his heart to seek a remission of his sins through prayer.
>
> Jacob refers to "life eternal" and "eternal life" three times, always in the context of the need for repentance: "Remember, to be carnally-minded is death, and to be spiritually-minded is life eternal" (2 Nephi 9:39); "Therefore, cheer up your hearts, and remember that ye are free to act for yourselves—to choose the way of everlasting death or the way of eternal life" (2 Nephi 10:23); and, "O then, my beloved brethren, repent ye, and enter in at the strait gate, and continue in the way which is narrow, until ye shall obtain eternal life" (Jacob 6:11). As in these passages, Enos' use of the phrase "eternal life" very likely refers to his immediate concern about eternal life, repenting and gaining a remission of his sins. . . .
>
> Much of the terminology Enos uses to describe his spiritual upbringing, which he attributes to his father, can be found in his father's teachings. At the core of the teachings of Jacob is the need for repentance, a need expressed and acted upon by Enos.[49]

Enos did act upon the inspired words of his father. Let's return to the narrative. We learn from his account that though Enos had started this familiar journey the way he had undoubtedly done so many times previously, he would learn that there was something markedly different this time; indeed, it was to be a completely different journey.

President Spencer W. Kimball explained that Enos's initial purpose had been to hunt beasts in the forest, "but no animal did he shoot nor capture. He was traveling a path he had never walked before. He was reaching, knocking, asking, pleading; he was being born again. He was seeing the pleasant valleys across the barren wastes. He was searching his soul. He might have lived all his life in a weed patch, but now he envisioned a watered garden."[50]

It is not happenstance that as Enos discussed this process of being born again, he referred to it as "*the wrestle* which I had before God, before I received a remission of my sins" (Enos 1:2; emphasis added). The Merriam Webster dictionary defines the word *wrestle* as, "to struggle to move, deal with, or control something."[51] Perhaps Enos's wrestle before God was a struggle to move away from sin and toward the Lord. Perhaps he used the word *wrestle* to try to describe his efforts in dealing with the guilt and pain brought on by his past transgressions. Maybe this wrestle was one for control, as he likely felt the need to turn his life over to the Lord but perhaps had not yet surrendered his pride or desire for power. Whatever the reason for Enos including the word *wrestle*, it effectively helps us to see and feel the struggle he felt as he sought the divine gift of forgiveness. This struggle is underscored as he described how his "soul hungered" and how he engaged in "mighty prayer and supplication for [his] own soul" (Enos 1:4) all the day long, and even throughout the night. President Kimball helps us engage with this experience as he provided the following insightful commentary:

> Here is no casual prayer; no worn phrases; no momentary appeal by silent lips. All the day long, with seconds turning into minutes, and minutes into hours and hours. But when the sun had set, relief had still not come, for repentance is not a single act nor forgiveness an unearned gift. So precious to him was communication with and approval of his Redeemer that his determined soul pressed on without ceasing. Could the Redeemer resist such determined imploring?[52]

Seeking divine approval became the consuming focus for this great man. He *had* to have it! Elder Bruce C. Hafen profoundly expressed, "We can have eternal life if we want it, but only if there is *nothing else* we want more."[53] As Enos wrestled and struggled and persisted to gain approval in the sight of God, it was clear that there was nothing so precious to him as "eternal life, and the joy of the saints" (Enos 1:3). President Kimball explained that Enos "was self-convicted. He was remorseful for his transgression, eager to bury the old man of sin, to resurrect the new man of faith, of godliness. . . . This was no silent, unexpressed wish or hope, but a heart-wrenching, imploring, begging, and pleading. It was vocal and powerful prayer."[54] He went on to ask,

> How many have thus persisted? How many, with or without serious transgressions, have ever prayed all day and into the night? Have many ever wept and prayed for ten hours? For five hours? For one? For thirty minutes? For ten? Our praying is usually measured in seconds and yet with a heavy debt to pay we still expect forgiveness of our sins. We offer pennies to pay the debt of thousands of dollars.
>
> How much do you pray, my friends? How often? How earnestly? If you have errors in your life, have you really wrestled before the Lord? Have you yet found your deep forest of solitude? How much has your soul hungered? How deeply have your needs impressed your heart? When did you kneel before your Maker in total quiet? For what did you pray—your own soul? How long did you thus plead for recognition—all day long? And when the shadows fell, did you still raise your voice in mighty prayer, or did you satisfy yourself with some hackneyed word and phrase?[55]

Why the Lord Allows Us to Wrestle

But why is such imploring required? Why such a steep price to be paid? Could the Redeemer resist such strugglings from Enos? Could he resist such strugglings from us? Isn't He the God who took upon Himself such infirmities so "that he may know according to the flesh how to succor his people according to their infirmities" (Alma 7:12)? We know that the Savior will never resist or ignore such sincere cries for help. And yet, we know that He will manifest Himself "in his own time, and in his own way, and according to his own will" (D&C 88:68).

Consider, for example, the following experience of the Savior with His Apostles on the Sea of Galilee. Shortly after Jesus miraculously fed the five thousand with two fish and five loaves of bread, Matthew tells us that Jesus sent His disciples to get into a ship and go to the other side of the sea. "And when he had sent the multitudes away, he went

up into a mountain apart to pray" (Matthew 14:23). Matthew then returned to the narrative with the Apostles and described how "the ship was now in the midst of the sea, tossed with waves: for the wind was contrary" (Matthew 14:24). According to John's account of this story, we learn that the disciples were laboriously toiling and rowing for about twenty-five to thirty furlongs (see John 6:19). This distance equates to somewhere between fifty-five to sixty-six lengths of a football field.

So we see this image of the disciples arduously rowing for their very lives! Perhaps they remembered the experience they had earlier where Jesus calmed the storm that had threatened their lives. Judging from the righteousness of the valiant Apostles, I would imagine that they were prayerful and earnestly sought heaven's help. But help did not seem to be coming. In fact, Matthew tells us that the divine help they sought did not come until the fourth watch of the night (which is between three and six in the morning). Now, it is safe to say that they probably did not begin this journey in the early hours of the morning. While we do not know exactly when they set out to sea, let's just imagine for a moment that they began their journey during the first watch of the night (between six and nine at night). These frightened disciples had now been rowing all through the night and into the morning. They were surely exhausted and wondering why, amidst their labor and fear, the Lord had still not come.

Mark's account provides an important statement that I believe teaches a profound principle. The record says that while the disciples struggled on the sea and the Lord sat up on the mountain, "*He saw them* toiling in rowing" (Mark 6:48; emphasis added). In other words, while they were fighting with every stroke of the oar, He sat on the mountainside watching them! Well, if He saw them struggling, then why did He wait until the fourth watch of the night to come and rescue them? This same question can be related back to the experience of Enos. It seems impossible to question the sincerity of Enos's heartfelt petitions. So, assuming he was sincere in his prayer, why would the Lord allow Enos to struggle, wrestle, and supplicate in mighty prayer all day and through the night?

The answer comes in the reality that, in His infinite wisdom, the Lord is not only interested in helping us return to live *with* Him, His work and glory is to help us become *like* Him. He allows each of us to pay an appropriate price because this is the process that leads to progression and eventual perfection. Through the wrestling, soul hungering, crying, and supplicating, we, like Enos, place the proper price on the blessings and approval of heaven. This process allowed him (Enos) to be made "at-one" with God, as he found himself "reconciled unto him through the atonement of Christ" (Jacob 4:11). As virtue would begin to garnish his thoughts through a remission of sins, he would begin to feel his confidence "wax strong in the presence of God" (D&C 121:45). Heaven does know how to set a proper price upon its goods. Enos helps us to see that, in the economy of heaven, the price to be paid to know your standing before God is to "offer your whole [soul] as an offering unto him" (Omni 1:26).

Having paid the price, the Lord accepted Enos's offerings with the divine declaration, "Enos, thy sins are forgiven thee, and thou shalt be blessed" (Enos 1:5). After hearing these soothing words, and knowing that God could not lie, Enos then experienced the sanctifying power of the Atonement of Jesus Christ as his guilt and impurities were "swept away" (Enos 1:6).

This divine cleansing elicited an inspiring question, which Enos asked: "Lord, how is it done?" (Enos 1:7). Anyone who has ever had a personal experience with the Savior's Atonement and felt of His redeeming power has likely asked some variation of this question. For example, after having felt the weight of the burden of sin, dealt with the uncomfortable and sickening feelings of being unclean, and felt the emptiness of having the Spirit temporarily withdraw, we can experience the redeeming grace of Christ. As we experience and rely on the influence of the Atonement, the burdens, guilt, and unclean feelings are taken. Everything changes. Burdens are made light. Guilt turns to peace. The Spirit is restored. In that moment, filled with deep emotion, we may ask, "Lord, how is it done?" Or, in other words, "Father, how did you do that? How did you take the pain, the hurt, and the bitter feelings, and replace them in an instant?" Our answer comes to us just as surely as it came to Enos: "Because of thy faith in Christ, . . . wherefore, go to, thy faith hath made thee whole" (Enos 1:8). Thus, if we pray as Enos prayed, wrestle as Enos wrestled, and trust as Enos trusted, we too can feel this divine change and immediately

look outward in striving to help others who seem to have become lost. Such is the miracle of the Atonement of Jesus Christ.

Our Experiences with Christ Bring a Divine Hope

We know from his record that Enos's experience led to "a desire for the welfare of [his] brethren, the Nephites," and that he "did pour out [his] whole soul unto God for them" (Enos 1:9). As he continued following the Lord's injunction to "go to," he began to pray "with many long strugglings for [his] brethren, the Lamanites" (Enos 1:11). Once again, we see the prophetic statement of Joseph Smith fulfilled as Enos became filled with the love of God and was no longer content with simply blessing his family alone but began to be anxious to reach out to the whole human race—even his perceived enemies.

As we study this miraculous experience and the faithful price paid by Enos, it would be useful for each of us to go through a self-evaluation in determining the "value" of our prayers. As we approach the throne of the Father, do we bring before Him "pennies to pay the debt of thousands of dollars," or are we offering "our whole souls as an offering unto him" (Omni 1:26)? Consider this prophetic invitation from President Kimball:

> If you have not, I sincerely hope that the time will soon come when, as others before you have, you will struggle in the spirit and cry mightily and covenant sincerely, so that the voice of the Lord God will come into your mind, as it did to Enos, saying: "Thy sins are forgiven thee, and thou shalt be blessed. . . . Because of thy faith in Christ . . . I will grant unto thee according to thy desires" (Enos 1:5, 8, 12). For this is the ultimate object of all prayer, to bring men closer to God, to give them a new birth, to make them heirs of his kingdom.[56]

What a profound statement! The object of prayer is to be brought closer to God, to become more like Him, and to prepare ourselves to one day return to His presence. As is so often the case, Enos's experience with the Lord led him to a lifetime of service in the kingdom until he felt his work was almost finished on this earth. He summarized his ministry by profoundly connecting his experiences with the Savior to his consecrated service in His kingdom. He wrote, "And I saw that I must soon go down to my grave, having been wrought upon by the power of God that I must preach and prophesy unto this people, and declare the word according to the truth which is in Christ. And I have declared it in all my days, and have rejoiced in it above that of the world" (Enos 1:26). Even after giving his life in the service of the Master, there is no sense that he had an ounce of regret. In fact, as he prepared to go down to his grave after offering a consecrated life to the Lord, we sense that he still considered himself to be an unprofitable servant. Nevertheless, this unprofitable servant taught one more significant lesson before closing his record.

Enos had experienced what it feels like to be unclean and to feel unworthy to stand in the presence of the Lord. However, after having sin and imperfection cleansed and purged from his soul, we sense his confidence began to, as stated earlier, "wax strong in the presence of God" (D&C 121:45). To conclude his record, he left us an undiluted testimony of having "hope through the atonement of Christ" (Moroni 7:41). *Preach My Gospel* defines hope as "an abiding trust that the Lord will fulfill His promises to you. It is manifest in confidence, optimism, enthusiasm, and patient perseverance. It is believing and expecting that something will occur."[57] Thus, this final testimony from Enos becomes an object lesson that we can all see and strive to emulate. As you read this final verse, pay particular attention to the words he used to demonstrate hope. He said, "And I soon go to the place of my rest, which *is* with my Redeemer; for *I know* that in him *I shall* rest. And I rejoice in the day when my mortal shall put on immortality, and *shall* stand before him; *then shall I see his face with pleasure*, and *he will* say unto me: Come unto me, ye blessed, there *is* a place prepared for you in the mansions of my father. Amen" (Enos 1:27; emphasis added).

What led to this divine assurance? Did Enos feel so confident before the Lord because of his works or some ecclesiastical résumé? Of course not. His confidence came to him in the same way that it can come to you and me. Confidence before God comes as we are "reconciled unto him through the atonement of Christ" (Jacob 4:11), as we rely on the "merits, and mercy, and grace of the Holy Messiah" (2 Nephi 2:8), and as we "press forward with a steadfastness in Christ, *having a perfect brightness of hope*" (2 Nephi 31:20; emphasis added).

Remember, the purpose of prayer—and the reason that God often allows us to wrestle before Him before we find the divine peace

we seek—is to be brought closer to Him, to be changed by Him so that we can one day become like and live with Him. Elder Jeffrey R. Holland promised,

> As you labor to know him, and to know that he knows you; as you invest your time—and inconvenience—in quiet, unassuming service, you will indeed find that "his angels [have] charge concerning thee: and in their hands they shall bear thee up" (Matthew 4:6). It may not come quickly. It probably won't come quickly, but there is purpose in the time it takes. Cherish your spiritual burdens because God will converse with you through them and will use you to do his work if you carry them well.[58]

Given the profound insight President Kimball provided into the life and experience of Enos, it seems appropriate to use an account from his life—indeed a wrestle that *he* had before God—to conclude this chapter. You may recognize the following struggle. The date was July 14, 1943. While this wrestle was not to receive a remission of sins, as Enos's was, President Kimball was, like Enos, wrestling to know his standing before God. In his own words, here is the account. Pay particular attention to the price he willingly paid in seeking divine approval.

> No peace had yet come, though I had prayed for it almost unceasingly. . . . I turned toward the hills. I had no objective. I wanted only to be alone. I had begun a fast. . . .
>
> My weakness overcame me again. Hot tears came flooding down my cheeks as I made no effort to mop them up. I was accusing myself, and condemning myself and upbraiding myself. I was praying aloud for special blessings from the Lord. I was telling him that I had not asked for this position, that I was incapable of doing the work, that I was imperfect and weak and human, that I was unworthy of so noble a calling, though I had tried hard and my heart had been right. I knew that I must have been at least partly responsible for offenses and misunderstandings which a few people fancied they had suffered at my hands. I realized that I had been petty and small many times. I did not spare myself. A thousand things passed through my mind. Was I called by revelation? . . .
>
> If I could only have the assurance that my call had been inspired most of my other worries would be dissipated. . . . I knew that I must have His acceptance before I could go on. I stumbled up the hill and

onto the mountain, as the way became rough. I faltered some as the way became steep. No paths were there to follow; I climbed on and on. Never had I prayed before as I now prayed. What I wanted and felt I must have was an assurance that I was acceptable to the Lord. I told Him that I neither wanted nor was worthy of a vision or appearance of angels or any special manifestation. I wanted only the calm peaceful assurance that my offering was accepted. Never before had I been tortured as I was now being tortured. And the assurance did not come. . . .

I mentally beat myself and chastised myself and accused myself. As the sun came up and moved in the sky I moved with it, lying in the sun, and still I received no relief. I sat up on the cliff and strange thoughts came to me: all this anguish and suffering could be ended so easily from this high cliff and then came to my mind the temptations of the Master when he was tempted to cast Himself down—then I was ashamed for having placed myself in a comparable position and trying to be dramatic. . . . I was filled with remorse because I had permitted myself to place myself . . . in a position comparable, in a small degree, to the position the Saviour found Himself in when He was tempted, and . . . I felt I had cheapened the experiences of the Lord, having compared mine with His. Again I challenged myself and told myself that I was only trying to be dramatic and sorry for myself.

Again, I lay on the cool earth. The thought came that I might take cold, but what did it matter now. There was one great desire, to get a testimony of my calling, to know that it was not human and inspired by ulterior motives, kindly as they might be. How I prayed! How I suffered! How I wept! How I struggled![59]

Eventually, peace came to this humble servant, even "the peace of God, which passeth all understanding" (Philippians 4:7). As President Kimball wrestled and wept, the Lord mercifully granted him a dream, perhaps even a vision. With this new experience, he said,

[The dream] came a calm like the dying wind, the quieting wave after the storm is passed. I got up, walked to the rocky point and sat on the same ledge. My tears were dry, my soul was at peace. A calm feeling of assurance came over me, doubt and questionings subdued. It was as though a great burden had been lifted. I sat in tranquil silence surveying the beautiful valley, thanking the Lord for the satisfaction and the reassuring answer to my prayers. Long I meditated here in peaceful quietude, apart, and I felt nearer my Lord than ever at any time in my life.[60]

Like Enos, President Kimball learned that those who desire divine assurance will come to understand that "there remaineth an effectual struggle to be made" (Mosiah 7:18). However, such devoted disciples will also come to know and experience the Lord's divine compassion as they experience a tender embrace, "encircled about eternally in the arms of his love" (2 Nephi 1:15).

And Thus We See

Let's conclude this chapter where we first began. Life has a way of teaching us that those things that are of greatest worth also require the greatest effort to obtain. Such was the case with Enos. Having sought a remission of his sins and a desire to know his standing before God, Enos showed the necessary investment to be made in order to obtain the riches of eternity. In so doing, Enos's story provides an example to follow for those of us who likewise seek to know our standing with God. As *we* wrestle, struggle, and beseech the Lord in prayer, we too can learn that the God of heaven will come to us, even run to us, and envelop us in His mercy and grace. Indeed, such consecrated imploring brings forth the closeness of heaven. And, having experienced this degree of heaven, we, like Enos, will not rest until we help the Father bring about heaven on earth.

Chapter 5: The People of King Benjamin

> King Benjamin's final address teaches us that when we enter places of worship and learn in the spirit of reverence and communion, we can experience an outpouring of divine grace. Through this experience, we learn that preparation precedes revelation, and that gaining an understanding of the Atonement can cause a mighty change in our hearts.

The Stewardship of Reputation

A couple of years ago, we had a visiting speaker at our stake youth standards night. This was a man who was extremely well known and, like Amulek, was "also a man of no small reputation among all those who know [him]" (Alma 10:4). In fact, we were actually his third fireside of the night. As this brother walked in, I observed the youth (a fascinating pastime if you are ever bored) and I could see their excitement as they watched this good brother make his way to the stand. Many of these youth had looked up to him for much of their young lives.

Having spoken with this brother on a few occasions, I know him to be an incredible priesthood holder, who in no way tries to draw attention to himself. It is clear that when he speaks at firesides and youth conferences, his primary motivation is to bless the lives of the individual members who attend. So when I saw this congregation of youth fix their eyes on him as he stood to begin his remarks, I knew that there was no pretention, no selfishness, and certainly no ulterior motives in his heart. As an educator, I could not help but notice what we refer to as "learner readiness." These young men and women had excitedly looked forward to this fireside for weeks, arrived early to make sure they were able to get a good seat, and now were ready to hear whatever message this brother had prepared to deliver.

As I sat in the congregation that night, I pondered this experience from a pedagogical perspective. It was clear to me that this group of youth was extremely excited for this talk. They had prepared their hearts and minds for this experience, and I was convinced that many lives were going to be blessed. Because of the previous efforts and reputation of this good brother, these "seedling saints"[61] sat cultivated and ready to be nourished by the Spirit.

As I pondered this situation, I had an interesting thought. I thought to myself, *This teacher's reputation has become a sacred and significant stewardship in which he is now expected by the Lord to deliver a powerful and scripturally substantive talk. Truly, where much is given, much is required, and as these students have now opened up their hearts, this teacher stands on holy ground.*

I learned that night that a person's reputation can become a significant stewardship. I also felt the truth that the only way to feed those who come to a class or a meeting hungry for things of the Spirit is to help them partake of the Bread of Life and to drink of the Living Water (see John 6 and 4).

There is a story about a man who was interested in being offered a position to teach in the Church Educational System. As part of the hiring process, prospective teachers are required to have an interview with a General Authority (I can say from personal experience that such opportunities are both extremely nerve-racking and edifying). As if the idea of an interview with a General Authority did not cause enough anxiety, this particular man was assigned to meet with Elder Joseph Fielding Smith. The story goes that Elder Smith asked this man what he intended to teach his students. Possibly thinking that this was a test of some sort, the man went on to mention several important gospel

principles. "Elder Smith looked at him lovingly but sternly and said, 'You teach Jesus Christ and him crucified.'"[62]

When given the stewardship to teach a group of people the restored gospel, we need to remember that whatever other gospel principles we are asked to teach, we must help the students "know to what source they may look for a remission of their sins" (2 Nephi 25:26). The story of King Benjamin's address demonstrates the "revelatory reciprocity"[63] that can happen when an inspired teacher and an inspired student understand and experience the doctrine of the Atonement of Jesus Christ together.

As the Book of Mormon narrative continues, Mormon tells us that the small plates were handed down from Enos and eventually were delivered into the hands of King Benjamin (who then put them with the large plates already in his possession). King Benjamin was a man beloved by his people. His reputation and relationship with his people likely played a significant role in the powerful experience recorded in chapters one through five of Mosiah (King Benjamin's famous address).

These chapters provide some of the most doctrinally substantive and inspiring passages in all of scripture. As is often the case when studying the scriptures, the context illuminates the content. This final address by this faithful prophet-king represents a profound meeting of the man, the moment, the message, and the multitude. What was said about another significant scriptural revelatory experience could be said of this experience shared by King Benjamin and his people: "The stage was set: preparation of a lifetime and preparation of the moment were recompensed with a heavenly endowment."[64] As we study this experience, looking at each of these key elements (the man, the moment, the message, and the multitude), we learn some important truths about how we can experience the Atonement of Jesus Christ in our own lives.

The Man

King Benjamin was clearly a man of "no small reputation" (Alma 10:4) and had earned the love and respect of his people. Perhaps it was the way he wielded the sword of Laban in defending his people and driving out the Lamanites (see Omni 1:34; Words of Mormon 1:11–18).

Or maybe it was the fact that he labored with his own hands in serving his people and thus became the epitome of a "servant leader" (see Mosiah 1:14). He was a king who insisted that his people not be "laden with taxes" and that he should not inflict them with anything that "was grievous to be borne" (Mosiah 2:14). King Benjamin labored "with all the might of his body and the faculty of his whole soul" in leading, teaching, and protecting his people (Words of Mormon 1:18).

King Benjamin was a man who loved the Lord and recognized his absolute reliance on heaven. It was Benjamin who helps us understand that we are "kept and preserved" by a merciful Father, who lends us breath from day to day (Mosiah 2:20–21). He helps us understand that we can never break-even with the Lord and can never repay Him for His kindness and mercy, or the blessings He so generously provides. Indeed, He helps us understand the reality that we are unprofitable servants who must "always retain in remembrance, the greatness of God, and [our] own nothingness" (Mosiah 4:11).

Even with all his power and influence, Benjamin magnified his stewardship by directing his people to their true King. "And behold also, if I, whom ye call your king, who has spent his days in your service, and yet has been in the service of God, do merit any thanks from you, O how you ought to thank your heavenly King!" (Mosiah 2:19).

This was a good man, a faithful man, even a man of Christ. Indeed, "King Benjamin also knew his own life was merely a type and shadow of Christ. He knew each person listening must turn his or her own heart, might, mind, and strength to God. Like the prophets before him, Benjamin realized that 'in every work that [one] began in the service of the house of God, and in the law, and in the commandments, to seek his God, he did it with all his heart'" (2 Chronicles 31:21).[65] While this section is not intended to be a complete biography of King Benjamin, it *is* intended to be a tribute to his faithfulness, and to introduce the idea that effectively studying and teaching the doctrine of the Atonement can often be the catalyst for an individual to seek the Lord and experience His grace.

The Moment

It is against this powerful backdrop that we read of Benjamin's conversation with his son Mosiah, in which he recognized that he had "waxed old, and he saw that he must very soon go the way of all the earth" (Mosiah 1:9). He spoke with his son and asked him to make a proclamation "unto all the people who were in the land of Zarahemla that thereby they might gather themselves together, to go up to the temple" so that he could speak to them before his death (Mosiah 1:18).

Because of the way that King Benjamin lived and ruled among the people, he had earned their trust and gained a strong reputation. The people loved and even revered this good man, and when they learned that he wanted to speak with them before his death, they came out in great numbers, even so great that they could not be numbered. Because "King Benjamin was a holy man, and he did reign over his people in righteousness" (Words of Mormon 1:17), his reputation and ability to righteously influence had perhaps become a more important stewardship than the kingdom itself.

This surely must have been an emotional moment for everyone as this beloved prophet-king stood atop a newly erected tower and, with his frame trembling before them, declared, "I say unto you that I have caused that ye should assemble yourselves together, that I might declare unto you that I can no longer be your teacher, nor your king" (Mosiah 2:29). Perhaps this announcement had the same effect that Joseph Smith's must have had as he spoke at the funeral of Ephraim Marks in Nauvoo in 1842.

Joseph said, "Some have supposed that Brother Joseph could not die, but this is a mistake: it is true there have been times when I have had the promise of my life to accomplish such and such things, but, having now accomplished those things, I have not at present any lease of my life. I am as liable to die as other men."[66] In both cases, the people surely thought that their beloved leaders would be spared, unable to even fathom the idea that there would be someone else who could teach, mentor, or lead them. And yet, for the people of King Benjamin, here was their prophet and king announcing his successor.

This emotional moment was only intensified as this beloved man declared, "I have not commanded you to come up hither to trifle with the words which I shall speak, but that you should hearken unto me, and open your ears that ye may hear, and your hearts that ye may understand, and your minds that the mysteries of God may be unfolded to your view" (Mosiah 2:9). He made clear that his purpose in speaking to them was not just to make an announcement, as important as that might be. From the beginning of this speech, from the hallowed ground on which he chose to hold this gathering, King Benjamin made clear that his intent was to have their hearts and minds touched that their conversion might deepen and that his people would rely more fully on their true, heavenly King.

The Message

While there are a variety of doctrines taught in this masterful sermon, the clear focus is the Atonement of Jesus Christ and our need to rely more fully upon His merits, mercy, and grace. Indeed, in his introductory comments, King Benjamin underscored the Lord's enabling grace as he declared that he has "been kept and preserved by his matchless power, to serve you with all the might, mind and strength which the Lord hath granted unto me" (Mosiah 2:11).

Perhaps better than anywhere else in all the scriptures, King Benjamin walks his people through what President Uchtdorf referred to as "a paradox of man," which is simply that "compared to God, man is nothing; yet we are everything to God."[67] King Benjamin helped them to identify and feel God's love as he explained that He "has created you, and has kept and preserved you, and has caused that ye should rejoice, and has granted that ye should live in peace one with another" (Mosiah 2:20). He would go on to teach that the Lord was preserving them from day to day, "lending [them] breath," even "preserving [them] from one moment to another" (Mosiah 2:21); but even if they were to "serve him with all [their] whole souls yet [they] would be unprofitable servants" (Mosiah 2:21). He taught, "Ye are eternally indebted to your heavenly Father, to render to him all that you have and are" (Mosiah 2:34).

This emphasis on the need to "always retain in remembrance, the greatness of God, and your own nothingness" (Mosiah 4:11) is laced

throughout this entire sermon. How does all of this relate to the Atonement of Jesus Christ?

Well, King Benjamin clearly understood that "just as a man does not really desire food until he is hungry, so he does not desire the salvation of Christ until he knows why he needs Christ."[68] And, as a master teacher, he also must have understood that "no one adequately and properly knows why he needs Christ until he understands and accepts the doctrine of the Fall and its effect upon all mankind."[69] Thus, King Benjamin effectively helped his people understand and feel their fallen state so that they were prepared to feel and believe that "there shall be no other name given nor any other way nor means whereby salvation can come unto the children of men, only in and through the name of Christ, the Lord Omnipotent" (Mosiah 3:17).

With his people in a deep state of readiness, King Benjamin provided a doctrinally drenched sermon on the Atonement, of our need to call in His name, "begging for a remission of [our] sins" (Mosiah 4:20), and our need to continually "grow in the knowledge of the glory of him" (Mosiah 4:12). The following are some of the powerful truths King Benjamin taught about the Atonement of Jesus Christ:

- "He shall suffer temptations, and pain of body, hunger, thirst, and fatigue, even more than man can suffer, except it be unto death; for behold, blood cometh from every pore, so great shall be his anguish for the wickedness and the abominations of his people" (Mosiah 3:7)
- "He cometh unto his own, that salvation might come unto the children of men even through faith on his name" (Mosiah 3:9)
- "And he shall rise the third day from the dead; and behold, he standeth to judge the world; and behold, all these things are done that a righteous judgment might come upon the children of men" (Mosiah 3:10)
- "His blood atoneth for the sins of those who have fallen by the transgression of Adam, who have died not knowing the will of God concerning them, or who have ignorantly sinned" (Mosiah 3:11)
- "Salvation cometh to none such except it be through repentance and faith on the Lord Jesus Christ" (Mosiah 3:12)

- "Whosoever should believe that Christ should come, the same might receive remission of their sins, and rejoice with exceedingly great joy, even as though he had already come among them" (Mosiah 3:13)
- "The law of Moses availeth nothing except it were through the atonement of his blood" (Mosiah 3:15)
- "Even if it were possible that little children could sin they could not be saved; but I say unto you they are blessed; for behold, as in Adam, or by nature, they fall, even so the blood of Christ atoneth for their sins" (Mosiah 3:16)
- "There shall be no other name given nor any other way nor means whereby salvation can come unto the children of men, only in and through the name of Christ, the Lord Omnipotent" (Mosiah 3:17)
- "Men drink damnation to their own souls except they humble themselves and become as little children, and believe that salvation was, and is, and is to come, in and through the atoning blood of Christ, the Lord Omnipotent" (Mosiah 3:18)
- "The natural man is an enemy to God, and has been from the fall of Adam, and will be, forever and ever, unless he yields to the enticings of the Holy Spirit, and putteth off the natural man and becometh a saint through the Atonement of Christ the Lord, and becometh as a child, submissive, meek, humble, patient, full of love, willing to submit to all things which the Lord seeth fit to inflict upon him, even as a child doth submit to his father" (Mosiah 3:19)
- "None shall be found blameless before God, except it be little children, only through repentance and faith on the name of the Lord God Omnipotent" (Mosiah 3:21)
- "If the knowledge of the goodness of God at this time has awakened you to a sense of your nothingness, and your worthless and fallen state—I say unto you, if ye have come to a knowledge of the goodness of God, and his matchless power, and his wisdom, and his patience, and his long-suffering towards the children of men; and also, the atonement which has been prepared from the foundation of the world, that thereby salvation might come

to him that should put his trust in the Lord . . . this is the man who receiveth salvation, through the atonement which was prepared from the foundation of the world" (Mosiah 4:5–7)

- "Believe that ye must repent of your sins and forsake them, and humble yourselves before God; and ask in sincerity of heart that he would forgive you" (Mosiah 4:10)
- "If ye have known of his goodness and have tasted of his love, and have received a remission of your sins . . . even so I would that ye should remember, and always retain in remembrance, the greatness of God, and your own nothingness, and his goodness and long-suffering towards you, unworthy creatures, and humble yourselves even in the depths of humility, calling on the name of the Lord daily, and standing steadfastly in the faith . . . if ye do this ye shall always rejoice, and be filled with the love of God, and always retain a remission of your sins" (Mosiah 4:11–12)
- "Because of the covenant which ye have made ye shall be called the children of Christ, his sons, and his daughters; for behold, this day he hath spiritually begotten you; for ye say that your hearts are changed through faith on his name; therefore, ye are born of him and have become his sons and his daughters" (Mosiah 5:7)
- "There is no other head whereby ye can be made free. There is no other name given whereby salvation cometh" (Mosiah 5:8)
- "I would that ye should be steadfast and immovable, always abounding in good works, that Christ, the Lord God Omnipotent, may seal you his, that you may be brought to heaven, that ye may have everlasting salvation and eternal life" (Mosiah 5:15)

President Boyd K. Packer taught that "true doctrine, understood, changes attitudes and behavior," and that "the study of the doctrines of the gospel will improve behavior quicker than a study of behavior will improve behavior."[70] We can combine this idea with Joseph Smith's statement that the most fundamental doctrines of our religion are "concerning Jesus Christ, that He died, was buried, and rose again the third day, and ascended into heaven; and all other things which pertain to our religion are only appendages to it."[71]

In other words, if we want to experience the mighty change spoken of by King Benjamin, we need to understand and experience the doctrine he taught about the Atonement of Jesus Christ. What makes these chapters of the Book of Mormon so powerful is that they not only provide the doctrinal substance that is at the heart of the change, but they also provide an example of hearts actually *being* changed when individuals understand these divine doctrines.

The Multitude

The experience of King Benjamin's people and how they prepared themselves for this pivotal experience is both instructive and inspiring. There are many lessons we can learn from their actions as we consider our responsibility to actively participate in the learning process and prepare our hearts and minds for a revelatory experience. As we study some of the actions taken, I would invite you to consider how we can prepare ourselves for these moments as we enter hallowed places of learning and worship.

Upon hearing the proclamation from Mosiah, we are told that "the people gathered themselves together" (Mosiah 2:1). This language is important because it indicates the exercise of agency as these people acted rather than being acted upon. This language is similar to that used when Helaman feared the people of Ammon would break their covenant and thus lose their souls.

You know what happened next: "But behold, it came to pass they had many sons, who had not entered into a covenant that they would not take their weapons of war to defend themselves against their enemies; *therefore they did assemble themselves together at this time*" (Alma 53:16; emphasis addded). In both accounts, it is clear that the people were anxious to do what was right and act for themselves in standing with the prophet. Are we proactive in putting ourselves in a position to stand with the prophets? Do we "gather ourselves" and our families together when the prophets invite us to act?

As the people arrived on the consecrated grounds of the temple, we are told that, according to the law of Moses, "they also took of the firstlings of their flocks, that they might offer sacrifice and burnt offerings" (Mosiah 2:3). These people entered this place of learning with obedient and submissive hearts.

Furthermore, they offered sacrifice unto the Lord "that they might give thanks to the Lord their God . . . that they might rejoice and be filled with love towards God and all men" (Mosiah 2:3–4). While King Benjamin's people were obedient unto the law of Moses in their burnt offerings, the Savior would later teach His people that they were no longer to offer up "the shedding of blood" but that they "shall offer for a sacrifice unto [Him] a broken heart and a contrite spirit" (3 Nephi 9:19–20).

He then promised that "whoso cometh unto me with a broken heart and a contrite spirit, him will I baptize with fire and with the Holy Ghost" (3 Nephi 9:20). Thus, if we seek revelatory experiences when we gather ourselves together to places of learning and worship, we must likewise offer our whole hearts and souls unto the Lord. After all, "The real act of personal sacrifice is not now nor ever has been placing an animal on the altar. Instead, it is a willingness to put the animal that is in us upon the altar—then willingly watching it be consumed!"[72] As we offer such divine sacrifice, we are promised the sanctifying experience of being "baptized with fire and with the Holy Ghost" (3 Nephi 9:20). What an important promise as we gather ourselves together to learn and worship our God.

The record indicates that "when they came up to the temple, they pitched their tents round about, *every man according to his family*" (Mosiah 2:5; emphasis added). Families are the fundamental unit in the kingdom of God, and the greatest responsibility for gospel teaching and learning rests firmly upon the shoulders of parents. The scriptures are clear that "inasmuch as parents have children in Zion, or in any of her stakes which are organized, that teach them not to understand the doctrine . . . the sin be upon the heads of the parents" (D&C 68:25).

It is significant that the parents brought their children to hear the words of the prophet. They seemed to understand that their children were "spiritually working on toward a maturity which they will early reach if [they] but feed them the right food."[73] Indeed, the record goes on to indicate that this experience deeply impacted the hearts of the entire congregation, and that it was the children who were too young to understand King Benjamin's words who would later fall into apostasy. This seems to suggest that the youth and those old enough to understand the words spoken in this great sermon remained converted to the gospel. It was surely such a blessing for these faithful parents who had the spiritual foresight to gather their families together on this sacred occasion.

One final note on the preparation of the people. As they gathered themselves together in families, "they pitched their tents round about the temple, every man having his tent with the door thereof towards the temple" (Mosiah 2:6). While the primary purpose of facing their tents toward the temple was clearly a practical decision (to remain in their tents while they heard King Benjamin speak), the symbolism is too good to ignore.

President Howard W. Hunter invited us to "establish the temple of the Lord as the great symbol of [our] membership." He went on to express that as we proverbially pitch our tents toward the temple, we can "be consistent and loyal in every walk of life, for we will be committed to a single, sacred standard of conduct and belief. Whether at home or in the marketplace, whether at school or long after school is behind us, whether we are acting totally alone or in concert with a host of other people, our course will be clear and our standards will be obvious."[74]

The temple is designed to point our souls to the Savior and to bring us into communion with Him. With the vision of the temple as the backdrop, the Christ-centered message from their feeble yet dedicated prophet, and with the people's hearts and minds prepared to receive his message, the stage was set for an immensely powerful, revelatory experience. Indeed, with the meeting of the man, the moment, the message, and the multitude would come a wonderful, marvelous miracle.

The Miracle

The Savior promised that "where two or three are gathered together in my name . . . behold, there will I be in the midst of them" (D&C 6:32). King Benjamin made clear that they were indeed gathered together in His name, as his primary purpose for this meeting was to "give [the] people a name" (Mosiah 1:11), and they were later invited to "take upon [themselves] the name of Christ" (Mosiah 5:8). The Lord's promise was fulfilled as these faithful people felt the Lord's

presence and experienced a divine communion with the Master. As King Benjamin taught pure doctrine, the congregation experienced what Paul describes as being sanctified and cleansed "with the washing of water by the word" (Ephesians 5:26).

The record states that "when King Benjamin had made an end of speaking the words which had been delivered unto him by the angel of the Lord, that he cast his eyes round about on the multitude, and behold they had fallen to the earth, for the fear of the Lord had come upon them" (Mosiah 4:1).

They had also fallen to the earth because "they had viewed themselves in their own carnal state, even less than the dust of the earth" (Mosiah 4:2). Perhaps they understood Mormon's commentary in the book of Helaman as he proclaimed, "O how great is the nothingness of the children of men; yea, even they are less than the dust of the earth. For behold, the dust of the earth moveth hither and thither, to the dividing asunder, at the command of our great and everlasting God" (Helaman 12:7–8).

It is not happenstance that, as this experience was transpiring, King Benjamin invited his people to "always retain in remembrance, the greatness of God, and [their] own nothingness" (Mosiah 4:11). We know that they remembered the greatness of God as they cried out, "O have mercy, and apply the atoning blood of Christ" (Mosiah 4:2). They knew of His mercy and trusted in His grace. Perhaps they remembered their former years when they were battling the Lamanites and conquered their enemies "in the strength of the Lord" (Words of Mormon 1:14). Elder Bednar invited us to think of the enabling and strengthening power of the Savior's grace each time we read the phrase *in the strength of the Lord* in the scriptures.[75] Surely their previous experiences with the Lord led them to cry out for His mercy in this moment of tender contrition.

The specific prayer of the people of King Benjamin was to "apply the atoning blood of Christ that we may receive forgiveness of our sins, *and* our hearts may be purified" (Mosiah 4:3; emphasis added). One of the most interesting words in that prayer is the word *and*. The people not only desired to have a forgiveness of their sins but also sought to have their hearts purified and changed. After all, their prophet had just taught them that they were to both put "off the natural man *and* [become] a saint through the atonement of Christ the Lord" (Mosiah 3:19; emphasis added). The scriptures further declare that the Atonement leads to our being justified (forgiven and made clean) and sanctified (changed and made whole), and that we are to have both "clean hands, *and* a pure heart" (Psalm 24:4; emphasis added).

Elder Bednar commented on this doctrine:

> Let me suggest that hands are made clean through the process of putting off the natural man and by overcoming sin and the evil influences in our lives through the Savior's Atonement. Hearts are purified as we receive His strengthening power to do good and become better. All of our worthy desires and good works, as necessary as they are, can never produce clean hands and a pure heart. It is the Atonement of Jesus Christ that provides both a *cleansing and redeeming power* that helps us to overcome sin and a *sanctifying and strengthening power* that helps us to become better than we ever could by relying only upon our own strength. The infinite Atonement is for both the sinner and for the saint in each of us.[76]

It is clear that when these people offered their heartfelt prayer, they sought real change. They sought divine change, the kind of permanent change that would both root out the natural and carnal and lead them to become men and women of Christ. As they experienced this change, their hearts "were filled with joy, having received a remission of their sins, and having peace of conscience" (Mosiah 4:3). They movingly testified that "because of the Spirit of the Lord Omnipotent, which has wrought a mighty change in us, or in our hearts, that *we have no more disposition to do evil, but to do good continually*" (Mosiah 5:2; emphasis added).

The Atonement of Jesus Christ helps us to remove the natural and the ungodly while enabling us to "act in doctrine and principle" (D&C 101:78), according to the will of God. Such was the case with the people of King Benjamin. The mighty change spoken of seems to have taken hold upon their hearts and led them to a lifetime of consecrated discipleship.

I recently had a humbling experience that led me to my knees in gratitude for the doctrine of the Atonement and for the spiritually

hungry young people I am fortunate enough to teach. We had been studying the doctrine of the Atonement together and had just read Elder Holland's quote mentioned earlier: "After an encounter with the living Son of the living God, nothing is ever again to be as it was before."[77] After reading this quote together, it was clear that the youth were in a state of readiness. We felt the Spirit and the closeness of heaven strongly. At such times, we as teachers especially feel our own nothingness and the greatness of God.

I had the distinct impression to take our discussion to a deeper level by asking the students a question. The only challenge with this prompting was that I did not know exactly how to ask the question I felt to ask and, as we all sometimes do, I hesitated to put such a precious topic in front of the students. After several minutes of grappling with these feelings, I finally followed the prompting and was honest with the class. I told them that I did not know how to ask the question I felt, and so I was just going to put my seemingly disconnected thoughts out there and hope that they would be able to discern what I was asking.

What I said to them was that there were probably several students in this class who thought about the Savior in a grateful manner and who genuinely appreciated the lessons, the miracles, and the Atonement of Jesus Christ. I then said that there were likely others in the class who had truly experienced one of these divine encounters with the Savior and have felt the truth that, after such an encounter, nothing was again to be as it was before. I then asked them the question, "For those of you who have had these experiences, what is the difference between the two?"

After having asked the question, I will confess that I was still a little bit nervous because I was not sure if they would understand my question or, even if they did, if they would be willing to be open enough to share such personal thoughts and feelings.

I cannot adequately describe the emotions that came as student after student shared powerful experiences in which they had come to know Christ on a personal and intimate level. They shared questions and doubts they had that led to their personal witnesses, and challenges they faced and how the Savior reached out with His encircling arms of love. They even shared about how they felt His grace when they repented and were made whole. When we wrapped up the class for the day, the only thing I could do was thank them for the feelings we had shared and add my simple testimony to their profound witnesses.

As we studied the doctrine of the Atonement of Jesus Christ together, many of us felt and experienced the power of His grace in that moment. Indeed, many of us experienced a mighty change that led us to have "no more disposition to do evil, but to do good continually" (Mosiah 5:2).

And Thus We See

King Benjamin was a man of God, and his people had come to respect and obey their beloved king. This relationship became a sacred stewardship. He clearly understood this as he prepared himself for this monumental gathering. Furthermore, this prophet-king chose the better part, as he focused his teachings on the Atonement of Jesus Christ and our need to rely on Him. The people had gathered themselves together in families and had opened their ears, their hearts, and their minds to hear the words that would be declared that day. The Lord rewarded their preparations with an outpouring of His divine grace.

Elder David A. Bednar spoke about his desire to remove the word *meeting* from the vocabulary of the Latter-day Saints. He said, "If members of families, as they come together, would think in terms of 'I'm preparing to participate in a revelatory experience with my family' instead of going to a meeting . . . I think we would prepare and act much differently."[78]

Such was certainly the case with King Benjamin and his people. From the experiences of these devoted Saints, we see that when an inspired teacher and a prepared student gather in the name of the Lord, His grace will attend them as they experience revelatory reciprocity. We see that gaining an understanding of—and acting upon—the doctrine of the Atonement can both cleanse our hearts and change our nature. We have seen that "when you choose to follow Christ, you choose to be changed,"[79] and that "no man can sincerely resolve to apply to his daily life the teachings of Jesus of Nazareth without sensing a change in his own nature. The phrase 'born again' has a deeper significance than many people attach to it. This *changed feeling* may be indescribable, *but it is real.*"[80]

Ryan H. Sharp

Like the people of King Benjamin, we too can experience firsthand "the atoning blood of Christ" (Mosiah 4:2) and be found with both clean hands *and* a pure heart.

Chapter 6: Alma the Elder and His Followers

> As a priest in King Noah's court, Alma confessed to being "caught in a snare" and doing many things that caused him "sore repentance" (Mosiah 23:9). As he and his people experienced the mercy of Christ, they felt "their hearts knit together in love one towards another" (Mosiah 18:21). Places become sacred because of what happens there. Alma and his people help us to see the beauty and sanctity of the places in which we come to know the Savior.

Sacred Places

About six or so months ago, I was working as a full-time seminary teacher and was right in the middle of teaching the Book of Mormon—one of the ultimate delights for all seminary teachers.

One night, my wife and I were in the kitchen cleaning up after dinner when I received a message from a former mission companion of mine. We had served together in New Zealand, but he was from Australia.

The message said, "Hey mate, I just bought a college. What would it take to get you to come down here to help me expand it?" I immediately showed it to my wife, and we initially had a good laugh about it, thinking how moving our little family to Australia seemed way too farfetched. However, after a lot of thought and even more prayer, we felt that the Lord wanted us to take this opportunity. Within just a few weeks of making this decision, we were packed up and ready to head Down Under!

This experience proved to be rewarding for our family, as we were able to do things we would have never dreamed of doing together. After we had been in the country for three months, however, my short-term visa was about to expire. This became an issue because our application for the long-term work visa was not even close to being processed, and we could not apply for another short-term visa while living in Australia. My wife and I decided that I would take our two older boys (ages seven and five) to New Zealand, where we would apply for a visa with hopes of coming home in just a couple of days (it had, after all, only taken a day for us to be given our initial visa).

Though I would have enjoyed returning to Auckland, where I served my mission, we decided to save a few dollars and fly into the Wellington Airport. We arrived on Wednesday night just before midnight. I decided to get the boys in bed and then get the application submitted immediately, with hopes of expediting the processing time. We spent the next two days living like vagabonds as we waited to get word from the department of immigration. In fact, because my Australian phone did not work overseas, each morning we would pack up all of our luggage and go back and forth to the library all day (the only place I could get Internet), hoping to get word that the visas were granted and that we were authorized to reenter the country. Because we had already booked a ticket to fly out on Friday, we decided to "plan with faith" and show up at the airport, anticipating that the approval would be granted. As we approached twenty minutes before takeoff, it was clear that we were not going to be going home when we had expected.

Fortunately for us, there was a shuttle back to the hotel, and I was able to get the boys in bed shortly thereafter. I, however, could not sleep. I was frustrated, annoyed, confused, and exhausted. It was now late Friday night. I knew there was no way the department would be working on this over the weekend, so I decided to try to make the most of the trip. I found a flight from Wellington to Auckland for under ninety dollars, and Saturday morning we hopped on a plane, then rented a car upon arrival in Auckland.

It was an interesting feeling to be standing in the exact airport and in the exact spots where I had stood some eleven years prior as I concluded my mission in this wonderful country. After getting the boys lunch, I decided to take them on a little mission tour. As we drove around, I talked with them about what my mission had been like, the people I came to know and love, and the memorable experiences I had while serving the Lord as a full-time representative. I took the boys to several of the chapels I met in and was able to tell them about some of the people whom we were able to meet and had the opportunity to teach and baptize. I showed them a couple of the missionary apartments we had stayed in and shared with them some of the rich experiences I had during my morning studies. I even took them to the homes of some the converts from my mission and told them about the experiences we shared together.

During some of these stops, it was difficult for me to control my emotions as I thought back to the profound experiences I had while serving these people whom I came to adore. I felt I had stood on sanctified and holy ground those days as I was reminded of how merciful the Lord had been to me as a missionary and how merciful He was being still. I was privileged to be with my boys at those holy sites. Thus, what I thought to be an inconvenience turned out to be one of the more spiritual experiences I have had and generated a special bond between my boys and me. Even now, as I stumble in my efforts to adequately describe this tender experience, I am left to say, with Ammon, "I cannot say the smallest part which I feel" (Alma 26:16).

Elder Marlin K. Jensen taught that "there are places on this earth that have been made sacred by what happened there."[81] Think of Moses as he approached the burning bush on Mount Sinai. You will recall that the Lord instructs him to "put off thy shoes from off thy feet, for the place whereon thou standest is holy ground" (Exodus 3:5). Or consider a small grove of "towering beeches, oaks, maples, and other trees, about one quarter of a mile west of the Joseph and Lucy Mack Smith family home near Palmyra."[82] It was in this grove of trees, and in response to the fervent prayer of a fourteen-year-old boy, that God the Father and the Son, Jesus Christ, appeared and once again rent the heavens that many thought had been forever sealed. It is because of this experience that this small grove of trees became appropriately known as the Sacred Grove. As we have personal encounters with divinity, the very places in which these experiences occur become precious and special to us. These places remind us of the love, mercy, and influence of the Almighty, and, like my experience tracing the steps from my mission with my boys, they also elicit deep spiritual feelings of gratitude. Such was certainly the case with the divine experiences of Alma and his followers in the land of Mormon.

The Conversion of Alma and the Power of One

While we do not know a lot about Alma's life prior to Abinadi's ministry, he does make mention of the iniquity of King Noah and his priests and humbly confesses that he himself was caught in that snare and "did many things which were abominable in the sight of the Lord" (Mosiah 23:9). We know that when Zeniff conferred the kingdom upon King Noah, one of the first points of business was to "put down all the priests that had been consecrated by his father and, [consecrate] new ones in their stead, such as were lifted up in the pride of their hearts" (Mosiah 11:5). We know these priests were supported by the people "in their laziness, and in their idolatry, and in their whoredoms" (Mosiah 11:6). Furthermore, we are told that Noah "placed his heart upon his riches, and he spent his time in riotous living with his wives and his concubines," and that his priests also spent "their time with harlots" (Mosiah 11:14). Once again, we do not know the degree to which Alma was involved in this gross iniquity, but we do know that he was numbered among those in transgression. This time period was the personification of Ralph Waldo Emerson's insightful observation: "It is the old story again: once we had wooden chalices and golden priests, now we have golden chalices and wooden priests."[83] However, with the impactful message and ministry of the prophet Abinadi, all of that was about to change.

Abinadi came into the land with a message of hope to this fallen people. He had such confidence in his calling that he boldly stood up to these wicked people and explained that the Lord would protect him until he had delivered his message (see Mosiah 13:2, 9). While the Lord's preservation of Abinadi's life was surely in part to cleanse

his garments of their blood, it is hard to imagine a more important purpose than giving the Spirit an opportunity to touch the heart of a particular young priest.

Though Abinadi took this opportunity to testify of the law, it seems that his focus was to give glory to the Creator of the law. While he spoke of sin and the consequences of sin, it seems that he did so to help his listeners more fully understand the mission of Him who provides redemption from sin. He spoke of the "sting of death" to help them understand that it is "swallowed up in Christ" (Mosiah 16:8). To make his point absolutely clear, he told these priests, "If ye teach the law of Moses, also teach that it is a shadow of those things which are to come—teach them that redemption cometh through Christ the Lord" (Mosiah 16:14–15).

We are told that not only did the people disregard these profound prophetic declarations; they took him and would "cause that he should be put to death" (Mosiah 17:1). After boldly declaring that he would not recall the words he had spoken, Abinadi *was* taken and *was* bound. He ultimately "suffered death by fire; yea, having been put to death because he would not deny the commandments of God, having sealed the truth of his words by his death" (Mosiah 17:20). So ended the life and ministry of this mighty messenger, destined to teach a hardened people and to die a martyr's death without eliciting any change in their sinful hearts—or so it would seem.

As King Noah commanded the priests to take Abinadi and put him to death, we are told that "there was one among them whose name was Alma . . . *and he believed* the words which Abinadi had spoken" (Mosiah 17:2; emphasis added). His heart had been pricked, and he now understood the wickedness of which Abinadi had testified. As the Spirit began to work upon this young man, he was led to courageously stand up to the corrupt king and plead with him that he might allow Abinadi to go in peace. But the prophet's fate was sealed. He had delivered the message he was sent to declare. Indeed, his time had come.

But lest this story end in somber tones, we must remember that though Abinadi would die a martyr's death, his message would live. King Noah's anger was so hot that when Alma pleaded for the release of Abinadi, he was banished from the kingdom and threatened with the same fate as the prophet. As Alma fled for his life, we are told that he "hid himself that they found him not. And he being concealed for many days *did write all the words which Abinadi had spoken*" (Mosiah 17:4; emphasis added), thus preserving Abinadi's matchless message. Furthermore, we are told that after Alma had repented, he went about the people and began to "teach the words of Abinadi" (Mosiah 18:1; see also Mosiah 18:19). Thus, it was the words of Abinadi that would lead to the conversion of about 450 souls![84]

In a great scriptural representation of learning by faith, we are told that "as many as believed him went thither to hear his words" (Mosiah 18:6). Those who gathered themselves together were taught about repentance, redemption, faith, the baptismal covenant, and much more. Alma taught them that the covenant of baptism included a willingness to "bear one another's burdens," "mourn with those that mourn," "comfort those that stand in need of comfort," and "stand as witnesses of God at all times and in all things, and in all places" (Mosiah 18:8–9). He promised his people that if they would cleave to God's covenants, they would "be redeemed of God, and be numbered with those of the first resurrection, that [they] may have eternal life" (Mosiah 18:9). Alma invited them to witness their desire to follow the Son by entering into the waters of baptism. But, like any great teacher, his invitation ended with a divine promise. He promised them that if they would enter this covenant, then the Lord would "pour out his Spirit more abundantly upon [them]" (Mosiah 18:10). When the people heard this, they "clapped their hands for joy, and exclaimed: This is the desire of our hearts" (Mosiah 18:11).

Before moving on with the rest of the story, I want to highlight a significant phrase from one of Alma's promises. Note that the final promise was that the Lord would pour His Spirit out upon the people in even greater abundance. Perhaps it was this promise that elicited the joyful excitement demonstrated by this Nephite flock. You may recall in 3 Nephi 19, when the Lord departed and the people knelt in prayer. Do you remember what they prayed for? The record says that "they did pray for that which they most desired; and they desired that the Holy Ghost should be given unto them" (3 Nephi 19:9). Just like those later Nephites in the land Bountiful, Alma's people sought this divine companionship. Alma clearly understood the sanctifying

effect of such an outpouring as he took Helam into the water and pleaded before the Master, saying, "O Lord, pour out thy Spirit upon thy servant, *that he may do this work with holiness of heart*" (Mosiah 18:12; emphasis added). Alma not only sought the comfort of the Spirit, but he also desired that he and his people be "sanctified by the reception of the Holy Ghost" (3 Nephi 27:20).

The Power of Godliness Is Manifest in Priesthood Ordinances

I believe there is an important doctrinal lesson to be learned here. The scriptures teach that it is in the ordinances of the priesthood that the power of godliness is manifest (see Doctrine and Covenants 84:20). Among other things, the power of godliness is the power "to make you holy, and your sins are forgiven you" (D&C 60:7). Nephi taught that his seed would "come to the knowledge of their Redeemer and the very points of his doctrine [the doctrine of Christ], that they may know *how* to come unto him and be saved" (1 Nephi 15:14; emphasis added). What is the doctrine of Christ? Simply stated, it is faith in the Lord Jesus Christ, repentance through the Atonement of Christ, baptism by immersion for the remission of sins (through the Atonement of Christ), being sanctified in Christ by the reception of the Holy Ghost, and finally "endurance of faith on his name to the end" (Moroni 3:3). There is a reason that a missionary's purpose is to "invite others to come unto Christ by helping them receive the restored gospel through faith in Jesus Christ and His Atonement, repentance, baptism, receiving the gift of the Holy Ghost, and enduring to the end."[85] Ordinances are not just an outward expression of an inner commitment, though that is part of it. Participating in saving ordinances is what provides an individual with the opportunity to experience the power of godliness and to fully lay hold upon the blessings of the Atonement! If this is done with "full purpose of heart, acting no hypocrisy and no deception before God, but with real intent . . . then cometh a remission of your sins by fire and by the Holy Ghost" (2 Nephi 31:13, 17).

Now, in this doctrinal context, let's return to Alma and his people. With the promise that by obedience to the covenant and ordinance of baptism they could have the Spirit of the Lord poured out upon them, they clapped their hands and came forward to accept this opportunity. We are told that Alma first took a man by the name of Helam into the water and there, "having authority from the Almighty God" (Mosiah 18:13), immersed both himself and Helam. When they both came forth out of the water, they rejoiced as they were filled with the Spirit of God. Indeed, the power of godliness had been manifest. Alma then remained in the water to baptize a total of 204 people in the waters of Mormon (though the number of followers would reach 450 by the end of the chapter). As final evidence of the outpouring of the Spirit, the record says that those who came forth and were baptized by this authorized priesthood holder were "filled with the grace of God" and would experience a mighty change of heart (Mosiah 18:16).

This band of believers became living evidence of the statement that once an individual experiences an "encounter with the living Son of the living God, nothing is ever again to be as it was before."[86] So powerful was this cleansing and sanctifying that there was no contention among them, "having their hearts knit together in unity and in love" (Mosiah 18:21). They observed the Sabbath day, gave thanks to the Lord on a daily basis, gathered themselves together in worship and fellowship as often as was possible, and imparted of their substance—both temporally and spiritually—that there might be no poor among them. Their experience with the power of godliness was so complete that they were, by scriptural definition, living a Zion lifestyle (see Moses 7:18).

All of this provides the context for the final principle I wish to stress from the experiences of Alma and his followers. You will recall that we began this chapter by talking about the power of place, and that there are some places that have become hallowed and sanctified by virtue of what transpired there. The Book of Mormon states that all of the experiences shared by Alma and his followers were "done in Mormon, yea, by the waters of Mormon, in the forest that was near the waters of Mormon; yea, the place of Mormon, the waters of Mormon, the forest of Mormon, *how beautiful are they to the eyes of them who there came to the knowledge of their Redeemer; yea, and how blessed are they, for they shall sing to his praise forever*" (Mosiah 18:30; emphasis added). This forest became more than a place of physical

refuge from King Noah and his servants. Because of the divine experiences shared in the land of Mormon, it became a spiritual refuge for these Saints, who there came to the knowledge of their Redeemer. Thus, like the Sacred Grove, the waters and land of Mormon were made holy because of what happened there.

Cleansed by Coming unto Christ

Perhaps one other story will help to tie all of this together. As I mentioned previously, I had the opportunity to serve in the Auckland New Zealand Mission. In one of my areas, we began working with and teaching a less-active single mother and her children. After visiting the family a couple of times, we learned that there was another young single mother in the home with her little two-year-old daughter. We learned that she was not a member of the Church, and she let us know that she was not interested in becoming one. Whenever we would come around, she would say hello and head back to her room with her daughter. Over time, however, she would walk down the hallway, as if she were going to her room, but would then sit around the corner, listening in on our lessons. After listening from a distance, she became more interested and agreed to let us teach her. She quickly accepted the message of the Restoration and, after overcoming a Word of Wisdom issue, committed to be baptized.

This young lady was extremely insecure and anxious. In fact, if she had it her way, there would have only been three people at the baptism: herself, my companion, and me. Having arrived early, we made sure the font was filled and everything was in place. This young mother sat in the front row in her white clothes, anxious to get started. Just before we were about to start, an older brother randomly approached me and said (in broken English), "Elders, maybe you could baptize my granddaughter?" We spoke to his bishop, who said that this little eight-year-old girl was ready to be baptized. Though random and unexpected, we agreed to baptize this little girl first.

As the service began, we sang and prayed together and heard a couple of powerful talks about the first principles and ordinances of the gospel. In the middle of the second talk, I heard someone loudly whisper, "Elder!" I looked over and saw that it was the second counselor in the bishopric, who was a massive Tongan fellow. His "whisper" turned out to be quite loud and caused everyone to look at me. As I looked at him, he again whispered, "Elder, the water." I thought, *Yeah, there is water . . . it is a baptism after all.* Sensing my confusion, he said, "No, the water . . . it's gone!" As we all know, water is a pretty significant part of the service. Somehow most of the water had drained out. There was less than a foot left in the bottom of the font.

Nervous, frustrated, and feeling the pressure of the moment, we called the man who had the key to the font and explained the situation. He hurried down and began to fill the font. However, this was a brand new chapel, and thus the font was constructed with an automatic fill feature. There was a little knob that you would put the key in, and as soon as you turned the key, it would automatically fill the font with enough water for a baptism. Unfortunately, the man with the key was feeling anxious himself and began to turn the key again and again and again until he had turned it five times. So each time he turned the key, the font would begin a brand new cycle! Thus, the jets unloaded water and continued doing so for the next several hours.

Knowing of the anxiety of our timid investigator, we approached her and asked if she wanted to reschedule for later that night when things had calmed down a bit. She said that everyone was already there, so she wanted to proceed with the service. As we opened the double doors to the font, we found the glass to be completely fogged over. We quickly squeegeed the glass so that everyone in the congregation could watch. We also unplugged the drain so that we could at least maintain a status quo with the water level and avoid flooding. I then invited the little eight-year-old girl to come into the font. It was actually a little funny because the water level was so high by then, it came up to her neck. All I had to do to baptize her was simply lean her to the side a little bit and she was fully immersed. I then invited our investigator in, and she seemed to be relatively calm. As we entered the water to perform the ordinance, we were both being blasted by the jets. After the baptism, we had one more speaker, a hymn, and a prayer. It is safe to say that from my finite, mortal, and fallen perspective, this would potentially go down as the least impressive baptismal service in the history of the Church (and

with the Church having been around for over 170 years at that point, I thought that was really saying something). However, I learned a lesson that night that continues to have deep significance in my life.

As we walked out of the chapel, I embarrassingly and almost apologetically asked this recent convert what she thought of the baptism. I will confess that I fully expected her to laugh or feel angry or even a little embarrassed. However, there was none of that. In fact, her response taught us more than we could have ever hoped to teach her. She turned to us and said, "Elders, I finally feel clean!" Here was a woman who had overcome a Word of Wisdom issue, had a child out of wedlock, and battled a number of other personal challenges. Whereas my perspective had been distorted by the physical setting of the ordinance, her heart was riveted by the miracle of the Atonement of Jesus Christ. She had felt the purging and its sanctifying effects and experienced the power of godliness. As I walked away from that experience, I learned for myself that it is in the ordinances of the priesthood that the power of godliness is manifest, and that even if we mortals sometimes get in the way, the Lord is still able to do His work. While she did not clap her hands in joy like the people of Alma, she did come "forth out of the water rejoicing, being filled with the Spirit" (Mosiah 18:14). She was "filled with the grace of God" (Mosiah 18:16), and we all felt that she had come to a knowledge of her Redeemer and experienced firsthand of His rescuing power.

The Power of Place

To bring this full circle, let's return to the experience I had with my two little boys as we toured my mission together. I will never forget the excitement I felt as we approached the chapel where that baptism took place. As we got out of the car, I almost instinctively returned to the spot where we had the conversation with that recent convert. While the surroundings had changed a bit over the past ten years, this particular spot seemed even more beautiful than it did that night so many years ago. Indeed, this particular spot had become my "waters of Mormon," as I there came to a deeper knowledge of my Redeemer and of His holy work.

Before concluding this chapter, I want to return to the account of Alma and his people in the land of Mormon, because this story has a deeper significance than we sometimes understand. We know the Book of Mormon is named after Mormon because he had the divine responsibility of abridging the plates. But where did Mormon's name originate? In 3 Nephi 5:12, Mormon is autobiographical as he states, "And behold, I am called Mormon, being called after the land of Mormon, the land in which Alma did establish the church among the people." Not only did the events that took place in the land of Mormon become hallowed to the people of Alma, they have by extension become holy to everyone who reads the Book of Mormon. Members of the Church are often referred to as *Mormons*. While this stems from our belief in the Book of Mormon, we need to remember that the Book of Mormon is named after the prophet Mormon, and that he is named after the land of Mormon that became significant because of the experiences with the Lord that took place there. Commenting on this, Elder Joseph B. Wirthlin said:

> Just as the land of Mormon became beautifully sacred to those "who there came to the knowledge of their Redeemer," so the Book of Mormon becomes divinely sacred to those millions of people who come "to the knowledge of their Redeemer" as they study, ponder, and pray about its powerful testimony of Jesus Christ.
>
> I hope, as we pay appropriate tribute to Mormon, Moroni, and Joseph Smith for their great work in preparing and bringing forth the Book of Mormon, that we will also remember the part Alma the Elder played in giving us the sacred name of the book. Whenever you think of the Book of Mormon or hear the name Mormon, I hope you will remember not only Alma the Elder but also the sacred significance of a holy place, a place sanctified by the Spirit, which burned in the hearts of "them who there came to the knowledge of their Redeemer" and which made the waters, and the forest, and the place of Mormon eternally beautiful to their eyes. How marvelous that the Book of Mormon, the most powerful instrument upon the face of the earth today for bringing all who will heed its message to "the knowledge of their Redeemer," should bear the name of this hallowed place![87]

Elder Withlin concluded his commentary by suggesting that when we are referred to as *Mormons*, we should remember the beautiful land of Mormon and think of the "stalwart life and ministry of Alma the Elder."[88] He suggested that when we think about the

experiences that took place there and remember the miracle of the Book or Mormon and its invitation for all of us to come to the knowledge of our Redeemer and experience His power to cleanse, change, and save.

And a Thus We See

The overarching invitation of the Book of Mormon is to "come unto Christ, and be perfected in Him" (Moroni 10:32). When, where, and how that happens can sometimes look different from person to person. What remains constant, however, is the role of ordinances and the deep impact of our experiences with the Lord. As we experience the grace of Christ, our hearts are changed, our minds are lifted, and our desires are refined to focus on serving others.

Another important lesson we can take from Alma and his people is the impact these experiences have with regard to the power of place. Just as the Sacred Grove became sacred by what took place there, so too did the Waters of Mormon become hallowed because of the outpouring of grace experienced by Alma and his people. This experience was so impactful and meant so much to this people that Mormon's father named his son after that holy land. As we experience the power of Christ's Atonement in our own lives, we tend to remember where we were when we felt His love and sang His praise. Let us remember these precious places, and as we remember them, let us remember the mercy we felt, the closeness of heaven, and the motivation to do and become better. Indeed, let us continue to "sing the song of redeeming love" (Alma 5:26) and to "sing to his praise forever" (Mosiah 18:30).

Chapter 7: Alma the Younger

The story of Alma the Younger is a story of hope. As we see him redeemed from his rebellious and sinful life, we learn that it is almost impossible for any of us to sin beyond the scope of the Savior's atoning grace. We learn that, as Neal A. Maxwell taught, "Christ's Atonement, of course, is for super sinners and the midrange sinners and then good people who make a lot of mistakes but are not wicked!"[89]

Christ's Mercy Knows No Bounds

In a recent conference talk, Elder Jeffrey R. Holland provided invaluable insight into one of the Savior's parables. He spoke of the Lord's parable of the laborers in the vineyard.[90] In this parable, the Lord told how a householder went out early in the morning to find people who would labor in his vineyard. He came multiple times throughout the day, hiring a new group at six a.m., nine a.m., noon, three p.m., and then a final group at around five p.m. To the great surprise of everyone involved, the householder paid everyone the same wage, regardless of how long they had labored. Elder Holland provided the following insight into this great parable:

> First of all it is important to note that *no one* has been treated unfairly here. The first workers agreed to the full wage of the day, and they received it. Furthermore, they were, I can only imagine, very grateful

to get the work. In the time of the Savior, an average man and his family could not do much more than live on what they made that day. If you didn't work or farm or fish or sell, you likely didn't eat. With more prospective workers than jobs, these first men chosen were the most fortunate in the entire labor pool that morning.

Indeed, if there is any sympathy to be generated, it should at least initially be for the men *not* chosen who also had mouths to feed and backs to clothe. Luck never seemed to be with some of them. With each visit of the steward throughout the day, they always saw someone else chosen.

But just at day's close, the householder returns a surprising fifth time with a remarkable eleventh-hour offer! These last and most discouraged of laborers, hearing only that they will be treated fairly, accept work without even knowing the wage, knowing that *anything* will be better than nothing, which is what they have had so far. Then as they gather for their payment, they are stunned to receive the same as all the others! How awestruck they must have been and how very, very grateful! Surely never had such compassion been seen in all their working days.[91]

This insightful commentary on the Lord's parable helps us to see and understand that Christ's mercy knows no bounds. Through this parable, we learn that the invitation to come unto Christ does not have an expiration date while we work through this probationary state, nor does it have a limit in its eternal scope. Speaking to all who would listen, Elder Holland pleaded that we would understand this lesson:

> I do not know who in this vast audience today may need to hear the message of forgiveness inherent in this parable, but however late you think you are, however many chances you think you have missed, however many mistakes you feel you have made or talents you think you don't have, or however far from home and family and God you feel you have traveled, I testify that you have *not* traveled beyond the reach of divine love. It is not possible for you to sink lower than the infinite light of Christ's Atonement shines.[92]

This truth is entirely personified in the life and ministry of Alma the Younger.

The Rebellion and Conversion of Alma the Younger

At a pivotal time in Nephite history, we learn that many in the rising generation did not believe in the traditions of their fathers

and, over time, determined to not just forsake the faith, but also to persecute the believers. Foremost among these rebellious dissenters were the sons of King Mosiah and Alma the Younger, the son of the prophet. You can imagine the drama as both the son of the prophet and the heirs of the throne went about, seeking to destroy both the Church and kingdom. We are told Alma "became a very wicked and an idolatrous man. And he was a man of many words, and did speak much flattery to the people; therefore he led many of the people to do after the manner of his iniquities. And he became a great hinderment to the prosperity of the church of God; stealing away the hearts of the people; causing much dissension among the people; giving a chance for the enemy of God to exercise his power over them" (Mosiah 27:8–9). A prophet's son, trying to destroy the church his father had given his life to, and four sons of the king, rebelling against the laws instituted by their fathers; this was a high drama indeed.

As these young men were going about, rebelling against the Lord, an angel appeared before them and began to speak. His voice was so powerful that it caused the earth to shake, and the young men fell to the earth in fear. After delivering his message of repentance, the angel departed and the boys remained on the ground. In fact, we are told that "the astonishment of Alma was so great that he became dumb, that he could not open his mouth; yea, and he became weak, even that he could not move his hands" (Mosiah 27:19). Seeing Alma in this helpless state, the four sons of Mosiah carried him unto his father. Alma the Elder, knowing that the Lord was doing a great work with his son, rejoiced in this experience and caused that the priests should gather together so they might open a collective fast for his son—and for the eyes of the people to "be opened to see and know of the goodness and glory of God" (Mosiah 27:22).

After three days, Alma's strength was restored. He stood before the people and testified that he repented of his sins and was redeemed of the Lord and born again of the Spirit. He then explained that except we become new creatures through the Atonement, none of us can gain entrance into the kingdom of God. He told how he felt he would be cast off, but that "after wading through much tribulation, repenting nigh unto death, the Lord in his mercy [saw] fit to snatch [him] out of an everlasting burning," and thus redeemed him from the darkest abyss to "behold the marvelous light of God" (Mosiah 27:28–29).

While this explanation of the experience is insightful and inspiring, we should forever be grateful to Alma for his willingness to provide a more thorough account as he later counseled his son Helaman. Here, he gives us a glimpse into what he went through during those three days and nights. He spoke of fear and of pain, describing how he was "racked with torment" and his soul "was harrowed up to the greatest degree," being "racked with all [his] sins" (Alma 36:12). As he remembered his sins and iniquities, he was "tormented with the pains of hell" and "even with the pains of a damned soul" (Alma 36:13, 16). Opening up his heart, Alma confided, "So great had been my iniquities, that the very thought of coming into the presence of my God did rack my soul with inexpressible horror" (Alma 36:14). So great was his pain and so real was his guilt that he wished to be completely annihilated from existence so he would not have to face his God. He said, "Oh, thought I, that I could be banished and become extinct both soul and body, that I might not be brought to stand in the presence of my God, to be judged of my deeds" (Alma 36:15).

Why Suffering?

Doctrinally speaking, suffering is an important and necessary part of repentance. Anyone who thinks otherwise is not familiar with the story of Alma the Younger—and likely has not attempted sincere repentance. President Spencer W. Kimball implored, "We must remember that repentance is more than just saying, 'I am sorry.' It is more than tears in one's eyes. It is more than a half a dozen prayers. Repentance means suffering. If a person hasn't suffered, he hasn't repented. I don't care how many times he says he has. If he hasn't suffered, he hasn't repented. He has got to go through a change in his system whereby he suffers and then forgiveness is a possibility."[93] Sometimes the young people of the Church do not understand this truth and even question why a merciful and loving God would require such suffering. Alma's son Corianton struggled with this concept (see Alma 42:1). Having been through a harrowing experience himself, Alma was perfectly qualified to help his son understand the mercy of God in allowing His children to suffer. In his concluding

counsel to Corianton, Alma taught, "And now, my son, I desire that ye should let these things trouble you no more, and only let your sins trouble you, with that trouble which shall bring you down unto repentance" (Alma 42:29). In other words, "Godly sorrow worketh repentance" (2 Corinthians 7:10). Perhaps this is why Elder Dallin H. Oaks would say that Alma the Younger's experience "is our best scriptural illustration of the fact that the process of repentance is filled with personal suffering for sin."[94]

In speaking about the Fall of Adam, President Ezra Taft Benson taught, "Just as a man does not really desire food until he is hungry, so he does not desire the salvation of Christ until he knows why he needs Christ."[95] The Book of Mormon teaches that we need Christ to redeem us both from the Fall of Adam and our own fall. Because of the Fall of Adam, "all mankind were fallen, and they were in the grasp of justice; yea, the justice of God, which consigned them forever to be cut off from his presence" (Alma 42:14). But Christ came to "redeem the children of men from the fall" so that they can be free "to act for themselves and not to be acted upon" (2 Nephi 2:26). Thus we see that because of the Atonement of Jesus Christ, we are not accountable for Adam's transgression but are rather to be "punished for [our] own sins" (Articles of Faith 1:2).

Because we all sin and come short of the glory of God, we periodically find ourselves in a lost and fallen state. Were it not for our repentance, we would unavoidably perish, as we would remain unclean, hardened, fallen, and lost (see Alma 34:9). As Dr. Robert L. Millet explained, "We have thoughts that are unclean, feelings that are un-Christian, desires that are unholy, attitudes that are divisive, inclinations that are disruptive to order and decency. We manifest pride and arrogance and too often filter our decisions through the lenses of ego. We are consumed with judgmentalism and tend to look more harshly upon the flaws and misdeeds of others than is wise or charitable. We complain and murmur when things do not go as we had hoped or when they go slower than we had anticipated."[96] We must remember that this hopeless and fallen condition is not because of the Fall of Adam, but because of our own fall. Alma's experience masterfully illustrates that President Benson's statement of not desiring the salvation of Christ until we know why we need Him has just as much bearing on our own fall as it does the Fall of Adam. Having viewed himself in this natural and carnal state, and having felt the deep personal suffering associated with sincere repentance, Alma was prepared to reach out and up for the rescuing hand of Jesus.

As Alma suffered through the pain and punishment, he gave the following account: "While I was harrowed up by the memory of my many sins, behold, I remembered also to have heard my father prophesy unto the people concerning the coming of one Jesus Christ, a Son of God, to atone for the sins of the world. Now, as my mind caught hold upon this thought, I cried within my heart: *O Jesus, thou Son of God, have mercy on me,* who am in the gall of bitterness, and am encircled about by the everlasting chains of death" (Alma 36:17–18; emphasis added).

Alma clearly felt and understood that "Christ is the power behind all repentance. . . . [He] had been touched by the teaching of his father, but it is particularly important that the prophecy he remembered was one regarding 'the coming of one Jesus Christ, a Son of God, to atone for the sins of the world.' (Alma 36:17.) That is the name and that is the message that every man must hear. . . . *Whatever other prayers we offer, whatever other needs we have, all somehow depends on that plea: 'O Jesus, thou Son of God, have mercy on me.'* He is prepared to provide that mercy. He paid with his very life in order to give it."[97]

The Great Pivot and the Brilliant Morning of Forgiveness

This heartfelt plea represents what Elder Maxwell called "the great pivot."[98] Alma's guilt and suffering led him to turn away from sin and toward the Lord. Once his mind caught hold of the thought that he could apply the atoning blood of Christ, he had a glimmer of hope and thus desperately pled for mercy and grace. "And now, behold, when I thought this, I could remember my pains no more; yea, I was harrowed up by the memory of my sins no more. And oh, what joy, and what marvelous light I did behold; yea, my soul was filled with joy as exceeding as was my pain! Yea . . . there could be nothing so exquisite and so bitter as were my pains. Yea, and . . . on the other hand, there can be nothing so exquisite and sweet as was my joy" (Alma 36:19–21).

Relief had come! The pain and fear that seemed to overcome his entire person subsided. At that moment, Alma was not only freed from the burden of his sins but also the pain, the torment, and the harrowing feelings, all of which were now replaced with feelings of hope, peace, light, and joy. Indeed, Alma had experienced the miracle of forgiveness and had, in his own words, "a mighty change wrought in his heart," which led him "to sing the song of redeeming love" (Alma 5:12, 26). He had awoken to a brilliant morning of forgiveness.

President Boyd K. Packer shared the following story from Church history, which highlights a couple of important insights to be drawn from the experience of Alma the Younger:

In April of 1847, Brigham Young led the first company of pioneers out of Winter Quarters. At that same time, sixteen hundred miles to the west the pathetic survivors of the Donner Party straggled down the slopes of the Sierra Nevada Mountains into the Sacramento Valley.

They had spent the ferocious winter trapped in the snowdrifts below the summit. That any survived the days and weeks and months of starvation and indescribable suffering is almost beyond belief.

Among them was fifteen-year-old John Breen. On the night of April 24 he walked into Johnson's Ranch. Years later John wrote:

"It was long after dark when we got to Johnson's Ranch, so the first time I saw it was early in the morning. The weather was fine, the ground was covered with green grass, the birds were singing from the tops of the trees, and the journey was over. I could scarcely believe that I was alive.

"The scene that I saw that morning seems to be photographed on my mind. Most of the incidents are gone from memory, but I can always see the camp near Johnson's Ranch."

At first I was very puzzled by his statement that "most of the incidents are gone from memory." How could long months of incredible suffering and sorrow ever be gone from his mind? How could that brutal dark winter be replaced with one brilliant morning?

On further reflection I decided it was not puzzling at all. I have seen something similar happen to people I have known. I have seen some who have spent a long winter of guilt and spiritual starvation emerge into the morning of forgiveness.[99]

Alma the Younger had been a wicked and idolatrous man and, with the sons of Mosiah, was among "the very vilest of sinners" (Mosiah 28:4). The angel's visit struck him with such great fear and amazement that he felt that he would be destroyed. As he fell to the earth, his soul was tormented, racked, and harrowed up because of the sins he had committed. In God's justice, Alma had to suffer both body and spirit.

However, Alma had learned firsthand that Christ knows "according to the flesh how to succor [run to] his people according to their infirmities" (Alma 7:12). After he crossed the difficult plains of repentance and suffered in the snow banks of his own sins, from his, as President Packer said, "long winter of guilt and spiritual starvation" he had emerged into this "brilliant morning of forgiveness."

The story of Alma the Younger underscores the truth that "relief from torment and guilt can be earned through repentance. Save for those few who defect to perdition after having known a fulness, there is no habit, no addiction, no rebellion, no transgression, no offense exempted from the promise of complete forgiveness."[100] The Savior taught that true repentance would be manifest as we confess and forsake our sins (see D&C 58:43). As soon as Alma received strength, he "did manifest unto the people that [he] had been born of God" (Alma 36:23) by the permanence of the change that had been wrought in his heart. From the time he experienced the cleansing and strengthening power of the Atonement of Jesus Christ to the year he left mortality,[101] he said, "I have labored without ceasing, that I might bring souls unto repentance; that I might bring them to taste of the exceeding joy of which I did taste; that they might also be born of God, and be filled with the Holy Ghost" (Alma 36:24).

The Long-Term Effects of Alma's Experience

Alma would eventually become both the high priest of the Church and the first chief judge of Zarahemla. In his ministry he would, among other things, confound the false teachings of at least two anti-Christs (see Alma 1 and 30), put an end to priestcraft and rebellion among the Amlicites, Ammonihahites, and the Zoramites (see Alma 2–4, 12–16, 30–34), sacrifice political prominence and position in order to "pull down, by the word of God, all the pride and craftiness

and all the contentions which were among his people" (Alma 4:19), cleanse and set in order the Church in Zarahemla (Alma 5–6), provide powerful and delicious doctrinal sermons (see Alma 7, 11–14, 29–33, 36–42), enjoy the sweet reunion with the sons of Mosiah—who were his brothers in the work of the kingdom—(Alma 17), provide intimate and doctrinally drenched counsel to his three sons (Alma 36–42), and even direct the war efforts of Captain Moroni (see Alma 43–44).

In short, Alma's influence on the kingdom of God cannot be overstated. We are told that "when Alma had done this he departed out of the land. . . . And it came to pass that he was never heard of more; as to his death or burial we know not of. Behold, this we know, that he was a righteous man; and the saying went abroad in the church that he was taken up by the Spirit, or buried by the hand of the Lord, even as Moses" (Alma 45:18–19).

What a leader! What a legacy! Alma the Elder poured the footings for the infant Church and Alma the Younger strengthened that foundation further. It was through his ministry that the Church eventually increased by tens of thousands. Knowing of his imminent departure, Alma prepared his son Helaman for the work of the kingdom and for his prophetic role. Helaman would then go on to influence his own son, Helaman. He would prepare and influence his son, Nephi, for the same prophetic role. Nephi would do the same for his son, Nephi. And so it went that Alma the Younger's prophetic ministry and legacy would continue to be felt and would prepare the way for the coming of the true High Priest, even Jesus Christ (see 3 Nephi 11).

Think of the masterfully orchestrated irony in this story. Alma the Elder was touched by the powerful testimony of Abinadi and led to repent and partake of the fruit of the Atonement. Having tasted of the fruit, Alma was led to speak and prophesy often "concerning the coming of one Jesus Christ, a son of God, to atone for the sins of the world" (Alma 36:17). It was this thought that would penetrate the heart of his rebellious son and lead him to experience the power of Christ's mercy. Cleansed and changed, Alma the Younger labored without ceasing in helping others taste as he had tasted. This legacy would continue until Alma the Younger's second great-grandson would have the humbling opportunity to kneel at the feet of the resurrected Christ and feel the prints of the nails in His hands and feet. And thus we see a powerful example of what can happen when an individual experiences the life-altering grace of the Lord Jesus Christ.

Alma the Younger as a Great Object Lesson

The story of Alma the Younger begins in Mosiah 27 (199) and continues until Alma 45 (321), spanning over 120 pages of a 531-page book. In other words, Alma's story covers approximately 23 percent of the Book of Mormon. To this point, Elder Holland taught, "More pages are devoted to the span of his life and ministry than to any other person in the Book of Mormon, and the book that bears his name is nearly 2 1/2 times longer than any other in the record. He strides with prophetic power onto the great center stage of the Book of Mormon, appearing near the precise chronological midpoint of the record—500 years after Lehi leaves Jerusalem, 500 years before Moroni seals up the record."[102]

So here is the question: If space on the abridged plates was relatively sparse, why would the Lord inspire Mormon to include so much of Alma's story? The self-stated purpose of the Book of Mormon is to help the remnant of the house of Israel to know "that they are not cast off forever" and also "to the convincing of the Jew and Gentile that Jesus is the Christ" (Title Page). Alma the Younger serves as the ultimate object lesson to this point. Sometimes we feel like we have sinned too many times or committed sins that are too grievous to be forgiven. One significant message of Alma the Younger's story is that no matter how far you think you have strayed, no matter how serious your sins may be, you can "come boldly unto the throne of grace" (Hebrews 4:16) and trust in "Jehovah's unrelenting refrain, '[My] hand is stretched out still.'"[103]

"More Longing for Home"

Let's look at one final lesson from this conversion story. As Alma was suffering through the repentance process, being "racked with eternal torment," "harrowed up to the greatest degree," and "racked with all [his] sins" (Alma 36:12), he said, "The very thought of coming into the presence of my God did rack my soul with inexpressible horror"

(Alma 36:14). He would go so far as to wish he "could be banished and become extinct both soul and body" so he would not have to stand in the presence of God to be judged of his deeds (Alma 36:15). His pain was so deep and his guilt so complete that he knew he "would be more miserable to dwell with a holy and just God, under a consciousness of [his] filthiness before him, than [he] would to dwell with the damned souls in hell" (Mormon 9:4). But he experienced a great pivot and caught hold upon the hope planted in his heart by his faithful father. As Alma's hope turned him to Christ, he learned firsthand of His reaching, rescuing, and redeeming power. After experiencing this divine change, Alma said, "Yea, methought I saw . . . God sitting upon his throne, surrounded with numberless concourses of angels, in the attitude of singing and praising their God; yea, and *my soul did long to be there*" (Alma 36:22; emphasis added).

One of the sweetest fruits of the Atonement of Jesus Christ is the deep motivational feeling of returning home to the Father. As we experience the power of godliness in our lives, we desperately seek "more freedom from earth-stains" and "more longing for home."[104] When I was a missionary in New Zealand, my companion and I were conducting a zone meeting. At the conclusion, we opened it up for people to share their testimonies.

After a couple of inspiring testimonies, a Samoan missionary stood up and walked to the front of the room. This young man had tattoos on his shoulder, had been involved in gangs in high school, and had experienced some pretty scary things in his life. As he opened his mouth to speak, he began to cry. Choking back tears, he said, "I just want you all to know that this past week, I have been very homesick." My companion and I looked at each other in shock, as we had known nothing about this previously. From all we could see, he seemed to have immersed himself in the work and was finding great success as a result of it. Before we could say a word to each other, this powerful elder tearfully continued, "I know what you're thinking, but it is not that kind of homesick." He paused and began to weep as he cried out, "I am homesick for my heavenly home." He proceeded to emotionally tell us of his relationship with Heavenly Father and how deeply he had come to love and adore Him. He had felt the Lord's mercies and, as a result, wanted nothing more than to humbly fall at His feet and thank Him for His goodness. He had felt that same longing that Alma had felt: a longing for home that comes from knowing "that your garments have been cleansed and made white through the blood of Christ" (Alma 5:27).

President Ezra Taft Benson taught, "Nothing is going to startle us more when we pass through the veil to the other side than to realize how well we know our Father and how familiar his face is to us."[105] As we experience divine grace, we feel ourselves "reconciled unto [the Father] through the Atonement of Christ" (Jacob 4:11). This reconciliation helps us know and feel the character of God. The more we know of Him, the more we come to love Him. The more we come to love Him, the more we long to be with Him. Indeed, this is one of the sweetest fruits of repentance and one of the blessings of that brilliant morning of forgiveness.

And Thus We See

In an *Ensign* article published in March, 1977, Elder Jeffrey R. Holland summarized what he hoped we would take from the story of Alma the Younger. Rather than me diluting his powerful prophetic prose, I have decided to just let him have the final word in this chapter:

> From the depths of sin Alma repented and became a prophetic model of virtue and valor . . . but [this] all came after—and finally only because of—his willingness to undergo what one twentieth-century writer has called "the ordeal of change"—movement from night to day, from pain to peace, from sin to the joy of salvation—that monumental process of the soul called repentance. "O Jesus, thou Son of God, have mercy on me" is the cry that changed Alma's world forever. . . . Perhaps no personal journey gives more encouragement to you or me that peace and joy are possible, that it can—and must—be so.
>
> There are multitudes of men and women—in and out of the Church—who are struggling vainly against obstacles in their path. Many are fighting the battle of life—and losing. Indeed, there are those among us who consider themselves the vilest of sinners. . . .
>
> How many broken hearts remain broken because those people feel they are beyond the pale of God's restorative power? How many bruised and battered spirits are certain that they have sunk to a depth at which the light of redeeming hope and grace will never again shine?

Ryan H. Sharp

To these the story of the younger Alma comes like water to a parched tongue, like rest to a weary traveler. From the depths of hellish iniquity, from rebellion and destruction and utter wickedness the younger Alma returned—and therein lies again the "miracle of forgiveness." It is a miracle. In fact, it is the greatest of all miracles. It is the miracle at the heart of the atonement of Jesus Christ.

Surely that is the "good news" of the gospel—that there is a way back, that there is repentance and safety and peace because of Christ's gift to us.[106]

Chapter 8: The Sons of Mosiah

The Lord has invited all of us to participate in the work of salvation and open our mouths in sharing the good news of the gospel with those around us. The experiences of the four sons of Mosiah teach us that success in missionary work begins and ends with the Atonement. They show us how the change wrought by sincere repentance immediately leads to enhanced spiritual vision and a desire to reach out and rescue those around us. Further, their experience teaches us invaluable lessons to remember as we immerse ourselves in the His work.

The Mormon Moment

In recent months and years, there has been an interesting connection in the national media. For example, think for a moment what the following people have in common: Mitt Romney (2012 presidential candidate), Stephanie Meyer (author of the *Twilight* series), Bryce Harper (2013 MLB Rookie of the Year), Glenn Beck (TV and radio host), Jabari Parker (number two pick in 2014 NBA draft), Harry Reid (Senate Majority Leader), Ziggy Ansah (number five pick in 2013 NFL Draft), David Archuletta (singer), Manti Te'o (Heisman runner-up), Jimmer Fredette (2011 NCAA National Player of the Year), and Clayton Christenson (named the World's Most Influential Business Management Thinker in 2011 and 2013). So what is the connection?

Everyone mentioned is a member of the Church and has spent a lot of time in the public eye. All of these examples, and many more, show us that we are experiencing what *Newsweek Magazine* called "the Mormon Moment." While this is certainly not the first time there have been members of the Church who have gained media attention, there seems to be a large confluence of members of the Church being discussed in the media.

As a result of this "Mormon Moment," the Church has also been getting a lot of publicity in the media and is being discussed more and more. Surely in such a moment, those "who are only kept from the truth because they know not where to find it" (D&C 123:12) will be given ample opportunity to have open dialogue with members of the faith. In addressing this unique opportunity, Elder Quentin L. Cook recently said, "In this so-called Mormon Moment, where there is more attention being paid to the Church and its members, we will need to be the best examples we can possibly be. Collectively our example will be more important than what any single member or leader proposes. . . . You must not be in camouflage as to who you are and what you believe."[107] In other words, while the door to dialogue is opening more and more because of this "Mormon Moment," it will be up to the individual members of the Church to reach out, join in the discussion, and thus ensure that the door stays open enough to allow those earnest seekers of truth to catch a glimpse of who we are and what we *really* believe.

Overcoming the Fears of Sharing the Gospel

In his landmark talk on missionary work, President Spencer W. Kimball taught, "Perhaps the greatest reason for missionary work is to give the world its chance to hear and accept the gospel. The scriptures are replete with commands and promises and calls and rewards for teaching the gospel. I use the word *command* deliberately for it seems to be an insistent directive from which we, singly and collectively, cannot escape."[108] Over the past couple of years, the Brethren have repeatedly spoken of the Lord's promise to "hasten [His] work in its time" (D&C 88:73). Most recently, Elder M. Russell Ballard said, "My message this afternoon is that the Lord is hastening His work. In our day this can be done only when every member of the Church reaches out with love

to share the truths of the restored gospel of Jesus Christ. . . . We know from our research that most active members of the Church want the blessings of the gospel to be part of the lives of others whom they love, even those whom they have never met. But we also know that many members hesitate to do missionary work and share the gospel."[109] Why is it that we sometimes hesitate to share the message of the Restoration with others? The biggest reason for such hesitation seems to be fear.

As one who loves missionary work and has tried to be actively engaged in sharing the gospel, I have spent a lot of time pondering this dilemma. I have concluded that these are some of the fears we have as we consider opening our mouths to share our message with others:

- We are afraid of what people will think of us
- We are afraid of offending the person we are talking to
- We are afraid that we might damage a relationship, or that it might make the relationship awkward
- We are afraid people will reject the message that we feel deeply about
- We are afraid we will not know what to say when such opportunities do come or, even if we do have a pretty good introductory script, that they might ask us a question that we don't know the answer to
- We are afraid that our testimony is not strong enough yet
- We are afraid that we will not have the words to express the deep and poignant feelings of our hearts

While this does not claim to be an exhaustive list, it does cover most of the fears I have encountered personally or have heard from others. Elder Holland shared the following true account that underscores some of the emotions we feel as we engage in this great work:

> Some time ago I was invited to speak at a youth conference, which is the kind of invitation that I have had to decline routinely for years. But something about this one kept gnawing at me, and I answered that I would come. It seemed a foolish thing to do. It meant a morning drive of about four hours into a neighboring state and then the same drive back that night. But I felt I should go, and I did. I put my wife and children in the car with sandwiches and a Scrabble board, and off we went.

After I dropped them off at the local city park and swimming pool, I went over to the youth conference held at a local stake center. The trip was worth it all to me for one brief testimony that I heard there. At this very moment I honestly cannot tell you what I said to that group as their invited speaker. It's gone from my memory and undoubtedly gone from all of theirs. But this young convert's testimony is still with me, and I leave it with you today.

She described her conversion to the Church and what the gospel of Jesus Christ had come to mean in her life. Her home life was something out of a horror story—broken marriage, mother living with a man not her husband, brother on drugs, sister expecting a baby. It was as bizarre as any social worker would ever need to see. But into her life had come the Church, and for this young fourteen- or fifteen-year-old girl it was everything, and she was hanging on. She described opening her school locker one day, only to have her paperback edition of the Book of Mormon fall to the floor. She used it in seminary, and to her it was a prized possession. She was still a little insecure about all of this, however, for the world around her had made her pretty insecure. And she was not yet certain what her new faith and friends held in store for her. She was happy but still tentative and very anxious to be stronger in the faith. She was embarrassed. She had not wanted anyone to see the book.

She hastily stooped down to pick it up before someone noticed. But someone had noticed, and they were standing right next to her. Three girls looked first at the book and then at her. Her heart sank, and she clutched at the little blue paperback cover. She said nothing, and neither did they for a moment. But then one of them asked, "Is that a church book?"

She said, "Yes."

The other girl said, "What church is it?"

And my young friend stuttered, "The Church of Jesus Christ of Latter-day Saints."

"Is that the Mormons?" shot back the inquirer.

"Yes," whispered the frightened little Latter-day Saint, "that's the Mormons."

There was a long pause, and then her interrogator said, "Are you true?"

After a pause that was both instantaneous and eternal, my little friend said, with her head slightly more erect and her back slightly straighter and her hands trembling a little less, "Yes, I'm true."

I must confess that when I first heard that young girl's testimony, I did not quite understand all that I was hearing. I've thought about it since, and obviously what the one girl, in her own way, was asking was, "Are you active?" That's the way we would have phrased it. But what a tragic loss to so phrase it. How much more meaning there is in the straightforward inquiry, "Are you true?"

There was no reprisal. The heretofore undisclosed copy of the Book of Mormon in a school locker had not brought on physical torture or social ostracism. A little confidence came, and a little conviction increased. There was just one young soul saying to another, "Are you true?" "If you are a Latter-day Saint, are you a good one?"

My beloved brothers and sisters, I testify to you this morning that the questions are no longer, "Is the Church true?"; "Is God true?"; "Is Christ or Joseph Smith . . . true?" All of that and a lot more was decided a long, long time ago. It is not now subject to popular ballot, yours or mine. In a word, all that remains for you and for me . . . is the simple inquiry, "Are you true?" May God bless us always to so be.[110]

Early in this dispensation, the Lord declared that this church has come forth out of obscurity and out of darkness and is a "true and living church" (D&C 1:30). For us to engage in this great work, we need to learn to overcome our fears and become "true and living" disciples of Jesus Christ. Yes, the fears associated with sharing the gospel are real, but "perfect love casteth out all fear" (Moroni 8:16). The conversion and ministry of the sons of Mosiah provides some key principles in helping us overcome our fears of sharing the gospel.

"Overhearing the Gospel"[111]

In the previous chapter, we recounted the rebellion and conversion of Alma the Younger and briefly mentioned that "the sons of Mosiah were numbered among the unbelievers" who went about secretly "seeking to destroy the church, and to lead astray the people of the Lord" (Mosiah 27:8, 10). We tend to think that the conversion story of the sons of Mosiah is the same as Alma the Younger. They were with Alma when the angel of the Lord appeared and did fall to the ground when they felt the earth shake beneath their feet. We are even told that these four young men heard more of the words of the angel than Alma did because he had, at that point, both fallen to the earth and fallen deaf. There is, however, an interesting distinction.

Reflect back on that experience, specifically the words of the angel. In fact, even more than the words of the angel, think about who the angel's audience was. We know that the words of the angel were heard by Alma, Ammon, Aaron, Omner, Himni and others (see Mosiah 27:11, 32–34). However, while the voice of the angel was heard by all of them, it is quite clear that the primary audience for this angelic discourse was Alma the Younger. For example:

- "He cried again, saying: Alma, arise and stand forth" (Mosiah 27:13)
- "Behold, the Lord hath heard the prayers of his people, and also the prayers of his servant, Alma, who is *thy* father" (27:14; emphasis added)
- "And now I say unto thee, Alma, go thy way, and seek to destroy the church no more" (27:16)
- "These were the last words which the angel spake unto Alma" (27:17)
- "The whole earth did tremble beneath our feet; and we all fell to the earth, for the fear of the Lord came upon *us*. But behold, the voice said unto *me:* Arise" (Alma 36:7–8; emphasis added)
- "And the angel spake more things unto *me*, which were heard by my brethren" (36:11; emphasis added)

After reading this, it might seem a bit strange to focus on the experience of Alma when discussing the conversion of the sons of Mosiah. But therein lies the lesson. It would seem that Alma the Younger's personal experience with the Savior was a catalyst in bringing the sons of Mosiah to recognize their own faults and repent. As is often the case, the conversion and growth of one person leads others to experience the same. While we do not have the full story, we do know that the experience with the angel both frightened the sons of Mosiah and helped them realize and feel the power of God (Mosiah 27:18). To the casual reader, it would seem that their conversion came because of this heavenly visit. If we look closer in the text, however, we learn that there was a much deeper and holier motivation. As they felt the earth shake, heard the thunderous words trumpeted by an angel of God, and saw their dear friend struck down into some kind of spiritual coma, it would seem that the Lord now had their attention as well. In that spirit, this experience seems to be the starting point, or the readying of the reservoir into which the Almighty could pour the wonders of His mercy and grace.

After seeing that Alma lay helpless on the ground, these young men carried their friend back to his father, the prophet, and "rehearsed unto his father all that had happened unto them" (Mosiah 27:20). Alma the Elder recognized this to be the work of God and rejoiced that God was lovingly responding to his deep and heartfelt petitions. Ever the missionary, he "caused that a multitude should be gathered together that they might witness what the Lord had done for his son, and also for those that were with him . . . that the eyes of the people might be opened to see and know of the goodness and glory of God" (Mosiah 27:21–22). Of this multitude who had gathered together to fast and pray and witness this miracle, surely the sons of Mosiah were there in the front row. One even wonders if Alma the Elder might have taken the opportunity during these few days to provide some private tutoring to these four young men, who seemed to be so prepared to hear a message of redemption. While we can't say entirely for sure what happened in the lives of these young men, let's take a moment and look at what the record *does* give us.

They Could Not Bear That Any Soul Should Perish

We know that after Alma arose and again received his strength, he and the sons of Mosiah traveled throughout the land, "publishing to all the people the things which they had heard and seen" (Mosiah 27:32). The record states further that "they traveled throughout all the land of Zarahemla, and among all the people who were under the reign of King Mosiah, zealously striving to repair all the injuries which they had done to the church, confessing all their sins, and publishing all the things which they had seen, and explaining the prophecies and the scriptures to all who desired to hear them" (Mosiah 27:35).

What was it that led to this mighty change in the hearts of the four sons of Mosiah? Was it the experience of Alma the Younger? Was it the trembling of the earth as the angel spoke? Or was it the days of fasting and praying that wrought so great a change? I submit that while all of these experiences played a part in opening the hearts of these young men, for so mighty a change to take full effect in the heart of a human soul, there must be a direct experience with the Master Healer. While we do not have the full account of their experiences, we *do* know that the Spirit of the Lord began to work upon them. We know that "they were the very vilest of sinners," and that "the Lord saw fit in his infinite mercy to spare them" (Mosiah 28:4). As was the case with Alma, such mercy did not come without a price, for "they suffered much anguish of soul because of their iniquities, suffering much and fearing that they should be cast off forever" (Mosiah 28:4). We learn that "after wading through much tribulation, repenting nigh unto death, the Lord in mercy" saw fit to snatch Ammon, Aaron, Omner, and Himni out of everlasting burning, just as He had done for Alma (Mosiah 27:28). Indeed, they had experienced the matchless power of the Atonement of Jesus Christ and had been led to praise His name and spread His word.

As these newly called missionaries went about the kingdom, "they were instruments in the hands of God in bringing many to the knowledge of the truth, yea, to the knowledge of their Redeemer" (Mosiah 27:36). Following this successful harvest, they "returned to their father, the king, and desired of him . . . that they might . . . go up to the land of Nephi that they might preach the things which they had heard, and that they might impart the word of God to their brethren, the Lamantites" (Mosiah 28:1).

Before continuing on with the narrative, it seems appropriate to take a brief moment to remind ourselves about the contemporary state of "their brethren," the Lamanites. They were a "wild and a hardened and a ferocious people; a people who delighted in murdering the Nephites, and robbing and plundering them; and their hearts were set upon riches, or upon gold and silver, and precious stones; yet they sought to obtain these things by murdering and plundering, that they might not labor for them with their own hands. Thus they were a very indolent people, many of whom did worship idols, and the curse of God had fallen upon them because of the traditions of their fathers" (Alma 17:14–15). From this description of the Lamanite people, it seems as if the sons of Mosiah do not quite understand the phrase: "the field is white already to harvest" (D&C 4:4).

Nevertheless, this did not shake the desire or the vision of these devoted disciples. Their greatest hope was to "bring [the Lamanites] to the knowledge of the Lord their God, and convince them of the

iniquity of their fathers; and that perhaps they might cure them of their hatred towards the Nephites" (Mosiah 28:2). Having experienced deliverance at the hand of their Redeemer, the sons of Mosiah sought to "bring them to know of the plan of redemption" (Alma 17:16); having known the fear of being cast off forever because of their vile sins, these young men had firsthand knowledge of the hope of salvation and the power of God's deliverance. With that knowledge, "they were desirous that salvation should be declared to every creature, for they could not bear that any human soul should perish; yea, even the very thoughts that any soul should endure endless torment did cause them to quake and tremble. . . . And it came to pass that they did plead with their father many days that they might go up to the land of Nephi" (Mosiah 28:3, 5).

The passion and zeal of Ammon, Aaron, Omner, and Himni for the work of salvation personifies the Prophet Joseph's declaration, "A man filled with the love of God, is not content with blessing his family alone, but ranges through the whole world, anxious to bless the whole human race."[112] And thus we see that as we continually experience the transformative power of the Atonement of Jesus Christ in our lives, and as we "rely on this Redeemer" (1 Nephi 10:6) to continue to touch our hearts, we can be filled with the love of God. As we "feast upon his love" (Jacob 3:2), we are able to begin overcoming our fears and anxieties of sharing the gospel. One of the sweet fruits of the Atonement is desperately wanting others to "taste of the exceeding joy of which [we] did taste" (Alma 36:24). Perhaps a relatively recent experience will help solidify this point.

A Changed Heart

There was a young man who had grown up in the Church and had always participated in whatever priesthood assignments came his way. In many ways, he was an ordinary young LDS boy. As he went through his teenage years, he struggled a bit with confidence but had a tendency to try to mask these insecurities by telling jokes and trying to make others laugh. While his tough guy, "I don't care what anyone thinks of me" attitude seemed to convince many, this young man knew that he lacked the confidence that comes from knowing who he really was and the work that he was meant to be engaged in.

As he went through high school, he attended seminary and appeared to really enjoy the lessons. While he seemed to feel the Spirit and have good experiences in both seminary and at church, the gospel had not taken root in his heart, and his private religious behaviors were left wanting. Because of this lack of depth in the soil of his soul, the temptations of the world came and scorched the seed, thus leading this young man to "frequently [fall] into many foolish errors, and displayed the weakness of youth, and the foibles of human nature; which, I am sorry to say, led [him] into divers temptations, offensive in the sight of God" (Joseph Smith—History 1:28).

During the last couple of months of his senior year, he took a challenge to read the Book of Mormon for himself. At first, it seemed as painful as it had been the many previous times he had started this seemingly impossible feat. But then something changed. As he read the experiences of the characters in the book, he felt like he could relate to the feelings they had. Over time, the reading became not only tolerable but also delicious! He began to spend more and more time in this incredible book of scripture. This diligence allowed the Spirit to prick his heart and lead him humbly to his knees in seeking forgiveness for his sins. As he petitioned the Almighty in prayer and supplication, the Lord, in His mercy and grace, reached down and snatched this young man from the grasp of sin. As he continued his study of the Book of Mormon, he began to feel the fire of the covenant, and the penetrating words became etched on his soul. He had felt of the Lord's rescuing power and continued to seek His guiding hand.

After experiencing this divine encounter with the living Son of the living God, this young man's life completely changed. The music he listened to, the movies he watched, the way he spoke to others, and the way he spoke *about* others all changed. His desires and motives changed. His conversations with his friends turned from girls, sports, and food to the gospel, missions, and the temple. In fact, nobody had to ask him to serve a mission because, at this point, there was nothing that could keep him from sharing his testimony of the Atonement of Jesus Christ with others.

The young man in this story . . . is me. I experienced the Atonement in a way and with a power I cannot describe. I wanted to share the gospel with others more than anything else in this world! When I

had read that the sons of Mosiah had been the "vilest of sinners. And the Lord saw fit in his infinite mercy to spare them" (Mosiah 28:4), I felt those same things in the deepest parts of my heart. I had felt the burden of sin and the guilt of being unclean. When forgiveness came, I did not know quite how to process it, other than to cry out in humility and profound gratitude that the Lord saw fit in His infinite mercy to "save a wretch like me."[113]

From that moment on, I remember the distinct impression that if the Lord could forgive me and sanctify my soul, then He could surely do it for everyone else. Furthermore, I thought and felt that if He could change my heart, and I could experience the exalting joy of forgiveness, then surely such a thing would be desirable to others if they could but feel what I felt. This led to a fire in my bones that drove me to want to share the gospel with everyone I saw. As I read the commentary that the sons of Mosiah "could not bear that any human soul should perish" and that "even the very thoughts that any soul should endure endless torment did cause them to quake and tremble" (Mosiah 28:3), I realized those were my exact feelings. This verse of scripture so resonated with me that when it came time to select the scripture to inscribe on my missionary plaque, it was a no-brainer as to what I would pick.

And so it is that one of the most important lessons we can learn about overcoming fear and sharing the gospel with others is that we need to minister and "teach out of our own changed hearts."[114] As we experience this divine change in our hearts, we will find, like the sons of Mosiah, that "the nearer we get to our heavenly Father, the more we are disposed to look with compassion on perishing souls; we feel that we want to take them upon our shoulders, and cast their sins behind our backs."[115]

It Is *His* Work, and We Are Simply Called to Assist

Even the most casual reader of the Book of Mormon is familiar with the inspiring missionary stories of the sons of Mosiah. While the next chapter will explore several of these experiences in detail, Ammon taught one overarching principle that is at the heart of overcoming our fears of sharing the gospel. To recognize this powerful lesson, let's first explore its doctrinal underpinnings.

Many of us who have tried sharing the gospel with others have experienced the roller coaster of emotions that can accompany this great work. These emotions come because we care so deeply about the gospel message and understand the impact that it can have on the people we love. If they reject the message, we often take it personally. We inappropriately think that if they do not accept our invitations, it must be our fault. After all, the gospel message is so good and is so attractive that nobody would willingly turn it down, right? President Dieter F. Uchtdorf recently said, "Sometimes we take upon ourselves too much credit or too much blame when it comes to others accepting the gospel. It's important to remember that the Lord doesn't expect us to do the converting."[116] When we blame ourselves for someone not accepting the gospel, we demonstrate our lack of understanding of one of the most important lessons regarding missionary work: this is God's work, and we are simply invited to act as instruments in helping Him.

In the Church, we are familiar with Moses 1:39: "For behold, this is my work and my glory—to bring to pass the immortality and eternal life of man." I am not sure how you read that verse or what words you emphasized, but I have personally come to read it this way: "For behold, this is *my* work and *my* glory—to bring to pass the immortality and eternal life of man." I believe the Lord is teaching the important truth that the work of salvation is *His* work. After all, He is the *Savior*. Not only is it important to understand that this is His work, but we must also remember that He has declared, "For I will show unto the children of men that I am able to do mine own work" (2 Nephi 27:21). Remember, He is omnipotent and can do all things.

Speaking to David Whitmer, the Lord underscored this truth when He said, "Wherefore, *I* must bring forth the fulness of *my* gospel . . . and behold, *thou* art David, and *thou* art called to assist" (D&C 14:10–11; emphasis added). There it is. That is our role. We are called to assist the Lord as He brings forth the fulness of His gospel among His children. He knew them long before you or I ever knew them. He knows them better than you and I could ever hope to know them. Indeed, He loves them even more than we could possibly love them, and He wants them to come unto Him even more desperately than we do. We need to remember this as we labor in the Lord's vineyard and trust that He really is intimately involved in this work. The Apostle Paul clearly understood this truth when he declared, "I have planted, Apollos watered; but God gave the increase" (1 Corinthians 3:6). It is for this precise reason that, as President Uchtdorf said earlier, we cannot take the blame when people don't accept our invitations, nor should we ever have the audacity to take the credit for God doing *His* work. Ammon taught this truth in a powerful way.

"In His Strength I Can Do All Things"

After their successful fourteen-year mission, Ammon took an opportunity to reflect with his brothers on the experiences they had together. He spoke of the thousands of Lamanites who had been "in the darkest abyss" and who had been "brought to behold the marvelous light of God" (Alma 26:3). As Ammon spoke of this immense harvest of souls, his brother Aaron feared that he was forgetting just whose work it really was and that Ammon was boasting in his own strength. While some may question the appropriateness of Aaron's accusations, how grateful we must be that it elicited Ammon's inspired response. As you read through these immortal lines, pay particular attention to Ammon's emphasis on exactly whose work it really is.

> I do not boast in my own strength, nor in my own wisdom; but behold, my joy is full, yea, my heart is brim with joy, and I will rejoice in my God. Yea, I know that I am nothing; as to my strength I am weak; therefore I will not boast of myself, but I will boast of my God, for in his strength I can do all things; yea, behold, many mighty miracles we have wrought in this land, for which we will praise his name forever. . . .
>
> Therefore, let us glory, yea, we will glory in the Lord; yea, we will rejoice, for our joy is full; yea, we will praise our God forever. Behold, who can glory too much in the Lord? Yea, who can say too much of his great power, and of his mercy, and of his long-suffering towards the children of men? . . .
>
> Now have we not reason to rejoice? Yea, I say unto you, there never were men that had so great reason to rejoice as we, since the world began; yea, and my joy is carried away, even unto boasting in my God; for he has all power, all wisdom, and all understanding; he comprehendeth all

things, and he is a merciful Being, even unto salvation, to those who will repent and believe on his name. Now if this is boasting, even so will I boast; for this is my life and my light, my joy and my salvation, and my redemption from everlasting wo. Yea . . . blessed be the name of my God, who has been mindful of us, wanderers in a strange land. (Alma 26:11–12, 16, 35–36)

Ammon and his brothers had learned of the mercy of God as they were snatched "from [their] awful, sinful, and polluted state. . . . Behold, he did not exercise his justice upon [them] but in his great mercy hath brought [them] over that everlasting gulf of death and misery, even to the salvation of [their] souls" (Alma 26:17, 20). Having experienced the mercy of the Master, these young men consecrated their hearts to the Lord and were made powerful instruments in His hands. Indeed, they had learned that success in the work of the vineyard comes as we put our trust in "the Lord of the harvest" (Matthew 9:38) and rely upon His guiding hand.

We are told that these sons of Mosiah "taught with power and authority of God" (Alma 17:3). This conviction, coupled with the timing of the Lord and the willing hearts of the Lamanites, brought about a conversion that was so deep and so complete that these converts "never did fall away" (Alma 23:6). As they experienced God's redemptive and cleansing power, they stayed true to the covenants they had made and were willing to sacrifice everything, even their own lives in some cases, to demonstrate their faithfulness to the Lord.

Neli Sasulu—A Life of Devoted Discipleship

In an effort to tie this chapter together, let's look at one more experience from New Zealand. I had been in the mission field for about nine months when I was transferred to a new city. My new area had a reputation of being quite difficult and had even been accused of being "dead." Naturally, I took this as a challenge, and my companion and I immersed ourselves in the work. After several weeks of labor—with little success to show for it—I felt discouraged and began to concede that perhaps the stereotypes were true. About five weeks into the transfer, I felt that I needed to humble myself, open a fast, and pray that we would find success.

As we opened a fast, we determined that we were going to show the Lord how committed we were going to be, and that we were going to go and tract all morning. The following day, we prayed to know which street we should tract. We both felt impressed that we were to get started on a street that was a few blocks away from where our apartment was. As we began knocking on doors, I looked down the road and noticed that there were two Jehovah's Witnesses knocking doors just a few houses in front of us. After knocking on the next door and finding the family visibly upset at having to deal with a second interruption, we decided that we were clearly not inspired and thus moved onto another road.

A couple of days later, however, we decided to return to this particular road. We decided that rather than starting at the same spot, we would start on the opposite end of the street. One of the first houses we knocked on was the home of a twenty-one-year-old young man named Neli Sasulu. He immediately let us in. He shared that he had a friend serving a mission for the Church and wanted to talk to us about our beliefs. As we proceeded through the first discussion, the Spirit filled the room and touched the heart of this young rugby player. His eyes were fixed on us as we spoke about Joseph Smith and about the coming forth of the Book of Mormon. We gave him a copy with a challenge to read a few select passages before our next visit. He was excited about the gift of the book and seemed even more excited to learn more about the restored gospel.

We soon returned for a follow-up visit and sat down to read a chapter from the Book of Mormon together. As we read, we talked about baptism and asked if Neli thought it was important to be baptized. He told us he did think it was important, and that he was baptized when he was a baby. We then taught him about priesthood authority and about baptism by immersion and asked, "Do you think it would be important for you to be baptized by someone holding this priesthood authority?" He said that he did. We then gave the invitation, "Neli, will you prepare yourself to be baptized by somebody holding the priesthood authority of God on November 23?" He excitedly responded with, "Yeah, heck yeah!"

Over the next couple of weeks, we saw a visible change in this young man. As he repented of his sins, he was filled with the light of the Spirit. Everyone who knew him could see something different about him and became interested in this change. He was baptized on November 23 (just three weeks after our invitation) and was confirmed the next day; he then received the Aaronic Priesthood and was ordained to the office of priest. The following week, he was called to be a ward missionary. From the moment Neli heard the message of the Restoration and felt the mighty change in his heart, he wanted to share the gospel with others. Immediately, he began to tell his friends and family of his experience and about his newly developed love for the Savior. Because they could all see this change, they were deeply interested in what he had to say.

Over the next several weeks and months, Neli's heart became more and more consecrated, and the Lord used him in remarkable ways. We were able to teach and baptize three of his brothers, and he reactivated his older sister. We taught dozens of his friends, many of whom entered into the covenant of baptism and received the gift of the Holy Ghost. In fact, about two weeks before completing my mission, I received a telephone call from one of his friends whom we had been teaching. He told me he had heard that I was leaving and wanted to get baptized before I left. We were able to schedule the rest of the lessons and set up his baptism to take place the morning I was to leave the mission field. As we made the preparations, this good brother asked Neli to perform the ordinance. What a powerful experience it was to see Neli and one of his good friends in their white clothes the day I wrapped up my mission.

I was able to participate as Neli was ordained an elder in the Melchizedek priesthood and spoke with him at length about his mission papers. A couple of months after returning home, I received a letter from Neli. Enclosed in this letter was a copy of another letter that said, "Dear Elder Neli Sasulu, you are hereby called to serve as a missionary for The Church of Jesus Christ of Latter-day Saints. You are assigned to labor in the Canada Calgary Mission." I couldn't believe it. Imagine a Samoan running around in Canada! He flew into Salt Lake City on the weekend and reported to the MTC on Wednesday. This meant I got to be "companions" with him for a few days. We met up with my companion whom I was serving with back then—the three of us had become close through our experiences together. We went to Temple Square and gave him a tour of everything there.

When Wednesday came, we dropped him off at the MTC. I felt like I was dropping off one of my own children as I tried reminding him to be obedient, work hard, and pray even harder. About a week later, I went to the MTC for a job interview and, as I pulled up, I offered a heartfelt—and perhaps selfish—prayer unto God. I simply said, "Heavenly Father, I know there are thousands of missionaries in there and dozens and dozens of buildings. But Neli is somewhere in here, and I would absolutely love it if there were any way that I could just happen to see him." As I walked in and turned one of the corners, I saw two missionaries walking down the hall. One of them was Neli. "Neli," I shouted. "Oh, I mean, Elder Sasulu." We embraced, and I asked him what he was doing. He said that they were sitting in class and his companion just happened to get sick. I thought, *I guess prayer really does work . . . but Lord, you did not have to smite this poor, innocent elder with sickness!* It was a tender mercy, and I will always remember the goodness of God and that sweet moment I was able to share with Elder Sasulu in the MTC. We kept in contact throughout his mission, and he became a well-known and well-respected missionary.

I was once attending a luncheon with a group of seminary teachers when I asked one student teacher where he had served his mission. He told me he served in Canada. My wife and I looked at each other and asked him which mission he had served in. He responded the Calgary mission. When he told us what years he was there, we concluded that it would have been about the same time as Neli. I asked, "Did you happen to know an Elder Sasulu?" He quickly responded, "How do you know Neli?" I shared that we had tracted into him in New Zealand and were able to teach and baptize him. He then asked, "Can I hug you?" He came over to me, gave me a hug, and said, "That man changed my life!" I told him that Neli had changed my life too. I asked him what Neli was like as a missionary. He told me that everyone knew who Neli was wherever he went in the mission. When he and Neli went tracting, he said that Neli would never just walk. He said that they would run from door to door and would always be on the move. Neli became one of the great leaders of his mission and influenced hundreds of other missionaries.

After his mission, Neli and his wife were sealed in the temple. They have been blessed with four beautiful children and are currently living in Australia. Last month, I happened to be in Australia and was able to catch up with Neli and his family. As we spoke, we reflected on our experiences together and on the changes that took place in his life. He shared with me something interesting that underscores the importance of remembering that God is in control of His work.

A couple of months before we tracted into Neli, he had felt impressed that he needed to change. He wasn't sure what that meant, but he decided to stop participating in the after-rugby game festivities. When his buddies would come over to his house to party, Neli would shut himself in his room and just mediate and pray. Then, a short time later, came a knock at the door from two missionaries, offering a message of hope and of change. The Lord was preparing the heart of this young man, even as He was guiding us to tract on that particular street. For us to take *any* credit for Neli's conversion and subsequent success would be like "the ax boast[ing] itself against him that heweth therewith" or "the saw magnify[ing] itself against him that shaketh it" (2 Nephi 20:15). Like the sons of Mosiah, Neli had been changed by the power of the Atonement and had become a new creature. The Lord knew Neli, just as He knew the sons of Mosiah, and, in both cases, saw fit in His infinite mercy to snatch them from their current states and shape and mold them into incredibly effective instruments in His hands.

A few years ago, I received an email from Neli. In this email, he shared an experience with me that I had not previously heard. He said,

> As I came to realize the rich blessings that come from living the gospel, I couldn't help but share it with all my friends. I knew that I needed to go on a mission! It brought so much joy and comfort as I thought and dreamt of one day being a missionary, then I was told that I had to wait a year after being baptized before I could even apply. I was devastated, but at the same time it was a time of training and preparation to help me become a better prepared missionary. While I was preparing, I was given the opportunity to represent Samoa at the Rugby World Cup 2003.
>
> I have wanted to go to the world cup and play for Samoa my entire life (this event is like the NBA finals or the NFL SuperBowl). But I wanted to serve a mission even more, because *I knew who had*

rescued me and who my life should be dedicated to, and that is God, so I turned down that *once-in-a-lifetime opportunity* to serve the Lord. I would never have had it any other way. Serving a mission has helped me in everything in my life!

I can't explain what the mission field is like; it's best if you go and serve and pave the way for your own family and have your own experiences to share with your children in the future. Now, the Lord has seen fit that I be blessed with the opportunity to play for Samoa, and so my brother, who is a recent convert of three months, and I have made the Manu Samoa team 2008. So the Lord will bless us in ways we cannot see, but as we just continue to serve faithfully and wholeheartedly, the Lord will bless us.[117]

In the strength of the Lord, Neli had become a powerful servant of the Lord and learned firsthand that "sacrifice brings forth the blessings of heaven."[118] His life had become dedicated to the Lord, and he and his wife have become refined and polished instruments in His hands. At one point, his social media page had the following:

- Religious views: "LDS through and through"
- Favorite book: "The Book of Mormon"
- Favorite TV show: "General conference"
- Favorite quote: "For the natural man is an enemy to God, and has been from the fall of Adam, and will be, forever and ever, unless he yields to the enticings of the Holy Spirit, and putteth off the natural man and becometh a saint through the atonement of Christ the Lord, and becometh as a child, submissive, meek, humble, patient, full of love, willing to submit to all things which the Lord seeth fit to inflict upon him, even as a child doth submit to his father" (Mosiah 3:19).

Their current social network pages are missionary tools, as they often share quotes and talks from the Brethren, and also what the gospel has come to mean to them. Neli and his sweet wife continue their faithful service and are truly inspiring examples of what can happen when all submit and allow the Lord to do His own work. As I reunited with Neli last month, I could not help but think of Alma's meeting with the sons of Mosiah after their missions. You will recall the joy that filled their hearts as they saw each other again. But "what added more to his joy, they were still his brethren in the Lord" (Alma 17:2). This is exactly how I felt as I observed that Neli had become a faithful father and a loving husband. I saw a righteous priesthood man who had "waxed strong in the knowledge of the truth" and who had become a man "of a sound understanding," having "searched the scriptures diligently, that [he] might know the word of God" (Alma 17:2). Because of the change in his heart, he felt a love for everyone and a realization that the hand of the Almighty is over all who embark in the great work of salvation. Like Ammon and his brethren, this realization gave Neli the confidence to reach out and share the gospel with everyone around him.

And Thus We See

The conversion of the sons of Mosiah is one of the most inspiring and instructive case studies in all of the Book of Mormon. Their conversion was initiated by the experiences of a good friend and the truths taught by a prophet. They were led to repent and had to endure "much anguish of soul because of their iniquities" (Mosiah 28:4). Nevertheless, in His mercy and grace, the Lord "snatched [them] from [their] awful, sinful, and polluted state (Alma 26:17). So sincere was their repentance and so complete was their change that they could not bear the thought that anyone would have to endure forever the type of suffering they experienced. They had concluded that if the Lord's grace could extend to them, being "the very vilest of sinners" (Mosiah 28:3), then surely there was hope for everyone else, including their brethren, the Lamanites.

Through the Atonement of Christ, these mighty sinners became mighty men of valor and were fashioned into "smooth and polished shaft[s] in the quiver of the Almighty."[119] Through their experience, we learn invaluable lessons relating to embarking in the work of salvation. We learn that success in missionary work begins with a change of heart wrought by the power of the Atonement.

In this way, we can, like the sons of Mosiah, teach and testify out of our own changed hearts. Furthermore, we learn that this is God's work, it is His glory, and He is indeed able to do His own work. We have seen that He invites us to assist Him in this great work and provides us the opportunity to become instruments in His hands. Like Ammon, we need to learn that we can do all things, even mighty miracles, as we recognize and rely on the enabling and emboldening power of the grace of Christ. And thus we see that the Atonement of Jesus Christ not only changes us as we experience these divine encounters but also forges a godly soul who is then led with an insatiable desire to help others to experience this same celestial change.

Chapter 9: King Lamoni, His Father, and the Anti-Nephi-Lehies

In a dramatic, Pentecostal-type outpouring, King Lamoni experienced a miraculous infusion of divine light. This transformation set in motion a series of conversions that would eventually impact this entire civilization. From these experiences, we learn that the grace of Christ not only roots out the natural tendencies of the flesh but also enables us to become men and women of Christ. As we lay down the weapons of our rebellion, we show God our willingness to be changed.

Pentecostal Experiences

The day of Pentecost has long been synonymous with spiritual outpourings, visions, and angelic visitations. In the second chapter of Acts, Peter gathered together with the fledgling flock of Saints shortly after the Ascension of Christ. Having just filled the vacancy in the Quorum of the Twelve Apostles, they had gathered themselves together in one place when "suddenly there came a sound from heaven as of a rushing mighty wind, and it filled all the house where they were sitting. And there appeared unto them cloven tongues like as of fire . . . and they were all filled with the Holy Ghost" (Acts 2:2–4). After some treated lightly and even mocked this experience, Peter stood and spoke with power and authority. He quoted scripture, prophesied, and testified of the Savior. As the people heard and felt this testimony, "they were pricked in their heart" (Acts 2:37) and around three thousand souls were brought to the waters of baptism.

In something of a latter-day Pentecost, the early Saints gathered themselves together for the dedication of the Kirtland Temple. In this gathering, similar to the experience of Peter and his people, the Prophet Joseph and the Saints saw visions, some prophesied, many saw angels, and most were touched by the Spirit of the Lord. In this meeting, "Brother George A. Smith arose and began to prophesy, when a noise was heard like the sound of a rushing mighty wind, which filled the Temple, and all the congregation simultaneously arose, being moved upon by an invisible power; many began to speak in tongues and prophesy; others saw glorious visions. . . . The Temple was filled with angels. . . . The people of the neighborhood came running together (hearing an unusual sound within, and seeing a bright light like a pillar of fire resting upon the Temple), and were astonished at what was taking place."[120] This outpouring came at a time of significant stress, poverty, and trial, and it ignited a resilience and determination in the hearts of these Saints to serve in the kingdom and stay true to the cause in which they had embarked.

As the sons of Mosiah embarked on their ministry to the Lamanites, they were able to experience this same kind of outpouring. We see the Spirit of the Lord pricking the hearts of a wicked, idle, and bloodthirsty people as they experienced visions, revelations, and ultimately complete changes of heart. Through this ancient American Pentecostal experience, we learn that thousands of Lamanites were "brought into the fold of God" (Alma 26:4). While the conversions of King Lamoni, his father, and their entire kingdom could deservingly have their own separate chapters, because they are so interdependent, I have decided to cluster them together into one.

The Conversion of King Lamoni

Our initial introduction to King Lamoni comes when Ammon was taken captive after he arrived in the land of Ishmael. We are told Lamoni was the king over the land of Ishmael and that he was a direct descendant of Ishmael (see Alma 17:21). We learn something

of the austere nature of King Lamoni as his servants literally feared for their lives after having lost some of the king's flock. As these Lamanite servants "began to weep exceedingly . . . because of the fear of being slain," Ammon's heart swelled with joy—he determined that the Lord had provided this opportunity for him to show forth His power in restoring the flocks unto the king (Alma 17:28–29). We remember well the story of Ammon defending the sheep as the men came again to scatter them. You will recall that Ammon *disarmed* these men and, after driving "them afar off, he returned and they watered their flocks and returned them to the pasture of the king" (Alma 17:39). So astounded were Ammon's fellow servants that they caused the arms to be taken to the king, with their testimony of the seemingly immortal strength of Ammon.

After hearing "of the faithfulness of Ammon in preserving his flocks, and also of his great power in contending against those who sought to slay him," Lamoni was astonished and seemed to immediately assume Ammon "[was] more than a man" and was more than likely "the Great Spirit" (Alma 18:27). His servants seemed to buy into this assumption, as they explained that a mortal man could not accomplish the feat they had witnessed, concluding that Ammon could not be slain.

From this exchange, we see that the Lamanites not only believed "in a Great Spirit" but they also "supposed that whatsoever they did was right" (Alma 18:5). However, notwithstanding this moral relativism, something seemed different now, and Lamoni was fearful as he thought of the many people he had unjustly caused to be slain. Being filled with a great desire to learn more, Lamoni sent for Ammon. In this exchange, we are told that Ammon was filled with the Spirit of the Lord and demonstrated that he could perceive the king's thoughts. This experience added to the king's wonder. Marveling at such a miraculous demonstration, the king asked the question that had been weighing on his mind and that had caused anxiety and fear to enter into his heart. He asked, "Art thou that Great Spirit, who knows all things?" (Alma 18:18). The exchange that follows is not only a model for missionaries and gospel teachers alike, but it also provides a vibrant example of how the Lord can chase away clouds of darkness with light and truth.

While we do not know a lot about Lamoni's life prior to this experience, what we do know seems to clearly indicate that he was a tyrant, who ruled by instilling fear in the hearts of his people. We know that "he had slain many" of his servants because they had lost some of his flocks (Alma 18:6). We know that the Lamanites were "a wild and a hardened and a ferocious people; a people who delighted in murdering the Nephites, and robbing and plundering them; and their hearts were set upon riches . . . yet they sought to obtain these things by murdering and plundering, that they might not labor for them with their own hands. Thus they were a very indolent people, many of whom did worship idols" (Alma 17:14–15). This darkness of perpetual unbelief blinded the eyes of Lamoni and his people. However, the record makes it clear that this condition was brought on largely "because of the traditions of their fathers," and the Lord promised to be merciful unto this people "on the conditions of repentance" (Alma 17:15). We will see that through the instrumentality of Ammon and his brethren, the Lord was reaching out and rescuing this idolatrous people and restoring them to the knowledge of their true God.

As Ammon began to teach the king, it quickly became apparent that the Spirit was working upon his hardened heart. Intrigued and astonished by Ammon's ability to know the thoughts of his heart, King Lamoni said, "Thou mayest speak boldly, and tell me concerning these things" (Alma 18:20). It seems that Lamoni was letting Ammon know that he did not just want to hear generalities. Rather, he was in a state of readiness and "in a preparation to hear the word" of the Lord (Alma 32:6). To that point, a few verses later, Lamoni assuringly said to Ammon, "I will believe all thy words" (Alma 18:23). What humility! With a prepared investigator, whose heart is contrite and armed with a sound desire to understand the word of God, Ammon then proceeded to teach Lamoni about the three great pillars of eternity: the Creation, the Fall, and the Atonement (Alma 18:34–36). As he spoke, "he expounded unto them all the records and scriptures" and also "expounded unto them the plan of redemption" (Alma 18:38–39). Believing all of the words Ammon spoke, King Lamoni began to cry unto the Lord for mercy and grace. In one of the purest and most humble prayers we have recorded in scripture, Lamoni pled, "O Lord,

have mercy; according to thy abundant mercy which thou hast had upon the people of Nephi, have upon me, and my people" (Alma 18:41). In answer to this fervent prayer, Lamoni was visited of the Lord. He fell into a spiritual trance and was motionless on the ground for two days.

The Effects of the King's Conversion

Not understanding what was happening, the people assumed their king was dead and thus began to prepare his body to be placed in a sepulcher. Ammon, however, "knew that King Lamoni was under the power of God" (Alma 19:6). Imagine Ammon's emotions at this moment, and likely the flashbacks he surely must have had, remembering Alma falling to the ground in similar fashion. In fact, I wonder if at this point Ammon just assumed that conversion was *always* accompanied by spiritual trances and visions.

After two days, Lamoni arose and said, "Blessed be the name of God, and blessed art thou. For as sure as thou livest, behold, I have seen my Redeemer; and he shall come forth, and be born of a woman, and he shall redeem all mankind who believe on his name" (Alma 19:12–13). So profound was his enthusiasm and so intense was the influence of the Spirit that after speaking these words to his wife and others, Lamoni slipped back into the trance—the queen with him. In a highly emotional moment, Ammon was overcome with the Spirit as he saw the spiritual outpouring "upon the Lamanites, his brethren, who had been the cause of so much mourning among the Nephites" (Alma 19:14). Overcome, "he fell upon his knees, and began to pour out his soul in prayer and thanksgiving to God for what he had done for his brethren; and he was also overpowered with joy; and thus they all three had sunk to the earth" (Alma 19:14).

In a powerful demonstration of faith and courage, a woman named Abish gathered the people together to see what had taken place. Seeing sharp contention among some of the people, Abish reached down and raised the queen from off of the ground. As soon as she felt the hand of Abish, the queen stood and cried out, "O blessed Jesus, who has saved me from an awful hell! O blessed God, have mercy on this people!" (Alma 19:29). This faith-filled woman had encountered the goodness of the Lord and felt His merciful hand. Having experienced the grace of the Lord, "she clasped her hands, being filled with joy, speaking many words which were not understood" (Alma 19:30), and took her husband by the hand and brought him out of his trance.

After rebuking the people and calming the contentious spirit, Lamoni began to teach and testify to them of what he had experienced. And when Ammon got back up, both he and Lamoni taught the people, and "as many as heard his words believed, and were converted unto the Lord . . . and they did all declare . . . the selfsame thing—that their hearts had been changed; that they had no more desire to do evil. And behold, many did declare unto the people that they had seen angels and had conversed with them; and thus they had told them things of God, and of his righteousness" (Alma 19:31, 33–34). Those who believed were invited into the waters of baptism, and they established the Church among themselves. In an important commentary, Mormon summarized, "And thus the work of the Lord did commence among the Lamanites; thus the Lord did begin to pour out his Spirit upon them; and we see that his arm is extended to all people who will repent and believe on his name" (Alma 19:36).

Why a Pentecostal-esque Experience?

I appreciate your patience in allowing me to review this narrative, for I believe it is essential to have the complete context in mind if we are to highlight the hand of the Lord in this scripture story. Perhaps the most significant takeaway from the experience with Lamoni and his people is the sheer drama and intensity. This clearly mirrors the Pentecostal experience from Acts 2 and what the early Saints experienced in Kirtland. This connection begs the question of why. Why such drama? Why such outpourings? Why did the Lord see fit to send angels, have people speak in tongues, and experience visions and trances and the like? The answer seems to be that, in each of these situations, His people were in a vulnerable and pivotal stage. Peter and his brethren had just witnessed the Ascension of Christ and likely felt the significant load that was being placed on their shoulders. Their experience was a testament that the Lord was going to remain with them and that they should continue to rely on Him. The Kirtland Saints were suffering persecution and poverty, and the Lord clearly knew that

neither would let up anytime soon. Perhaps He provided the miracles at the Kirtland Temple to show the Saints that He had not—nor would He ever—forsake them. He had accepted their sacrifices and offerings, and thus instilled in the hearts and minds of His Saints a determination to serve Him to the end.

Against that backdrop, let's now consider the dramatic experience of Lamoni and his people. Why the trances and visions and angels? One likely possibility is that the Lamanites had become so hardened and so blinded by the darkness of wicked traditions that such an overwhelming and penetrating infusion of light was necessary. An entire people was being introduced to ideas that were likely foreign to them or had been so distorted after running their course through the antagonistic, wicked Lamanite traditions that they were hardly recognizable. Through this experience, the Lord gave no room for doubt. Everyone who was there felt of His mighty power and witnessed the outpouring of His grace. The record says "the dark veil of unbelief was being cast away from [Lamoni's] mind, and the light which did light up his mind, which was the light of the glory of God, which was a marvelous light of his goodness—yea, this light had infused such joy into his soul, the cloud of darkness having been dispelled, and that the light of everlasting life was lit up in his soul, yea, he knew that this had overcome his natural frame, and he was carried away in God" (Alma 19:6).

Lamoni learned that "the heavens begin to part and the blessings of heaven begin to distill upon us with the very first steps we take toward the light."[121] Furthermore, he had experienced firsthand that "the very moment you begin to seek your Heavenly Father, in that moment, the hope of His light will begin to awaken, enliven, and ennoble your soul."[122] Infused with this divine light, Lamoni and his people had their hearts changed forever.

Elder Dallin H. Oaks once shared an insight that has deep relevance to this story. He said, "I was helping my wife wash dishes on one occasion (she would say one *rare* occasion). She had baked nut bread. When I got to the pans, she said, 'Don't try to wash those pans before you soak them in water. The residue is cooked on.' Many of our erroneous ideas about the things of God and the procedures we should follow to accomplish his purposes are also 'cooked on' by the heat and pressure of worldly traditions and professional practices. Those ideas will not yield to cleansing until they have been soaked in the living water of gospel principles."[123] As one reads the narrative of King Lamoni's conversion, the change in his countenance is clear. The wicked traditions were soaked off in the living water of the Savior. This initial change began a domino effect that will yield thousands of deeply converted Lamanites, including Lamoni's own father.

The Conversion of Lamoni's Father

As the narrative continues, we later see Ammon, accompanied by Lamoni, heading toward Middoni to deliver his imprisoned brethren. Making their way to the city, they stumbled across King Lamoni's father. Here, we learn just how deep the Lamanites' grudge ran, as Lamoni's father immediately began to question his son's decision to be with "one of the children of a liar" (Alma 20:10). Things escalated quickly as Lamoni's father became so angry with Ammon that he commanded Lamoni to kill him. He told Lamoni that Ammon was the son "of a liar" and that "he robbed [their] fathers" and now came to rob them (Alma 20:13). Seeing that Lamoni would not even consider hurting the man whom he esteemed to be a holy prophet of God, Lamoni's father drew his sword in an attempt to slay Ammon—once again, a clear sign of how corrupt the paradigm was among the Lamanite people. Ammon withstood the attempt and disarmed the king. When he saw that Ammon could slay him, he feared for his life and said, "I will grant unto thee whatsoever thou wilt ask, even to half of the kingdom" (Alma 20:23). As Ammon spoke to him, Lamoni's father realized Ammon "had no desire to destroy him, and when he also saw the great love he had for his son Lamoni, he was astonished exceedingly" (Alma 20:27). After listening to the words of Ammon and Lamoni, the king was desirous to learn more.

The king's desire was realized after Aaron and his brethren were released from prison and "went forth whithersoever they were led by the Spirit of the Lord" and eventually went to "the land of Nephi, even to the house of . . . the father of Lamoni" (Alma 21:16; 22:1). They introduced themselves as the brethren of Ammon and were invited into the king's palace. Upon offering to be the king's servants, the king responded by saying, "Arise, for I will grant unto you your

lives, and I will not suffer that ye shall be my servants; but *I will insist* that ye shall administer unto me" (Alma 22:3; emphasis added).

The king was now prepared and, like Lamoni, assured the missionaries that he would believe all they taught him. "When Aaron saw that the king would believe his words, he began from the creation of Adam, reading the scriptures unto the king" (Alma 22:12). He then proceeded to teach the king about the connection between the Creation, the Fall, and the Atonement, making clear to the king that "since man had fallen he could not merit anything of himself; but the sufferings and death of Christ atone for their sins" (Alma 22:14). As the truths regarding the Atonement sunk deep into the heart of this now-humbled king, he was filled with a desire to repent and change. Indeed, the teaching of true doctrine directly from the revealed word of the Lord ignited in this man a longing for a new birth. In a tender and heartfelt plea, Lamoni's father cried out to Aaron, "What shall I do that I may have this eternal life of which thou hast spoken? Yea, what shall I do that I may be born of God, having this wicked spirit rooted out of my breast, and receive his Spirit, that I may be filled with joy, that I may not be cast off at the last day?" (Alma 22:15). This man's plea provides a profound glimpse into the divine change that can happen when a humble heart calls on the name of the Lord in submissive, mighty prayer.

So powerful was the desire of this man to experience this mighty change that he declared a willingness to forsake everything that he possessed, including his palace and kingdom if necessary. As Aaron saw the king's contrition, he helped him to understand that the Lord does not want the palace or kingdom; after all, the entire earth is His. Rather, He invites all to bow down before Him in faith and repent. So great was the faith of the king that he did immediately "bow down before the Lord, upon his knees; yea, even he did prostrate himself upon the earth, and cried mightily, saying: O God, Aaron hath told me that there is a God; and if there is a God, and if thou art God, wilt thou make thyself known unto me, and I will give away all my sins to know thee" (Alma 22:17–18). This simple and yet sublime prayer provides poignant insight into the repentance process and the application of the Atonement of Jesus Christ. The king seemed to understand that the Lord did not want his property, his possessions, or his position. Rather, He wanted his sins so that He could sanctify his soul and perform a mighty work among His people.

Rooting Out the Natural Man

Elder Bruce C. Hafen taught, "We can have eternal life if we want it, but only if there is *nothing else* we want more. So we must willingly give everything, because God Himself can't make us grow against our will and without our full participation."[124] Lamoni's father demonstrated that he was willing to give up anything and everything to have this hope of eternal life. This powerful experience underscores the truth that "repentance must involve an all-out, total surrender to the program of the Lord."[125] As the king surrendered and consecrated his heart to the Lord, he fell, like Lamoni previously did, into a deep trance. When the queen saw her husband, she assumed he was dead and sent her servants to slay Aaron and his brethren. Seeing the danger, Aaron "put forth his hand and raised the king from the earth" (Alma 22:22). Everyone marveled as the king stood forth and began to minister unto the people. So great was his faith and so powerful was this experience "that his whole household were converted unto the Lord" (Alma 22:23). Through the Atonement of Jesus Christ and by the power of repentance, King Lamoni's father experienced a new birth. The natural man had been rooted out of his heart, and he walked in a newness of life, even having the mind of Christ.

C. S. Lewis effectively captured this "rooting out" of the natural man in one volume of his Chronicles of Narnia series. In this book, *The Voyage of the Dawn Treader*, Lewis told of a young boy named Eustace. This young boy was pompous, self-righteous, and thus extremely annoying to those around him.

In the story, there is a shipwreck and, rather than helping the others make the necessary repairs, Eustace wanders off to explore. He works his way down a large mountain, discovering a pool of water. Approaching the water, he hears a noise behind him. At that moment, a dragon comes out of its cave and it is clearly struggling in pain. Terrified, Eustace looks at the dragon as it goes over to the pool of water, takes a little drink, and staggeringly collapses to the ground. This young boy does not know what to think of this situation

and is not sure if the dragon is dead or alive. He hesitantly walks over to the dragon and realizes it is dead. At that moment, it begins to rain, and Eustace starts looking for shelter. He finds the dragon's cave and determines to make his way over to get out of the rain. As he enters the cave, he finds what any of us would expect to find in a dragon's cave: treasure! He begins reveling in the treasure, anticipating the power and influence he will have with his newfound wealth. As he sits on this treasure, thinking worldly thoughts, he finds himself exhausted and decides to take a nap. However, just before going to sleep, he places a golden ring on his arm. After falling asleep, he begins to hear a strange sound. As he peeks his eyes open, he sees two jet streams puffing up. Naturally, he finds himself terrified as he remembers that he is in a dragon's cave. He rebukes himself for being so thoughtless as to not consider that the dragon he previously encountered likely had a mate.

Doctor S. Michael Wilcox summarized the next part of the story:

> He holds his breath. But as he holds his breath, the steam stops. When he lets it out again, slowly, trying not to draw attention to himself, the steam issues forth in a straight steady jet. He reaches to the left, feeling for the wall to sneak out that way. Yet as he reaches out his hand, he sees a great dragon claw come into view. He freezes. It freezes. He lowers it. It lowers. The dragon is on the left side of him. He reaches his right out and as he does so another great claw comes into view. He freezes. It freezes. He drops it. It drops. The dragon must be over him with its paws around him and it is mimicking his every move.[126]

In shock and absolute terror, Eustace decides to run for safety toward the pool of water. When he arrives, he looks into the water and notices that the dragon he was running from was actually himself. He had become a dragon! Apparently, sleeping on a dragon's hoard while thinking greedy, dragonish thoughts in his heart caused him to become a dragon.

We are often taught that we become the product of our thoughts and desires. In the case of young Eustace, as the feelings, thoughts, and desires of the natural man overcame him, he became this symbolic representation of the natural man: a dragon.

As Eustace reunites with his party—after the shock of realizing that this dragon was indeed their shipmate Eustace—they are relieved to find him alive. In fact, they end up finding it quite helpful to have a dragon as part of their crew, with his strength and flying abilities. Eustace, however, finds himself discouraged, frustrated, and deeply alone. He yearns to be a boy again and be able to communicate with the others. Drawing from the language of Lewis,

> He wanted to get back among humans and talk and laugh and share things. He realized that he was a monster cut off from the whole human race. An appalling loneliness came over him. He began to see that the others had not really been fiends at all. He began to wonder if he himself had been such a nice person as he had always supposed. He longed for their voices. . . . When he thought of this the poor dragon that had been Eustace lifted up its voice and wept. A powerful dragon crying its eyes out under the moon in a deserted valley is a sight and a sound hardly to be imagined. At last he decided he would try to find his way back to the shore.[127]

Almost at this precise moment, he looks up and sees Aslan walking by. This symbolic representation of Christ invites Eustace to come and follow Him. This familiar invitation touches Eustace, and he is soon filled with hope. Aslan leads Eustace down to a beautiful pool of water and invites him to bathe in the water but instructs him that he must first undress. After overcoming some initial confusion, Eustace realizes that dragons are kind of like snakes and must therefore have several layers of skin. Feeling a new hope and encouragement, Eustace begins to claw and scratch at his outer layer of skin. Upon realizing that he still was not yet prepared for this bath, he determinedly scratches off another layer, and then another. At this point, he again becomes discouraged as he realizes that he cannot "undress" as he had been instructed to do.

Sensing his discouragement, Aslan asks Eustace if he would like help. Humbled, penitent, and hungry for change, Eustace submits to Aslan's offering, ready to do anything to be rid of the beast he has become and be transformed into a new person. Aslan invites Eustace to lay down on his back and warns him that this change is going to be painful. But at this point, Eustace is willing to do anything. In that moment, the great Lion takes his claws and begins to tear deeply into the dragon's skin until he reaches the little boy inside. In his own words, Eustace explained, "And when he began pulling the skin off,

it hurt worse than anything I've ever felt. The only thing that made me able to bear it was just the pleasure of feeling the stuff peel off. . . . Well, he peeled the beastly stuff right off—just as I thought I'd done it myself the other three times, only they hadn't hurt—and there it was lying on the grass: only ever so much thicker, and darker, and more knobbly-looking than the others had been. And there was I as smooth and soft as a peeled switch and smaller than I had been."[128]

Mercifully, tenderly, and with his loving paws, Aslan helps Eustace into the water, thus healing and transforming this natural man into a man of Christ. The entire character and nature of young Eustace is changed. Where he was once filled with selfishness, arrogance, and pride, he now found himself deeply humbled, graciously generous, and anxious to serve others. Drawing on this story and the imagery of this change, Dr. Wilcox observed:

> That comment of Eustace about the layers of dragon skin he had peeled off not hurting is an important idea for Lewis. Sometimes we go to the Savior and we want to get healed or helped in some little thing that is troubling us. We feel the pinch of the conscience. Something in our lives no longer fits comfortably. Maybe we are watching the wrong kind of movies. We scratch and peel and throw that bad habit at the Lord's feet and say, "Is that enough?" But we know in our hearts it is not. Maybe we're irritable. Maybe we get angry. Maybe we gossip. Maybe we have a little problem with the Word of Wisdom or tithing. Maybe we waste time. We continue to peel off the layers and lay them down. But the whole dragon skin has got to come off.[129]

Giving Away All Our Sins

The conversion story of King Lamoni's father highlights both the need for us to be willing to give away all of our sins, as well as the singular power of the grace of Christ to root out our natural tendencies and replace them with Christlike attributes. As the story of Eustace shows, eventually we all must learn that "only God can bless us. Only He can sustain us. Only He can cause our hearts to beat and give us breath. Only He can preserve and protect us. Only He can give us strength to bear up the burdens of life. Only He can give us power, knowledge, peace, and joy. Only He can forgive our sins. Only He can heal us. Only He can change us and forge a godly soul."[130] We all eventually learn that it is only in and through the Atonement of Jesus Christ that we become whom our Father intends for us to become.

I will never forget one of my most regretful moments as a religious educator. I was a student teacher in my first month of studying the Book of Mormon. The class and I had been talking about the story of King Lamoni's father and had just read his heartfelt commitment to give away all of his sins when a sixteen-year-old girl said, "That is so silly. It doesn't even make sense. What does that even mean, give away his sins? Of course he wants to give them away. I mean, why in the world would he even want to keep them?" The eyes of thirty-two students were riveted on me as this young woman almost defiantly folded her arms at what she considered to be an absurd scripture. While I do not recall exactly what I said, I remember fumbling around for a while, trying to come up with a meaningful way to respond. Unfortunately, and regretfully, I just nervously agreed with her and said that it did sound a bit strange, and we moved on.

Oh, how I wish I could have that moment back with those same students! This young woman had served up a proverbial softball for me, and I swung and completely missed! If I could go back, I would talk to both her and this class about how absurd it *does* sound to think that we would want to hold onto our sins. But that would only be the beginning. If I could go back, I may have posed questions like this to her: "You're absolutely right, that is crazy. So why do we do it? Why do we sometimes do things that we know we should not do? Why do we hold onto our sins instead of laying them at the feet of the Lord?"

I would then take the class to 2 Nephi 15:18 and read these words from Isaiah: "Wo unto them that draw iniquity with cords of vanity, and sin as it were with a cart rope." I would take them to the footnote in Isaiah 5:15, which provides the following insight: "They are tied to their sins like beasts to their burdens." Isn't that so true? We sometimes bind ourselves to our favorite sins and get uncomfortable if we begin to distance ourselves too much. I would most certainly talk about the significance of Lamoni's father's willingness to give away *all* of his sins, even his favorite ones, to know the Lord. If we had time, we could turn a few pages ahead and read of the Anti-Nephi-Lehies and their willingness to bury the weapons of *their*

rebellion deep in the earth so that they would no longer be tempted to fall short of their potential.

The conversation might be well served by inviting students to ponder and write in their journals about some of those little pet sins that they need to separate themselves from. I would then testify to them that when we feel the Spirit of the Lord, we lose any and all desire to sin, even with our favorite sins. I would promise them that they can have eternal life, but only if they are willing to give up anything ungodly or unholy and put on Christ and walk with Him.

The message for those early-morning seminary students—and the message for every one of us:

> The Christian way is different: harder, and easier. Christ says "Give me All. I don't want so much of your time and so much of your money and so much of your work: I want You. I have not come to torment your natural self, but to kill it. No half-measures are any good. I don't want to cut off a branch here and a branch there, I want to have the whole tree down. I don't want to drill the tooth, or crown it, or stop it, but to have it out. Hand over the whole natural self, all the desires which you think innocent as well as the ones you think wicked—the whole outfit. I will give you a new self instead. In fact, I will give you Myself: my own will shall become yours."[131]

King Lamoni's father is a powerful example of this. Through the grace of Jesus Christ, and because of his willingness to give up everything, he would become a significant instrument in setting up the conversions of thousands of Lamanites throughout his entire kingdom.

The Conversion of the Anti-Nephi-Lehies

Following his conversion, the king sent a proclamation throughout the land, decreeing that no hands should be laid upon these faithful missionaries and that they should "go forth preaching the word of God, in whatsoever place they should be" (Alma 23:1). There is an interesting idea in Alma 23:3 regarding political stewardship. We talked earlier about the notion of the stewardship of reputation; this seems to add a new look to the same idea. Both Lamoni and his father demonstrated the influence of political power, both for evil and for good. We have seen the tyranny demonstrated prior to their conversion and will now see their use of political power for good. The record says, "And thus they [the sons of Mosiah and their brethren] might go forth and preach the word according to their desires, *for the king had been converted unto the Lord* . . . therefore he sent his proclamation throughout the land unto his people, that the word of God might have no obstruction" (Alma 23:3; emphasis added). That phrase underscores the influence of the king's conversion on the gospel spreading forth, and thus to the conversion of these people. It is clear that prior to this conversion, there *was* an obstruction to the word of God, and thus the people were left in darkness as to things of the gospel.

Immediately following this proclamation, Aaron and his brethren got to work. It did not take long for them to see the significance of the king's conversion and his subsequent proclamation as "thousands were brought to believe" (Alma 23:5). Lamanites were converted in the lands of Ishmael, Middoni, Nephi, Shilom, Shemlon, and Lemuel, and in the city of Shimnilom. After reading of this great harvest amongst the Lamanites, we see this little jewel that is typically just a quick, passing read: "And the Amalekites were not converted, save only one" (Alma 23:15). I look forward to the day when I can hear the story of that one courageous Amalekite!

Interestingly—and not coincidently—following their conversion, these faithful Lamanites sought some way to distinguish themselves from their brethren. After much consultation, they determined that they would call themselves the "Anti-Nephi-Lehies; and they were called by this name and were no more called Lamanites" (Alma 23:17). It is important to note how anxious they were to remove themselves from their wicked traditions. Indeed, they were applying the divinely inspired invitation to "come ye out from the wicked, and be ye separate" (Alma 5:57). Having experienced the grace of the Savior, they were full of gratitude and were determined to show the Lord that they intended to remain steadfast in Him.

After All We Can Do

Because He has "granted unto [us our] lives," and because we all "depend upon the same Being, even God, for all the substance which we have," it is true that we can do nothing save it be by His kindness

and mercy (see Mosiah 2:23; 4:19). Nevertheless, true faith is always manifest in faithfulness, and these disciples of Christ greatly desired to demonstrate their faithfulness to the Lord. As King Anti-Nephi-Lehi met with his people, he movingly taught, "Oh, how merciful is our God! And now behold, since it has been as much as we could do to get our stains taken away from us, and our swords are made bright, let us hide them away that they may be kept bright, *as a testimony to our God at the last day . . . that we have not stained our swords in the blood of our brethren since he imparted his word unto us and has made us clean thereby*" (Alma 24:15; emphasis added). In a dramatic demonstration of sacrifice, trust, and consecration, these faithful converts "did lay down the weapons of their rebellion" (Alma 23:7) and did "bury them deep in the earth" (Alma 24:17). In so doing, they entered into a binding covenant with the Lord that "they never would use weapons again for the shedding of man's blood; and this they did, vouching and covenanting with God, that rather than shed the blood of their brethren they would give up their own lives" (Alma 24:18).

With his people gathered together, King Anti-Nephi-Lehi took this opportunity to both gracefully and gratefully testify of the Savior's mercy and grace. He said, "I thank my God . . . that our great God has in goodness sent these our brethren . . . to convince us of the traditions of our wicked fathers" (Alma 24:7). He then added, "I thank my great God that he has given us a portion of his Spirit to soften our hearts . . . we have been convinced of our sins, and of the many murders which we have committed" (Alma 24:8–9). Finally, he said, "I also thank my God, yea, my great God, that he hath granted unto us that we might repent of these things, and also that he hath forgiven us of those our many sins and murders which we have committed, and *taken away the guilt from our hearts, through the merits of his Son*" (Alma 24:10; emphasis added). This king was clearly overwhelmed at the goodness and grace of God and was fully aware that they were entirely undeserving of such mercy.

Earlier in the Book of Mormon, Nephi taught, "We know that it is by grace that we are saved, after all we can do" (2 Nephi 25:23). One author suggested we look at the preposition *after* in this verse as a preposition of separation rather than one of time. In other words, rather than thinking that we do not receive the Savior's grace until we have exerted all of our energy and efforts, Nephi could have been saying "we are saved by grace 'apart from all we can do,' or 'all we can do notwithstanding,' or even 'regardless of all we can do.' Another acceptable paraphrase of the sense of the verse might read, 'We are still saved by grace, after all is said and done.'"[132] Adding his prophetic tone to this same idea, Elder Ballard said, "It is ultimately by the grace of Christ that we are saved *even* after all that we can do. . . . No matter how hard we work, no matter how much we obey, no matter how many good things we do in this life, it would not be enough were it not for Jesus Christ and His loving grace. On our own we cannot earn the kingdom of God—no matter what we do."[133]

Continuing with his meek and contrite address to his people, the king of the Anti-Nephi-Lehies seemed to speak to Nephi's earlier *after all we can do* phrase. He taught, "And now behold, my brethren, since *it has been all that we could do* (as we were the most lost of all mankind) *to repent of all our sins* . . . *it was all we could do to repent sufficiently before God* that he would take away our stain—now, my best beloved brethren, since God hath taken away our stains, and our swords have become bright, then let us stain our swords no more with the blood of our brethren" (Alma 24:11–12; emphasis added).

Isn't that interesting? He made it clear that it is only through the merits, mercy, and grace of the Messiah that they had been cleansed and made whole. In fact, his explanation underscores that their determination to put away their swords had everything to do with their gratitude for the Atonement. This verse could be used in tandem with Nephi's statement that "we know that it is by grace that we are saved, after all we can do" (2 Nephi 25:23). In other words, for the Anti-Nephi-Lehies, all that they could do was repent and rely on the Redeemer. Perhaps this same idea is true for all of us. Robert L. Millet provided the following insight into this concept:

> This does not mean that we must do everything we can do *before* Christ can assist us. This is not about chronology. Further, who do you know who has or will ever do *all* they can do? Grace is not just that final boost into heaven that God provides at the end of a well-lived life, although we obviously will need all the help we can get. Rather, the Almighty assists us all along the way, every second of every minute of every hour of every day, all through our lives. It does not

mean that we will carry the bulk of the load to salvation and Jesus will fill in the gaps; he is not the God of the gaps. Our contribution to glory hereafter, when compared to his, is infinitesimal and minuscule. If I might be permitted a paraphrase of what the passage stated, "We are saved by grace, *above and beyond* all we can do, *notwithstanding* all we can do, *in spite of* all we can do.[134]

Recognizing that they were in fact doing all they could do as they repented and relied on the Savior, they were determined to stay true to the covenants they had made. Shortly after this dramatic moment of burying their weapons of war, these recent converts were given an opportunity to demonstrate their newfound conviction and determination. The Lamanites who had not been converted were stirred up to anger against the Anti-Nephi-Lehies. Lamoni, his brother, and the sons of Mosiah met in a council of war to determine how they should best defend themselves. The record states that "there was not one soul among all the people who had been converted unto the Lord that would take up arms against their brethren; nay, *they would not even make any preparations for war* (Alma 24:6; emphasis added).

Think of that! Their change of heart had run so deep that they did not want to even consider the possibility that they would take another human life again. Perhaps they understood that "the devil knows where to tempt, where to put in his telling blows. He finds the vulnerable spot. Where one was weak before, he will be most easily tempted again."[135] Feeling this truth surely led them to confidently agree, and later covenant, that they would not shed the blood of another as long as they should remain upon the earth.

The Weapons of Our Rebellion

As the wicked Lamanites approached these recent converts with rage and jealousy in their hearts, the Anti-Nephi-Lehies looked upon them and they "prostrated themselves before them to the earth, and began to call on the name of the Lord; and thus they were in this attitude when the Lamanites began to fall upon them, and began to slay them with the sword. And thus without meeting any resistance, they did slay a thousand and five of them; and we know that they are blessed, for they have gone to dwell with their God" (Alma 24:24–25). As these Lamanites saw the willingness of their converted brethren to lay down their lives rather than take up their swords again, "there were many whose hearts had swollen in them" (Alma 24:24), and they were led to repent of their sins. In defiance against the sins that they had committed, these newly touched Lamanites "threw down their weapons of war" (Alma 24:25) with the commitment that they too would willingly give up their lives rather than shed the blood of their brethren. This act of bravery and faith led to the conversion of more than a thousand Lamanites, thus demonstrating "that the Lord worketh in many ways to the salvation of his people" (Alma 24:27).

Commenting on this dramatic display of faithfulness, and helping us find application therein, Elder David A. Bednar recently taught, "They never did fall away and surrendered 'the weapons of their rebellion, that they did not fight against God any more.' To set aside cherished 'weapons of rebellion' such as selfishness, pride, and disobedience requires more than merely believing and knowing. Conviction, humility, repentance, and submissiveness precede the abandonment of our weapons of rebellion. Do you and I still possess weapons of rebellion that keep us from becoming converted unto the Lord? If so, then we need to repent now."[136] So deep was their love for the Savior and so complete was the converting influence of His Atonement that as many of them as believed "and were converted unto the Lord, never did fall away" (Alma 23:6). What a remarkable statement and what a miraculous demonstration of the lasting change that can happen when individuals lay hold upon the gospel of Jesus Christ and rely on His grace.

And Thus We See

We have covered a lot of ground in this chapter, analyzing the lives and conversion of Lamoni, his father, and their people. As we consider the experiences of these great Saints, it is important to remember that the Lord knew them and was aware of the harvest of souls that would take place as Ammon and his brethren embarked upon the work of the kingdom. These stories highlight the reality that God truly is in control of the work of salvation, and if we will turn to Him and rely on the direction, He will provide great success,

both personally and ecclesiastically. Just as He provided a Pentecostal experience when Peter was feeling the weight of the work that was to be required of him, the Lord provided a spiritual feast for these Lamanites who were blinded by the wicked traditions of their fathers. From Lamoni's experience, we can plainly see that the gospel light has the ability to penetrate the darkest places and can chase away darkness from among us (see D&C 50:25).

Lamoni's father illustrates the need to be willing to consecrate everything to the Lord. He learned that he *could* eventually inherit eternal life; he likewise learned that he needed to desire it more than anything else if he was to inherit that ultimate blessing. His experience teaches of the necessity of not only putting off the natural man but also having it completely rooted out of our hearts. In so doing, we learn that coming to know God the Father and His Beloved Son is worth any price we might be required to pay and any sacrifice we may need to make. Indeed, as we willingly give away all of our sins to know Him, His divine love is poured out upon us, and we are filled with a great desire to do good and help others experience this same miracle.

As Lamoni and his father opened up the land to the preaching of the gospel, we witness the power of the word and its ability to help us become clean through the Atonement of Jesus Christ (see Alma 24:15). These illustrious converts demonstrated their willingness to sacrifice as they buried the weapons of their rebellion and willingly gave up their lives rather than break the covenant they had made with God. Because of the change that had been wrought in their hearts, they knew that even if they did perish, they would be blessed, having "gone to dwell with their God" (Alma 24:22). Because of the experiences they had with the Savior, they developed a deep and abiding trust in Him and in His eternal promises.

Chapter 10: Captain Moroni

As the world around us drifts further and further from
the moral standards of the Lord, we find spiritual battles
becoming more and more heated. Captain Moroni and
his Nephite armies help us to remember that the battle
is really the Lord's. As we keep our covenants with Him,
trust in Him, and rely on His enabling grace, we can
experience divine hope and confidence.

Taking Satan Down

I am the father of five rambunctious, high-energy boys, who are
all eight years old and younger. As you can imagine, our house vacil-
lates between a wrestling mat, a football field, and an oversized artist
easel. During sacrament meeting, my wife and I sometimes feel like
we are referees who throw the proverbial flag, calling penalties for
unsportsmanlike conduct (such as throwing cereal or other objects,
hitting, kicking, and pinching), offsides (meaning having one of the
boys break through our tackles to escape down the aisle), and exces-
sive celebration (that is to say, the lack of concern for the people sitting
around us, evidenced by loud, boisterous behavior).

One of the things I love most about being a father to young children is the fact that there never seems to be a dull moment. I remember one experience we had when I was invited to speak at a meeting

where a young woman in my ward was receiving her Young Women's medallion. This was a particularly important evening for her because she was turning eighteen and had overcome a lot of major obstacles to achieve this award. The meeting was held in the Primary room and was a small, intimate group (around twenty people or so). As the meeting began, we sang "The Spirit of God," and the Spirit was there in abundance as we sang together. As the person offering the opening prayer concluded, the congregation offered a unified, "Amen." After that, and as the brother who offered the prayer was walking back to his seat, my five-year-old shouted out, "Aaamen to that prayer!" Needless to say, it elicited a lot of laughter, and everyone in attendance remembers well that night when our little boys made their presence quite known.

To try to help redirect the energy of our boys, we do a lot of wrestling in our home. They love to wrestle, but they especially love to wrestle their dad. Their ultimate goal at this stage in their lives is to be able to "take Daddy down." These little guys are getting quite creative now, and I often walk right into an ambush on my way into the house. (They even have the two-year-old getting involved in their conniving little plans.)

Like many small children, our little boys sometimes struggle to eat their dinner. One of the ways we have encouraged them to eat their food is to tell them that if they eat, their bodies will be healthy and strong, and then they will be able to "take Daddy down." As they take bites, we say things like, "Wow, look at how big your muscles are getting. I think if you keep eating, you're going to be strong enough to take Daddy down." Our little four-year-old works on reverse psychology, so I will say things like, "Uh oh, don't eat that, Caleb, because I don't want you to take me down." He will then pick up his fork and look up at me, and I will say, "No, don't do it! Don't do it, don't . . . oh no, you did it! Now I'm scared because you are going to be too strong for me!" It is an absolute delight to play with these little guys.

On one particular day, my wife was feeding the boys lunch while I was at work. As they sat eating their food, our then-five-year-old (while surely thinking of all of the ways he would be able to take me down after eating this meal), said, "Mommy, I want to take Satan

down." My wife was taken aback a bit and decided to make this a teaching moment. She said, "Well, buddy, Satan doesn't even have a body, so we can't physically take him down." Seeing the disappointed look in his eyes, she continued, "But do you want to know how we *can* take him down?" Immediately, his eyes beamed and he excitedly—with a giggle in his voice—shouted, "Yessss!" My wife then taught our boys that the way we take Satan down is by making good choices and following Heavenly Father and Jesus. They seemed excited about this newly discovered knowledge.

Later that night, we were sitting down to watch a movie as a family. Like most people, we have a coveted spot on the couch that always seems to be the most popular, and thus causes the most contention in our home. After cleaning up dinner, the race was on for the coveted spot. My oldest boy got there first, and his younger brother immediately began to throw a tantrum. Upon seeing the reaction of his little brother, my oldest said, "It's okay, you can have the spot." He then jumped up and moved over on the couch to make room. As he stood up, he looked up at us and said, "I just took Satan down!" We couldn't help but smile at his determination.

While that story is cute and shows the innocence and purity of a child, it does teach a profound lesson. President Howard W. Hunter underscored this lesson when he warned, "Our most deadly contest in life is not with human enemies."[137] To this point, Brigham Young said, "The men and women, who desire to obtain seats in the celestial kingdom, will find that they must battle every day."[138] Elder Ballard added to this idea when he said, "We battle literally for the souls of men. The enemy is unforgiving and relentless. He is taking eternal prisoners at an alarming rate. And he shows no sign of letting up."[139] Clearly this battle against the adversary is real, and it is certainly ongoing.

Captain Moroni's Strategy

Those who have given the Book of Mormon even a cursory reading are familiar with the chapters that have become popularly known as "the war chapters." In Alma 43, immediately after Alma's counsel to his sons, we are introduced to a man who is an absolute pillar in the second half of the book of Alma: Captain Moroni. In fact, "It is of interest to note that approximately one out of every ten pages of the Book of Mormon deals with the life and times of Captain Moroni."[140] Perhaps you have wondered why so much of the sacred space on these plates would be dedicated to war and, more specifically, to Captain Moroni and his experiences during such times. Elder Joe J. Christensen suggested that we live in a time where we need more authentic heroes. He then explained, "Captain Moroni provides young and old with the kind of hero the world so critically needs—a hero who deserves to be emulated. He possessed personal characteristics that set him apart as a remarkable individual. The prophet Mormon recognized the rare values found in Captain Moroni's life and experiences and generously chose to share them with us in our day and time."[141] Having seen our day and the imminent wars and rumors of wars in the last days, it would seem that Mormon wanted us to observe a model of how to prosper in times of war. Furthermore, as we read these chapters, we learn that they are overflowing with rich symbolism designed to help us as we battle the adversary in this great spiritual struggle.

In the war chapters, we are introduced to several exemplary disciples of Jesus Christ. Among them are Captain Moroni, Lehi, Helaman, Teancum, the stripling warriors, Lachoneus, Pahoran, and many others. Unfortunately, we are not given much with regard to the specific experiences that led them to develop their faithful resilience and commitment to Christ. We are shown, however, how Captain Moroni built his entire military philosophy on his firm and consecrated commitment to Christ. Think of what that would be like in our day. What would our society look like if we had a political system that remained true to Christian principles and relied on the Omnipotent One? As we look through the war chapters of the Book of Mormon, we can see various ways in which we can cleave to our covenants and inspire others to stay true to the cause of Christ. We will see that some of the lessons learned from these chapters are symbolic in nature, while others could be seen as more literal.

There is a powerful lesson demonstrated in the first war story in these chapters. We see a battle that has been brewing between Moroni with his army of Nephites and Zarahemnah and his Lamanite army, "who were a compound of Laman and Lemuel, and the sons of Ishmael,

and all those who had dissented from the Nephites, who were Ama-lekites and Zoramites, and the descendants of the priests of Noah" (Alma 43:13). This chapter describes the juxtaposition between the designs of both armies in going to battle. It was the wicked design of the Lamanites to "usurp great power over [the Nephites] . . . by bringing them into bondage" and the righteous desire of the Nephites to "support their lands, and their houses, and their *wives*, and their *children*, that they might preserve them from the hands of their enemies; and also that they might preserve their *rights* and their privileges, yea, and also their *liberty*, that they might *worship* God according to their desires" (Alma 43:9; emphasis added).

As the book of Alma describes the "wicked and murderous disposition" (Alma 43:6) of many of Lamanite leaders, their "hatred towards the Nephites" (Alma 43:7), and "the extreme hatred of the Lamanites towards . . . the people of Anti-Nephi-Lehi" (Alma 43:11), we are given a detailed account of the war that ensued. At the height of the first battle, we are told that the war was "more dreadful on the part of the Lamanites" (Alma 43:37) because of their glaring lack of armor. The Nephites, on the other hand, came off victorious because Moroni had armed his people "with swords, and with cimeters, and all manner of weapons of war . . . [and] had prepared his people with breastplates and with arm-shields, yea, and also shields to defend their heads, and also they were dressed with thick clothing" (Alma 43:19). As the story continues, it becomes clear that Moroni's inspired decision to properly prepare his people made the difference in this great battle.

The Power of the Word

Just as physical armor was crucial in leading the Nephites to victory over the Lamanites, the "whole armour of God" has been promised to help us overcome and "stand against the wiles of the devil" (Ephesians 6:11). Speaking of the armor of God, Elder Jeffrey R. Holland taught,

> In that description of preparing for spiritual battle, I have been impressed that most of the protection the Lord outlines for us there is somewhat defensive. The revelation speaks of breastplates and shields and helmets, all of which are important and protective but which leave us, in a sense, without an actual weapon yet. Are we only to be

on the defensive? Are we simply to ward off blows and see it through and never be able, spiritually speaking, to strike a blow? No.

We are supposed to advance in this and win a battle that started in heaven long ago. So we need some kind of even chance on the offense, and we are given it. You are given it. The weapon that is mentioned, the thing that allows us to actually do battle with the "darkness of this world," to use Paul's phrase, is "the sword of the Spirit, which is *the word of God*" (Ephesians 6:12, 17; italics added). May I repeat that? "The sword of the Spirit, which is the word of God." I love that marriage of spiritual concepts.

Coupled with prayer and the power of the priesthood that ought to be in all of our lives, I believe the greatest source of spirituality available to our youth (and everyone else) is the word of God, the scriptures, the revelations.[142]

Elder Holland's commentary is further enhanced when coupled with Alma's insight that the preaching of the word "had had more powerful effect upon the minds of the people than the sword, or anything else, which had happened unto them—therefore [he] thought it was expedient that [his people] should *try the virtue of the word of God*" (Alma 31:5; emphasis added). "Another word for *virtue* is *power*. [For example,] when the woman came to touch the hem of Christ's garment, in the scene in the New Testament, He said, 'Virtue [has] gone out of me' (Luke 8:46). The original Greek New Testament language for that is *power*."[143] When we speak of trying the "virtue of the word of God," what we are really talking about is experimenting on the *power* of the word.

President Ezra Taft Benson illustrated the power of the word when he said, "This is an answer to the great challenge of our time. The word of God, as found in the scriptures, in the words of living prophets, and in personal revelation, has the power to fortify the Saints and arm them with the Spirit so they can resist evil, hold fast to the good, and find joy in this life."[144] That phrase, *arm them with the Spirit*, has fascinating connotations! It underscores the imagery of spiritual battle and promises the protection and power provided by the word. For example, think of a time where you felt the Spirit, and there was no other explanation for those feelings. While you were "in the Spirit" (D&C 76:11), did you have any desire to sin?

Of course not. When you feel the Holy Ghost, there is no such thing as a temptation. A beloved hymn says, "I need thee every hour, stay Thou nearby; / Temptations lose their power when Thou art nigh."[145] When we feel the Holy Ghost, there is no temptation that Satan can offer that is beguiling to us. Perhaps this is what Paul had in mind when he instructed the Saints to "walk in the Spirit, and ye shall not fulfil the lust of the flesh" (Galatians 5:16). Thus, one of the ways in which the word of God provides power in our lives is by arming us with His Spirit.

As battles rage on throughout the remainder of the book of Alma, this imagery of the power of "the sword of the Spirit" in combating the wiles of the devil continues. As Moroni encircled the Lamanites in the final moments of this devastating battle, he actually testified of the power of the word of God. Speaking to Zerahemnah, he talked about "the maintenance of the sacred word of God," and then boldly testified that it is the blessing of the word of God "to which [they] owe[d] all [their] happiness" (Alma 43:5).

Shortly after Moroni's victory, we learn that because there were "many little dissensions and disturbances which had been among the people, *it became expedient that the word of God should be declared among them*" (Alma 45:21; emphasis added). Later on, we find out that while Amalickiah had been "obtaining power by fraud and deceit, Moroni, on the other hand, had been preparing the minds of the people to be faithful unto the Lord their God" (Alma 48:7). We learn that the people began to prosper "because of their heed and diligence which they gave unto the word of God" (Alma 49:30).

We read that Helaman "did take upon him again to preach unto the people the word of God; for because of so many wars and contentions it had become expedient that a regulation should be made again in the church. Therefore, Helaman and his brethren went forth, and did declare the word of God with much power unto the convincing of many people of their wickedness, which did cause them to repent of their sins" (Alma 62:44–45). Finally, following the wars recorded in Alma, we read of the prophetic promise that "whosoever will may lay hold upon the word of God, which is quick and powerful, which shall divide asunder all the cunning and the snares and the wiles of the devil, and lead the man of Christ . . . across that everlasting gulf of misery which is prepared to engulf the wicked—and land their souls . . . at the right hand of God in the kingdom of heaven" (Helaman 3:29–30). While we see that Moroni and the other great leaders in this section of the Book of Mormon were brilliant military strategists, we also see them relying upon the word of God in their efforts to strengthen their brethren.

Healing the Wounded Soul

Perhaps we can pull one more symbolic application from this idea of the sword of the Spirit and the power of the word. Throughout these passages, we find the wars growing more intense, leaving hundreds and even thousands of soldiers wounded or dead on the battlefields. Earlier in the Book of Mormon, the prophet Jacob provided a poignant application of the word of God. In what has become a personal favorite passage of mine, we read about Jacob speaking to his people and expressing how they had come up to "hear the pleasing word of God, yea, the word which healeth the wounded soul" (Jacob 2:8). As in all battles, our own personal struggles often leave us hurt and sometimes even deeply wounded. Elder Richard G. Scott recently stated, "Scriptures can calm an agitated soul, giving peace, hope, and a restoration of confidence in one's ability to overcome the challenges of life. They have potent power to heal emotional challenges when there is faith in the Savior."[146] I have come to know, feel, and trust in the power of the word of God to heal these wounds. Furthermore, as a religious educator, I have seen this healing come in the lives of many young people. As you read the following account, consider how the word provides the support and healing that this young lady desperately sought.

Several years ago, while studying in my office, I received a phone call from a student in one of my classes. It quickly became clear that this young lady was really shaken up—she was struggling to tell me what was going on. As the conversation continued, she explained that her home life had been pretty rough and that her parents always seemed to be fighting with each other. In fact, she said that when she went home, it sometimes felt like a battleground.

On this particular day, she had returned home from school and found her dad in an absolute rampage. Evidently, her dad had said

or done something that pushed her mom over the line, and she took off to go live with her sister. This young lady, understandably emotional as we spoke, then told me *she* had just left the house and was terrified to go back with her dad there and did not know what to do. I was not sure what to do or say, so I simply asked her if she had her bishop's phone number (I felt the best thing I could do was to direct her to the proper ecclesiastical channel). I also asked if she had other family around, and she said her grandparents lived close by. She decided to pick her two little brothers up from school and head to her grandma's house, where they would stay for several months.

To make a long story short, I received a letter from this young lady about six months after that phone call. In this letter, she described for me what had transpired over that time, and the profound spiritual experiences she had. She said that as she was hurt, confused, and emotionally struggling, she remembered how many times she had been told that to turn to the scriptures for help. She said she remembered many of her peers saying how they would randomly open their scriptures and turn to a verse that would be exactly what they needed to hear at that moment. She decided to try it, but the verse she read didn't seem to make sense, in light of her struggles. She tried again but ended up with the same disappointing result. After trying one more time with no answer coming, she felt like giving up. She said that she was not sure if Heavenly Father didn't know what was going on, or if He didn't love her, or if she wasn't worthy of such help.

Though she continued studying the scriptures, she continued this internal wrestle, and as she struggled, she had a precious experience with the divine. She said that during this time of doubt, discouragement, and despair, she realized it was not necessarily the words she was reading that were providing the help she needed. Rather, it was that, as she read the scriptures, she felt peace, comfort, hope, and love overpower the negative feelings she was experiencing.

She concluded her letter with this powerful testimony: "Through studying the scriptures, my relationship with my Heavenly Father has grown. I have received personal revelation and consolation from the Lord that couldn't have gotten to me any other way. The scriptures are truly the word of God. They allow you to talk to Heavenly Father, and they will, without a doubt in my mind, heal any wounded heart."[147] What a powerful example of Paul's promise that "we through patience and comfort of the scriptures might have hope" (Romans 15:4).

Sometimes these emotional challenges we face are personal, and we do not want to share them with others. Indeed, sometimes these wounds are hidden and unseen. During such times, it can be helpful to remember these inspired words: "As I search the holy scriptures, May thy mercy be revealed. Soothe my troubled heart and spirit; *May my unseen wounds be healed*."[148] I testify that even those deep, personal, unseen wounds can be healed by the power of the word of God.

In the Strength of the Lord

Another principle we can learn from the war chapters of the Book of Mormon comes from Moroni's steadfast adherence to basic gospel tenets, regardless of circumstance. We do not see any exact experiences that *led* Moroni down the covenant path of Christ, but we can be sure that he was deeply committed to remaining faithful to the celestial path. Elder David A. Bednar taught that when pondering the grace of the Savior, it is important for us to identify passages and phrases that the record keepers used to teach the principle of the enabling grace of the Lord. One of the phrases he emphasized was, *in the strength of the Lord*.[149] As you consider the following examples, keep your mind focused on the Lord remaining close to those who seek Him, particularly in times of trial, trouble, and tragedy:

- "But now, ye behold that the Lord is with us" (Alma 44:3)
- "Ye see that God will support, and keep, and preserve us" (Alma 44:4)
- "I command you, in the name of that all-powerful God, who has strengthened our arms that we have gained power over you" (Alma 44:5)
- "The Lord had again delivered them out of the hands of their enemies . . . and they did worship God with exceedingly great joy" (Alma 45:1)
- "Let them come forth in the strength of the Lord" (Alma 46:20)
- "There were many who died, firmly believing that their souls were redeemed by the Lord Jesus Christ; thus they went out of the world rejoicing" (Alma 46:39)

- "That they might live unto the Lord their God" (Alma 48:10)
- "[Moroni] was a man who was firm in the faith of Christ" (Alma 48:13)
- "God would make it known unto them whither they should go to defend themselves against their enemies, and by so doing, the Lord would deliver them" (Alma 48:16)
- "They were highly favored of the Lord" (Alma 48:20)
- "The people of Nephi did thank the Lord their God, because of his matchless power in delivering them" (Alma 49:28)
- "Moroni, with his armies, which did increase daily because of the assurance of protection" (Alma 50:12)
- "And thus we see how merciful and just are all the dealings of the Lord" (Alma 50:19)
- "I would not suffer them that they should break this covenant which they had made, supposing that God would strengthen us" (Alma 56:8)
- "Behold our God is with us, and he will not suffer that we should fall . . . if they did not doubt, God would deliver them" (Alma 56:46–47)
- "They had fought as if with the strength of God" (Alma 56:56)
- "Their preservation was astonishing. . . . And we do justly ascribe it to the miraculous power of God" (Alma 57:26)
- "Their minds are firm, and they do put their trust in God continually" (Alma 57:27)
- "Blessed is the name of our God; for behold, it is he that has delivered us" (Alma 57:35)
- "I was filled with exceeding joy because of the goodness of God in preserving us" (Alma 57:36)
- "We trust in our God who has given us victory" (Alma 58:33)
- "But, behold, it mattereth not—we trust God will deliver us" (Alma 58:37)
- "They have received many wounds; nevertheless they stand fast in that liberty wherewith God has made them free" (Alma 58:40)
- "Known unto God were all their cries, and all their sufferings" (Alma 60:10)
- "We will go forth against them in the strength of the Lord" (Alma 61:18)

- "See that ye strengthen Lehi and Teancum in the Lord" (Alma 61:21)
- "Because of the prayers of the righteous, they were spared" (Alma 62:40)
- "Neither were they slow to remember the Lord their God. . . . Yea, they did remember how great things the Lord had done for them" (Alma 62:49–50)
- "They did pray unto the Lord their God continually, insomuch that the Lord did bless them" (Alma 62:51)

From these examples, it is easy to see that Moroni was in fact "a man who was firm in the faith of Christ" (Alma 48:13) and that he made a significant contribution in helping many people to become "true believers in Christ" (Alma 46:15). His life, his service, and even his righteous indignation at times were all evidence of his consecrated commitment to the cause of Christ.

Not only did Moroni demonstrate such consecration, but he also was able to help instill that same spirit in his people. One of the fruits of a life in Christ is a firm hope in Christ. *Preach My Gospel* defines *hope* as "an abiding trust that the Lord will fulfill His promises to you. It is manifest in confidence, optimism, enthusiasm, and patient perseverance. It is believing and expecting that something will occur. . . . The scriptures often describe hope in Jesus Christ as the assurance that you will inherit eternal life in the celestial kingdom."[150] Thus, hope in Christ suggests that you have confidence, optimism, enthusiasm, *and* an expectation that you will receive eternal life.

Hope in Christ

I recently read a book by Dr. Alonzo Gaskill entitled *Odds Are, You're Going to Be Exalted*. While it was the clever title that captured my attention, the prophetic and scriptural substance of the book has left an indelible impression in my mind. Gaskill asserted, "We must remember—and we *must* firmly believe—that the plan of salvation, the great plan of happiness, was designed to work. . . . All too often we assume that only a small, select few will return to the Father's presence, there to dwell with Him for time and for all eternity. Yes, only the select will have the honor and privilege of so doing. But who is it that the Father has selected for this great blessing? Our answer—*all*

of his children! The Father desires that *all* be exalted. Not just saved, but exalted" (for scriptural support, see 1 Timothy 2:3–4; John 3:17; 2 Nephi 33:7, 12; 3 Nephi 27:13–15; D&C 29:5; 76:40–43).[151] Gaskill went on to quote Elder Bruce R. McConkie in an address given to Church Educational System employees, in which he said, "You tell your students that far more of our Father's children will be exalted than we think! . . . We ought to have hope [and] we [need] to be positive and optimistic about attaining that glory."[152] Indeed, it is the Father's "good will to give [us] the kingdom" (D&C 29:5).

Against that backdrop, consider the following scriptural symbolism as it relates to the hope of eternal life. Immediately following the inspiring account of the Lord protecting and preserving the stripling warriors, we read that the Nephites turned their attention to overtaking the land Manti. This particular area had become a significant stronghold for the Lamanites, and they were "receiving great strength from day to day" (Alma 58:5). To make matters even more difficult, this was the period in time when Pahoran was dealing with insurrection, and he was unable to send additional reinforcements to Helaman and his exhausted army. Consequently, this faithful army was left to commend themselves unto the Lord and to "pour out [their] souls in prayer to God, that he would strengthen [them] and deliver [them]" (Alma 58:10). As you read the following passages, pay particular attention to the italicized words, which describe the hope we have been speaking about:

> Yea, and it came to pass that the Lord our God did visit us with *assurances* that he would deliver us; yea, insomuch that he did speak *peace* to our souls, and did grant unto us great *faith*, and did cause us that we should *hope* for our *deliverance* in him.
>
> And we did take *courage* with our small force which we had received, and were *fixed with a determination* to conquer our enemies, and to maintain our lands, and our possessions, and our wives, and our children, and the cause of our liberty.
>
> And thus we did *go forth with all our might* against the Lamanites, who were in the city of Manti; and we did pitch our tents by the wilderness side, which was near to the city. (Alma 58:11–13; emphasis added)

We have the opportunity in our lives to put this same trust in the Lord and rely on Him and His power, no matter how bleak our opportunities may look. If we are looking, we will see that the Lord is providing us with "assurances" that He will eventually deliver us from our own personal struggles and sustain us as we battle against the challenges of mortality. He will, as he did to the aforementioned Nephites, speak "peace to our souls" and help us to be "fixed with a determination" to stay on the pathway of discipleship. Indeed, we can have this hope and this assurance if we will but "rely on this Redeemer" (1 Nephi 10:6) and look forward with joyful anticipation to the day when we will finally be reunited with Him again.

I believe that far too many of us forget that the plan of Salvation *really* is designed to save us and that Christ's grace *really* is sufficient. I also believe that we can and must overcome our salvation anxiety by relying upon "the merits, and mercy, and grace of the Holy Messiah" (2 Nephi 2:8) and by obtaining a deep and abiding "hope in Christ" (Moroni 7:41). Perhaps this is naïve, but I wholeheartedly believe that if we have continually repented of our sins and have met with the Lord's authorized servants, who have pronounced us worthy to enter into the house of the Lord, then we are worthy to enter into His rest in the celestial kingdom. After all, isn't the temple a symbol of God's presence and of His celestial glory? Furthermore, even as we enter His house, we understand that we are not worthy to be there because *we* are amazing; no, we are worthy to be there because *He* is amazing, and because His grace is amazing. Indeed, it is His grace that provides us with the "assurances," "peace," "faith," "hope," and "courage," "fixed with a determination" to "go forth with all our might" and overcome the natural man and become men and women of Christ. Empowered with such hope, we can—like Moroni and these faithful Nephites—firmly believe that our souls are redeemed by the Lord Jesus Christ and can thus rejoice in His salvation (Alma 46:39). In a day when we seem to be overwhelmed, anxious, and unsure about our standing before God, we need to rely more firmly on the hope that comes through the Atonement of Jesus Christ.

An Example of Hope in Christ: Elder Bruce R. McConkie

In an effort to help us understand and feel this important truth, let's consider a modern example of this hope. Elder Bruce

R McConkie remains one of the strongest doctrinal voices of this generation. His writings and sermons have impacted millions and continue to provide instruction and insights even now. Toward the end of 1983, he had been experiencing some pain and discomfort in his stomach. Not sure exactly what was happening, he went to the doctor for some tests. Many of the tests came back negative, but the doctors did find a spot on his liver. A surgery was scheduled for January 20, 1984. As the doctors went in to perform the procedure, they discovered that Elder McConkie had terminal cancer and that there was nothing they could do to help him. The doctors met with the family and told them he had only a short time to live.

While many of the Brethren in the Twelve and the First Presidency came to visit him, Elder Boyd K. Packer called and asked if he could give him a special blessing. "He came, saying that he had struggled with the matter for two days and that he was fighting mad: 'Bruce was not to be taken.' He gave [him] a blessing and told him that they were laboring on both sides of the veil to keep him here."[153] With this priesthood blessing, combined with the faith and prayers of thousands of Saints around the world, Elder McConkie was sent home from the hospital significantly earlier than expected.

In the ensuing weeks and months, Elder McConkie began chemotherapy. "In the course of some months, another scan was made of his liver, which showed that there were no new cancer spots and the old ones were shrinking. His doctor told him that this was medically impossible. A couple of days later his doctor, not a member of the Church, visited his office to explain, 'I don't think you understand. What has happened is not medically possible.' Dr. Russell M. Nelson confirmed that. 'No one recovers when the cancer has spread like it had in his liver.'"[154] His health and strength would be restored. In August 1984, he could jog five miles.

However, in early September, the cancer returned with a vengeance, and he began to lose strength again. Upon receiving this news, he asked a few of the Brethren to administer to him again. This time, Elders Faust and Oaks stood in with Elder Packer, again acting as voice. In this blessing, he reiterated the truth that members on both side of the veil were laboring for his recovery and even suggested that President Joseph Fielding Smith was foremost in this effort.

Miraculously, Elder McConkie was spared once again and would go on to deliver a few landmark talks over the next several months.

In all of this, he continued receiving appropriate medical treatment and likewise continued his work in the kingdom. While his strength seemed to be fading, he did as much as he was physically able in his weakened condition. He was determined to endure to the end. With this determination came an absolute conviction that the doctrines he had devoted his life to studying, writing, teaching, and living were indeed true. In early 1985, his son was called to be a stake president in a BYU stake. When he called Elder McConkie to describe his stake, he asked, "What do you think Joseph Smith would have done if he had had fourteen hundred returned missionaries with whom to begin the labors of this dispensation? [Elder McConkie] answered, 'I don't know, but in a few weeks I'll ask him.'"[155] He knew that his days were numbered. However, as April general conference was approaching, he also knew of his significant responsibility to deliver the message the Lord had given him. Elder McConkie's wife recounted the following experience that took place shortly before conference:

> [He] came into the kitchen and said, "Would you like to hear what I have prepared for general conference?" I was making him a pie, because his appetite had begun to go downhill, and I thought maybe he'd like an apple pie. I had the apples all ready to put in it, and I was rolling up the dough, the oven was on, everything was ready, and he came in and sat down and started to read me his talk and the tears streamed down his face. He didn't get more than a couple of sentences out and I thought to myself, "You don't make apple pies when somebody is saying these things to you." So I sat down, dropped everything, and listened to him. I asked him, "How are you going to be able to get up and read this?" Because there he was, having a hard time saying what he was saying because he was so touched. And he said, "I don't know, but I'm going to do it."[156]

On the Tuesday before general conference, he was told that he had only a few more days to live and that he should stay home and be as comfortable as possible. The doctors said that he would be too weak to speak at conference and that there was a serious chance that he would pass out at the pulpit. Nevertheless, he was determined to

stay the course and give one final witness to the world. This talk was to be the pinnacle of his ministry, since he would pass away thirteen days after it was delivered. As you read this grand testimony, please focus on the hope and confidence that he demonstrates because of the experiences that he has had with the risen Lord:

> And now, as pertaining to this perfect atonement, wrought by the shedding of the blood of God—I testify that it took place in Gethsemane and at Golgotha, and as pertaining to Jesus Christ, I testify that he is the Son of the Living God and was crucified for the sins of the world. He is our Lord, our God, and our King. This I know of myself independent of any other person.
>
> I am one of his witnesses, and in a coming day I shall feel the nail marks in his hands and in his feet and shall wet his feet with my tears.
>
> But I shall not know any better then than I know now that he is God's Almighty Son, that he is our Savior and Redeemer, and that salvation comes in and through his atoning blood and in no other way.
>
> God grant that all of us may walk in the light as God our Father is in the light so that, according to the promises, the blood of Jesus Christ his Son will cleanse us from all sin.
>
> In the name of the Lord Jesus Christ, amen.[157]

This moving testimony is a powerful witness of the hope we have been talking about in this chapter. This hope is manifest in an assurance and expectation that something is going to occur. In the case of Elder McConkie, his hope was in Christ and the reality of the long-awaited reunion that would take place when he passed through the veil. Moroni and his faithful people manifested this same hope. It is the same hope that strengthened the Anti-Nephi-Lehies as thousands of their innocent loved ones were slain. Nevertheless, they would testify that they "know that they are blessed, for they have gone to dwell with their God" (Alma 24:22) and that they "have no reason to doubt but what they were saved" (Alma 24:26).

I love their confidence in the salvation of God. We worship a God who is "mighty to save" (2 Nephi 31:19), and we need to always remember that His "grace is sufficient" (Ether 12:27). Let us have the hope, confidence, and assurance that if we are repenting often and are relying on the grace of Christ, when His authorized mortal servants declare us worthy to enter His house, we, by extension, are also worthy to enter into His presence in the eternities. Such is the ultimate hope of the Atonement of Jesus Christ.

And Thus We See

We live in "perilous times" (2 Timothy 3:1–7), where "all things [are] in commotion," "men's hearts [are failing] them (D&C 88:91), and "we hear of wars, and rumors of wars" (Joseph Smith—Matthew 1:28). Having seen our day, the prophet Mormon made provision in his abridgement of the plates to help us see how to maintain faith during times of significant distress. In his deep respect and adoration for Captain Moroni, Mormon gave us a powerful example of ways in which we can rely on the Savior and stay true to the cause of Christ.

In these war chapters, we see a wonderful demonstration of the protective effect of armor and, by extension, a powerful example of the significance of the armor of God. We must remember that the Lord does not expect us to just put this armor on, curl up, and simply be on the defensive side of this great battle. No, he expects us to wield the sword of the Spirit, even the word of God, and advance, progress, and win. We have received significant promises as we "rely upon the things which are written" (D&C 18:3). We know that "the words of Christ will tell you all things what ye should do" (2 Nephi 32:3) and can provide the direction we may be seeking. Elder Lawrence Corbridge said, "The Lord is not talking about just reading the scriptures but rather adopting His words to govern your life all of the time, so that they become the standard works—*the standard for your works*. As you do so His thoughts will become your thoughts and His ways will become your ways."[158] In addition to direction, the scriptures can also provide protection. The scriptures arm us with the Spirit. As we walk in the Spirit, temptations lose their power. Finally, as in all battles, this spiritual struggle sometimes causes us to be wounded and hurt. The scriptures provide the power to heal our wounded souls. Therefore, let us learn to wield the sword that Moroni testified had accounted for all of their happiness (see Alma 44:5).

From Captain Moroni, let us remember the necessity of relying on the strengthening power of Christ. Laced throughout the war chapters are verses that provide evidence of Moroni knowing the Lord and the

Lord knowing Moroni. We see Moroni and his army strengthened again and again *in the strength of the Lord*. If we are to come off conqueror in our own battles, we too need to learn to rely on the enabling power of the grace of Christ. Like Moroni and those faithful Nephites, we too can look to the Lord for help and strength. After all, has He not counseled, "Be not afraid nor dismayed by reason of this great multitude; for the battle is not yours, but God's" (2 Chronicles 20:15)? The Lord has promised, "I will fight your battles" (D&C 105:14). Therefore, "shall we not go on in so great a cause? . . . Courage, brethren; and on, on to the victory!" (D&C 128:22). Like Moroni, we can have courage in our battles because our cause is just. Like this Nephite army, we aim to protect our homes and our families, our freedoms and our God. We seek to defend ourselves from the onslaught of the adversary and maintain our own title of liberty as we stay true to our covenants.

Finally, we see these faithful Nephites developing and demonstrating the beautiful hallmark of hope. In the midst of their troubles and without any mortal assurance that they would receive reinforcements, the Nephites maintained hope and trust in Almighty God. Elder Maxwell insightfully observed, "In these times of widespread commotion, disorder, unrest, agitation, and insurrection, the hearts of many will fail. (D&C 45:26; 88:91.) Others will be sorely tried but will, in their extremities, seek succor from seers as did the anxious young man who approached the prophet [Elisha] as ancient Israel was surrounded: 'Alas, my master! how shall we do?' The answer of today's prophets will be the same: 'Fear not: for they that be with us are more than they that be with them.' Only when we are settled spiritually can we understand that kind of arithmetic. Only then will our eyes, like the young man's, be opened. (2 Kings 6:15–10.)"[159]

Moroni, Helaman, and other great Nephite leaders maintained that same hope and confidence in the Lord. As we seek eternal life, let us be filled with the hope and expectation that the Lord, who is indeed mighty to save, looks forward with joyful anticipation to the day when we can again be "encircled about eternally in the arms of his love" (2 Nephi 1:15). Let us likewise look forward with that same anticipation, that we shall again "see his face with pleasure" (Enos 1:27) and be welcomed back into His presence.

Chapter 11: The Nephites in the Land Bountiful

As the Nephites gathered themselves around the temple on that fateful and hallowed day, they were likely filled with anxiety, fear, hope, and humility. As they lifted their eyes toward heaven, they eventually recognized their Lord and immediately fell in reverence. They experienced the personal, intimate ministry of the Master as they felt of His divine touch. As He blessed and healed them, their anxieties and fears were replaced with an overwhelming desire to stay close to Him, follow Him, and become like Him.

Arms of Safety

Several years ago, there was a story in the *New Era* about a nineteen-year-old young man named Ian Bagley. Ian had decided last minute to take a trip with his family to see the Grand Canyon. Shortly after arriving, he and his family stood at the Grand Canyon's north rim when they heard screaming. According to the article, "a two-year-old girl, while looking over the railing, had fallen 35 feet to a ledge below. Her parents desperately searched for a way to save their daughter, while onlookers stood stunned. Not understanding the pleadings of her parents and family to stay still, her effort to climb back up resulted in her slipping further down until she was five feet from the next drop off—this one a terrifying 200 feet."[160]

The entire scene was shocking and terrifying for everyone involved, including young Ian. However, having become a trained EMT through his local community college, Ian was prepared. He later said, "'Immediately, it all came at me, and I just knew what I had to do. I set down my camera and went up the trail a little ways where it wasn't as steep, climbed over the rail, scrambled down a bunch of rocks and through brush, and found her.' Holding her in his arms for an hour, Ian waited until emergency teams could drop down with ropes. Ian's mother, waiting at the top, remembers seeing the little girl and her son as they ascended with the help of rescuers. 'I could see blond hair and a tiny face among all of the emergency equipment, and she held her hand out and it was wrapped around Ian's two fingers.'"[161] A tragic death was avoided, a new friendship was forged, and a miracle transpired.

Elder Jay E. Jensen, now an emeritus General Authority, once used this story to draw out a familiar scriptural phrase. He explained that when he read this story, he was impressed with the idea that this young man held the little girl in his arms for about an hour as they waited for the emergency teams to drop down. He said that this reminded him of the scriptural use of the word *arms*. The scriptures, particularly the Book of Mormon, talk about the Savior's "arms of mercy" (Jacob 6:5; Mosiah 16:12; Mosiah 29:20; Alma 5:33; Alma 29:10; D&C 29:1), His "arms of safety" (Alma 34:16), being "encircled about eternally in the arms of his love" (2 Nephi 1:15; D&C 6:20), and being "clasped in the arms of Jesus" (Mormon 5:11).

Elder Jensen highlighted the fact that when Jesus taught, he "used tangible things, such as coins, seeds, sheep, loaves, fishes, and body parts to teach gospel principles. Arms are tangible, and we use them to express affection and love. When I come home from the office, I am encircled in the tangible arms of my wife."[162] He then explained that he has found it helpful to use this imagery of arms of safety and arms of love to teach others about the Atonement. The Savior demonstrated His compassionate outstretched arms as he personally ministered to the Nephite Saints in Third Nephi.

The Light of the World

Ralph Waldo Emerson once wrote, "If the stars should appear one night in a thousand years, how would men believe and adore; and

preserve for many generations the remembrance of the city of God which had been shown [them]!"[163] Commenting on this thought from Emerson, Elder Holland invited us to "consider another startling—and much more important scene that should evoke belief and adoration, a scene which, like the stars at night, we have undoubtedly taken too much for granted."[164] He was speaking of the personal visit of the resurrected Christ to ancient America. He continued,

> Imagine yourselves to be among the people of Nephi living in the land of Bountiful in approximately A.D. 34. Tempests and earthquakes and whirlwinds and storms, quickened and cut by thunder and sharp lightning, have enveloped the entire face of the land.
>
> Some cities—entire cities—have burst into flames as if by spontaneous combustion. Others have disappeared into the sea, never to be seen again. Still others are completely covered over with mounds of soil, and some have been carried away with the wind.
>
> The whole face of the land has been changed, the entire earth around you has been deformed. Then, as you and your neighbors are milling about the temple grounds (a place that has suddenly seemed to many like a *very* good place to be), you hear a voice.[165]

On top of all of this geographical change, there was likewise a monumental solar change. The record says that "there was darkness upon the face of the land. And it came to pass that there was thick darkness upon all the face of the land, insomuch that the inhabitants thereof who had not fallen could feel the vapor of darkness" (3 Nephi 8:19–20). It seems clear that this was no ordinary darkness. This was a thick, vaporous darkness that seems to have enveloped the land.

While the primary point has been clearly made—it was really dark—the record actually goes on to belabor the point. As we continue in the passage, pay attention, in all of the references, to the lack of light. "And there could be *no light*, because of the darkness, neither *candles*, neither *torches*; neither could there be *fire* kindled with their fine and exceedingly dry wood, so that there could *not be any light* at all; And there was *not any light seen*, neither *fire*, nor *glimmer*, neither *the sun*, nor *the moon*, nor *the stars*, for so great were the mists of darkness which were upon the face of the land. And it came to pass that it did last for the space of three days that there was *no light* seen (3 Nephi 8:21–23; emphasis added). What is it that we are supposed to take from this account? Apparently, we are to understand that it was so dark that no light of any kind could be seen in the land.

The scene was set. The Master teacher was about to deliver one of the most powerful object lessons in recorded history. As the Nephites sat in thick darkness, scared as they surely must have been, the "tender but firm voice of the Lord Jesus Christ"[166] penetrated the silence: "I am the light and the life of the world" (3 Nephi 9:18). As they sat, surrounded in total darkness, Jesus identified himself as the Light of the World. He helped this people understand that without Him, they were destined to walk in darkness—but with Him as their guide, they could have hope, direction, and an abundant life.

As a Hen Gathereth Her Chickens

Among those things taught by Jesus came a divine invitation. Speaking to those who were spared, Jesus said, "Will ye not now return unto me, and repent of your sins, and be converted, that I may heal you? Yea, verily I say unto you, if ye will come unto me ye shall have eternal life. *Behold, mine arm of mercy is extended towards you*, and whosoever will come, him will I receive; and blessed are those who come unto me" (3 Nephi 9:13–14; emphasis added). As if to underscore His invitation for them to come unto Him and experience His arms of mercy, Jesus used apperception to help them feel of its importance. He drew on the imagery of nature to teach His willingness to lovingly protect His covenant children. "O ye . . . who are of the house of Israel, how oft have I gathered you as a hen gathereth her chickens under her wings, and have nourished you" (3 Nephi 10:4). In this verse, Christ showed them that He has been there for them in the past, therefore implying that they could trust in Him. In so doing, He helped them to remember how merciful He had been unto them and how they had already experienced His arms of mercy in their lives.

In the next verse, the Savior focused his attention on the times when he had invited them to repent and dwell safely in His covenant arms, but they chose not to come. He said, "How oft *would* I have gathered you as a hen gathereth her chickens, and ye would

not" (3 Nephi 10:5; emphasis added). Perhaps He highlighted these times when they chose not to follow Him to help them consider the contrasts in their lives. As they considered the times in their lives when they relied on Him, they most likely remembered the peace and safety they felt. As they remembered the times when they were more rebellious, or perhaps forgetful or distracted, they likely recalled the anxiety or unrest they experienced. As they reflected on these times, their hearts were surely turned toward Him with a greater desire and stronger trust in His invitation and promise.

Finally, having helped them see and feel the safety and hope that come in the protection of His merciful arms, He promised, "O ye house of Israel whom I have spared, how oft *will I* gather you as a hen gathereth her chickens under her wings, if ye will repent and return unto me with full purpose of heart" (3 Nephi 10:6; emphasis added). This final promise re-instilled a sense of hope in the hearts of these Nephite Saints. Jesus masterfully helped them recognize their reliance on Him and also remember their shortcomings of the past, yet still infusing hope for the present and future. From this, they remembered His past mercy and could now "come boldly unto the throne of grace" (Hebrews 4:16) and be gathered into the protection of the covenant.

There is a story that adds deep insight to the Savior's imagery of the mother hen, symbolizing His atoning grace. A fire once consumed a large field, and a small group of people went to inspect the damage. As they went about assisting one of the inspectors, they noticed several smoldering mounds throughout the field. One of the members of the group was intrigued by the mounds and asked the inspector what they were. The inspector suggested the young man kick one to see what it was. This young man did so. Just then, he saw several baby sage grouse chicks scatter around him. His initial thought was that these babies were smart enough to hide under this mound when the fire came to save themselves. But the inspector told him that the "natural" mound he had thought these babies hid under was actually the remains of their mother.

The inspector then took the moment to help the volunteers understand that when the mother hen saw there was a dangerous fire looming, she invited her young to gather under her wings for protection.

She gathered them close and gave them a refuge from the elements around them.[167] And so it is that the Savior of mankind invites all of us to be encircled in the arms of His mercy and find peace and refuge from the storms of our lives.

Stop, Look, and Listen

It is against this compelling backdrop of His promise to gather His people that we see the Savior descend from on high and personally minister to these humbled Nephites. You will recall that the Nephites had gathered themselves around the temple in the land Bountiful. As they gathered, they heard another voice, but this time they could not understand what the voice was saying. The voice was heard a second time, but again the people did not understand it. Mormon pointed out that this was "not a harsh voice, neither was it a loud voice," but it "did pierce them that did hear to the center . . . and did cause their hearts to burn" (3 Nephi 11:3). Having felt this burning as the voice spoke a second time, they finally "did open their ears to hear it; and their eyes were towards the sound thereof; and they did look steadfastly towards heaven, from whence the sound came" (3 Nephi 11:5). The voice was the voice of God the Father who, as His Beloved Son descended from heaven, introduced Him and invited His children to hear Him. As they steadfastly looked up to heaven, they fixed their eyes on the Redeemer. "A glorious, resurrected being, a member of the Godhead, the creator of innumerable worlds, the God of Abraham, Isaac, and Jacob, stood before their very eyes."[168]

Upon hearing Christ introduce Himself, the multitude fell to the earth in overwhelming reverence and humility. Commenting on this singular moment, Elder Holland explained,

> It is a dazzling display. He seems to emanate the very essence of light and life itself—a splendor in sharp contrast to the three days of death and darkness just witnessed. He speaks and says simply, with a voice that penetrates the very marrow of your bones, "I am Jesus Christ, whom the prophets testified shall come into the world" (3 Nephi 11:10). There it is—or, more correctly speaking, there *he* is! He is the focal point and principal figure behind every fireside and devotional and family home evening held by those Nephites for the last six hundred years, and by their Israelite forefathers for thousands of years before that. *Everyone* has talked of him and sung of him and dreamed

of him and prayed—but here he actually is. This is the day, and yours is the generation. What a moment! But you find you are less inclined to check the film in your camera than you are to check the faith in your heart.[169]

Many of us have been "called many times and [we] would not hear" (Alma 10:6). We are sometimes so caught up in the thick of thin things that when the call comes, we see no way of hearkening to the tender voice. Like these Nephites who were gathered around the temple in the land Bountiful, we are, at times, not quiet enough to hear the still small voice as it beckons us into communion. When overwhelmed by the busyness of our lives, we need to remember to stop, look, and listen. It is safe to say that in the rushing lifestyles of modern society, we all need more "stop, look, and listen" time if we are going to hear the still small voice of the Lord inviting us to draw nearer to Him. For these ancient covenant people, their willingness to stop their conversations, look up steadfastly to heaven, and listen to the voice of the Lord proved to be a catalyst in their hearing the voice of the Lord and experiencing His divine love. Similarly, we must find or create such moments of sacred silence, where the whispered voice of the Spirit can be heard and felt.

One by One

With the multitude humbled and prostrated before Him, the Savior invited them to arise and come unto Him to feel the prints of the nails in His hands and feet. The record says the people went forth *"one by one* until they had all gone forth, and did see with their eyes and did feel with their hands, and did know of a surety" (3 Nephi 11:15; emphasis added). Elder Merrill J. Bateman once taught that "although the multitude totaled 2,500 souls, the record states that 'all of them did see and hear, every man for himself'" (3 Nephi 17:25).[170] If each person had fifteen seconds to approach the Master and feel the prints of the nails, more than ten hours would have been required.[171] What a powerful example of the individual love that Christ has for each of us! While the Atonement of Jesus Christ is infinite in its scope, it is also personal and intimate in its application. Indeed, Jesus Himself was intimate and personal in His ministry, as He always seemed to follow this same pattern of ministering one by one.

The entire ministry of the Savior among this Nephite people underscores this merciful personal touch. You will recall when, after having taught and ministered unto the people for an entire day, Jesus said unto the multitude, "Behold, my time is at hand. I perceive that ye are weak, that ye cannot understand all my words which I am commanded of the Father to speak unto you at this time. Therefore, go ye unto your homes, and ponder upon the things which I have said, and ask of the Father, in my name, that ye may understand, and prepare your minds for the morrow, and I come unto you again" (3 Nephi 17:1–3). Interestingly, this experience in which Jesus invited them to feel those "five special wounds"[172] seems to have taken place relatively early in the day. What then followed was conferral of priesthood authority, and then theologically drenched teaching, in which He covered the following: baptism by immersion, the Godhead, the doctrine of Christ, the Beatitudes, the higher law, forgiveness, prayer, righteous judgment, the law and the covenant, the call to rescue, the last days, and many other topics. Is it any wonder that they looked a little overwhelmed at the end of class that day?

As the Master teacher, Christ exemplified the truth highlighted by Elder David A. Bednar when he said, "Teaching is not talking and telling. Rather, teaching is observing, listening and discerning so we then know what to say."[173] As He looked over the crowd, He initially perceived their weakness and, as any effective teacher would do, suggested they take a break so that they could come back with renewed energy. However, as He counseled them to go unto their homes and let them know of His intention to leave in order to visit the lost tribes of Israel, "he cast his eyes round about again on the multitude, and beheld they were in tears, and did look steadfastly upon him as if they would ask him to tarry a little longer with them" (3 Nephi 17:5). Once again, underscoring His personalized ministry, Jesus was completely unrushed in this moment.

As was noted earlier, His assignment next was to minister to the lost tribes; this was not a trivial matter. But even with the immediacy of this assignment, He seemed to have changed His plans, and "in so doing, he provided these people with one the spiritual highlights of his new world ministry, a testimony to the faith, devotion, and unspoken desire of these true disciples."[174] Their faithfulness was perceived as

Christ's bowels were filled with compassion. Perceiving their desire to experience the healings that were manifested in Jerusalem, Jesus beckoned any who were sick, lame, blind, halt, maimed, leprous, withered, deaf, or afflicted in any manner to come unto Him and be healed. "And it came to pass that when he had thus spoken, all the multitude, with one accord, did go forth with their sick and their afflicted, and their lame, and with their blind, and with their dumb, and with all them that were afflicted in any manner; *and he did heal them every one as they were brought forth unto him*" (3 Nephi 17:9; emphasis added).

So powerful was this moment and so humbled were these Nephite disciples that "they did all, both they who had been healed and they who were whole, bow down at his feet, and did worship him; and as many as could come for the multitude did kiss his feet, insomuch that they did bathe his feet with their tears" (3 Nephi 17:10). This overwhelming spiritual outpouring was intensified as Christ then "took their little children, *one by one,* and blessed them, and prayed unto the Father for them" (3 Nephi 17:21; emphasis added). "The scriptures do not indicate how many children were there, but one surmises that in a multitude of 2,500, there must have been a few hundred. Again, it would have taken hours to complete the blessings."[175] And again, Jesus here demonstrates His willingness and desire to reach us on an individual level.

The Touch of the Master's Hand

As Jesus patiently, charitably, and irresistibly ministered to each individual in attendance, they came to know for themselves of His goodness and power. They all knew that He was "the God of Israel, and the God of the whole earth, and [had] been slain for the sins of the world" (3 Nephi 11:14). They had experienced the tenderness of His voice, and their hearts had been touched by the penetrating power of His love. His healing touch had been felt; its effects upon this people would last through the eternities. President Howard W. Hunter reminded us that "whatever Jesus lays his hands upon lives. If Jesus lays his hands upon a marriage, it lives. If he is allowed to lay his hands on the family, it lives."[176] If He is allowed to touch the lives of those of us who are sometimes beaten down by the cruelties of mortality, then we shall live. In a recent general conference talk,

President Dieter F. Uchtdorf told of a dramatic situation in which the touch of Christ's healing hands brought new life and light into the heart of one young lady:

> I'd like to tell you about a woman who grew up in a room filled with darkness—I'll call her Jane.
>
> From the time Jane was three years old, she was repeatedly beaten, belittled, and abused. She was threatened and mocked. She awoke each morning not knowing if she would survive until the next day. The people who should have protected her were those who tortured her or allowed the abuse to continue.
>
> In order to protect herself, Jane learned to stop feeling. She had no hope of rescue, so she hardened herself to the horror of her reality. There was no light in her world, so she became resigned to the darkness. With a numbness that can come only from constant and unrelenting contact with evil, she accepted the fact that any moment might be her last.
>
> Then, at age 18, Jane discovered The Church of Jesus Christ of Latter-day Saints. The joy and hope of the restored gospel penetrated her heart, and she accepted the invitation to be baptized. For the first time, light entered her life, and she saw a bright path before her. She left the darkness of her world and decided to attend school a great distance away from her abuser. At last she felt liberated from an environment of darkness and evil—*free to enjoy the Savior's sweet peace and miraculous healing.*
>
> However, years later, after her abuser had died, Jane was again troubled by the horrible events of her youth. Profound sadness and anger threatened to destroy the wonderful light she had found in the gospel. She realized that if she allowed that darkness to consume her, her tormentor would have a final victory.
>
> She sought counseling and medical help and began to realize that, for her, the best path for healing was to understand and accept that darkness exists—but not to dwell there. For, as she now knew, light also exists—and that is where she chose to dwell.
>
> Given her dark past, Jane could easily have become vindictive, venomous, or violent. But she didn't. She resisted the temptation to spread the darkness, refusing to lash out in anger, hurt, or cynicism. Instead, *she held fast to the hope that with God's help she could be healed.* She chose to radiate light and devote her life to helping others. This decision enabled her to leave the past behind and to step into a glorious, bright future. . . .

Jane learned that healing comes when we move away from the darkness and walk toward the hope of a brighter light. It was in the practical application of faith, hope, and charity that she not only transformed her own life but forever blessed the lives of many, many others.[177]

What a powerful example of the power of the healing touch of the Master! This story underscores the truth learned by the ancient Nephites: Jesus Christ has the ability and the desire to heal those of us who endure trial, hardship, or are "afflicted in any manner" (3 Nephi 17:7). As we feel His divine touch, we become encircled in the perfect, pure arms of His love.

Always Remember Him

To put an absolutely ideal ending on a divinely directed day, Christ instituted the sacrament, with the instruction that this holy ordinance "shall be a testimony unto the Father that ye do always remember me" (3 Nephi 18:7). After teaching, ministering to, and healing the multitude, Christ seemed to be instituting the sacrament to help them to remember Him and the miracles they had experienced and witnessed.

Commenting on the connection between the Atonement and the sacrament, Elder Jay E. Jensen pointed out that many of us "come to sacrament meeting prayerfully, hungering for spiritual healing, hoping, pleading to hear in their minds and hearts these words: 'Behold, your sins are forgiven you; you are clean before me; therefore, lift up your heads and rejoice' (D&C 110:5)."[178] As we gather, we seek the rescuing hand of Christ to reach out and heal us with His immortal touch. Elder Jensen provided the following true account that helps illustrate this principle:

> While serving as a bishop, I witnessed the blessings of the Atonement in the lives of Church members who committed serious transgressions. As a judge in Israel I listened to their confessions and, when needed, placed restrictions upon them, such as not partaking of the sacrament for a time.
>
> A young single adult in our ward was dating a young woman. They allowed their affections to get out of control. He came to me for

counsel and help. Based on what was confessed and the impressions of the Spirit to me, among other things, he was not permitted to partake of the sacrament for a time. We met regularly to ensure that repentance had happened, and, after an appropriate time, I authorized him to again partake of the sacrament.

As I sat on the stand in that sacrament meeting, my eyes were drawn to him as he now partook of the sacrament worthily. I witnessed arms of mercy, love, and safety encircling him as the healing of the Atonement warmed his soul and lifted his load, resulting in the promised forgiveness, peace, and happiness.[179]

The Lord has declared that it is in the ordinances of the priesthood that the power of godliness is manifest (see D&C 84:20). Among other things, the power of godliness is the power to make us holy, clean, and pure. By this divine power, we too can be made whole. As we humbly and contritely partake of the sacrament, we experience the encircling arms of the Lord's love.

Returning to the account of the Nephites in the land Bountiful, the record says they "were all converted unto the Lord . . . and there were no contentions and disputations among them, and every man did deal justly one with another. And they had all things common among them" (4 Nephi 1:2–3). We learn that the primary reason there was no contention was "because of the love of God which did dwell in the hearts of the people . . . and surely there could not be a happier people among all the people who had been created by the hand of God" (4 Nephi 1:15–16).

And because of Christ's personal ministry, "there were no robbers, nor murderers, neither were there Lamanites, nor any manner of -ites; but they were in one, the children of Christ, and heirs to the kingdom of God" (4 Nephi 1:17). So complete was the change in the hearts of these disciples that the entire people stayed faithful throughout their lives, and it wasn't until over 160 years later that their descendants began to be lifted up in the pride of their hearts, leading to iniquity. Elder Bateman observed, "On occasion, speakers note that the impact of his appearance produced a season of peace that lasted two hundred years. The truth is that his appearance and teachings had an eternal impact on the lives of those present and for generations to come."[180] Such was the eternal change brought about

by experiencing the personal transforming and healing touch of the Lord Jesus Christ.

And Thus We See

The Savior's ministry among the Nephites is the pinnacle of the Book of Mormon and is likewise the ultimate divine encounter outlined in this special record. What began as an invitation from a voice on high to come unto Christ while his "arm of mercy is extended" (3 Nephi 9:14) ended with the transformation of over 2,500 disciples as they experienced firsthand the touch of the Master's hand. So uniquely sacred was this experience that "no tongue can speak, neither can there be written by any man, neither can the hearts of men conceive so great and marvelous things as [they] both saw and heard Jesus speak" (3 Nephi 17:17).

This account clearly highlights the reality that the Savior seeks to teach and bless on an individual level. His one-by-one ministry is exemplified in His willingness to invite the mass of people to come up one by one and feel the prints in His hands and feet and wet His feet with their tears. Furthermore, we learn that as we come unto Him with our sins, weaknesses, pains, sicknesses, heartaches, and other afflictions, we can experience divine healing. Elder Jeffrey R. Holland once told a story that illustrates our need to trust in and rely on the Savior's mercy and grace. He said, "Katie Lewis is my neighbor. Her father, Randy, is my bishop; her mother, Melanie, is a saint. And her older brother, Jimmie, is battling leukemia." He went on to explain the struggle and heartache the parents experienced, trying to process their little boy's deadly disease. Elder Holland described how this faithful family prayed, fasted, and attended the temple often as they sought divine direction. One day, Sister Lewis came home from the temple tired and worn out. Perhaps this was one of those moments that she wanted nothing more than to collapse on the couch and cry, hoping to just be left alone for a while. Elder Holland recounted:

> As she entered her home, four-year-old Katie ran up to her with love in her eyes and a crumpled sheaf of papers in her hand. Holding the papers out to her mother, she said enthusiastically, "Mommy, do you know what these are?"

Sister Lewis said frankly her first impulse was to deflect Katie's zeal and say she didn't feel like playing just then. But she thought of her children—all her children—and the possible regret of missed opportunities and little lives that pass too swiftly. So she smiled through her sorrow and said, "No, Katie. I don't know what they are. Please tell me."

"They are the scriptures," Katie beamed back, "and do you know what they say?"

Sister Lewis stopped smiling, gazed deeply at this little child, knelt down to her level, and said, "Tell me, Katie. What do the scriptures say?"

"They say, 'Trust Jesus.'" And then she was gone.

Sister Lewis said that as she stood back up, holding a fistful of her four-year-old's scribbling, she felt near-tangible arms of peace encircle her weary soul and a divine stillness calm her troubled heart.[181]

Trust Jesus. How simple yet sublime! As we trust in the Savior, we too can feel those "near-tangible arms of peace" encircle our weary and sometimes discouraged souls. The Nephites in the land Bountiful learned that Christ could help them and rescue them, no matter what their concerns or challenges were. We can, as Elder Maxwell once said, trust in "the omniscience of an omnipotent and omniloving God."[182]

So intimate and perfect are His empathy and His love that He understands what we are going through, and He knows precisely how to help and sustain us. Consider your own life as you analyze the following:

- He understands what it is like to suffer through the death of a loved one (both when it happens, as well as those important moments later in your life when you wish they were there).
- He understands what it is like to struggle financially. He understands what it is like to lose your job, or have a dad or husband lose his job, and the effects that has on the entire family.
- He understands what it is like for those who desperately want to be married, but who feel the loneliness of going through this mortal life alone.
- He understands what it is like to struggle in your marriage.
- He understands what it feels like to have your parents go through a divorce.

- He understands what it is like to have a spouse or a parent have an affair and the accompanying feelings of pain, hurt, and betrayal.
- He understands what it is like to feel like you have no friends, or that you don't fit in.
- He understands the anxiety of a young father trying to carve out a living to provide for his young family.
- He understands what it is like to fail an exam (even after hours of study).
- He understands what it is like to feel completely alone and unknown.
- He understands what it is like to see a loved one stray from the gospel path.
- He understands what it is like to get cut from a team or fired from a job and the feelings of rejection.
- He understands the feelings of a young mother who is absolutely overwhelmed, feeling like she is insignificant and inadequate.
- Through His Atonement, He understands what it feels like to have the Spirit withdraw because of sin and rebellion.
- He understands what it is like to have to move to a new home and ward.
- He understands what it is like to strike out, miss the shot, or commit an error when the game was on the line.
- He understands what it is like to have people gossip about you behind your back or spread rumors that taint your reputation.
- He understands what it is like to feel the pains of abuse (physical and emotional).
- He understands the pain of both the repentant abuser who has recognized his or her wrong and committed to be better, and the victim of the abuse who has to carry that baggage with him or her.
- He understands what it is like to have someone you love and trust turn against you.
- He understands what it is like to have spent many years in dedicated service and feel underappreciated or underused.
- He understands what it is like to have doubts about a doctrine of the gospel and the fear and emotion that often accompany these doubts.

- He understands what it feels like to be depressed, discouraged, and hopeless.
- He understands what it is like to feel lost, hopeless, tired, and terrified.
- He understands what it is like to not be able to trust someone you loved because he or she has hurt you so many times, and in so many ways.

In short, He knows *you*! He loves *you*! He is aware of *you*! He suffered for *you*! And He did all of that so He could help, lift, comfort, direct, protect, heal, and eventually exalt *you*! As Elder Maxwell said, "Indeed, we cannot teach Him anything! But we can listen to Him. We can love Him, we can honor Him, we can worship Him! We can keep His commandments, and we can feast upon His scriptures! Yes, we who are so forgetful and even rebellious are never forgotten by Him! We *are* His 'work' and His 'glory,' and He is *never* distracted!"[183]

As we come to know Jesus in this way, we will, like these ancient Nephite disciples, experience the same transformative peace that puts an end to contention and spreads the love of God abroad in the hearts of all who will trust in Him.

One night shortly after one of our little boys was born, he started screaming in his crib, which awoke us. It was around two in the morning, and I went in to check on him and see what was the matter. He was around two months old at the time. As I picked him up and set him on my chest, he immediately stopped crying. I sat down in the rocking chair and held the little guy in my arms, rocking back and forth. Feeling the tenderness of this special experience, I offered up a silent prayer, letting Heavenly Father know how grateful I was for the precious gift of this little boy.

As I sat there that night and held my son, I tried to comfort him so that he could feel the love and security of being encircled in my arms. As I concluded my prayer, I told Father that this was my favorite part of being a dad. I felt a soft reply simply say, "Ryan, that is my favorite part of being a dad too."

What a blessing it is that both the Father and the Son invite us to come to Them and experience their personal and divine love. Even

"while we gaze in awe at His majesty, He does not ask us to stay our distance but bids us to come unto Him."[184] As we follow this invitation, we can, like the Nephites, be "encircled about eternally in the arms of his love" (2 Nephi 1:15).

Chapter 12: Mahonri Moriancumer

The Lord desperately wants us to be close to Him. He invites us to draw near unto Him so that He may draw near unto us. From the brother of Jared, we learn that "ordinary people with ordinary challenges can rend the veil of unbelief and enter the realms of eternity."[185] Through this account, we learn that simple, pure faith can lead to miraculous experiences with the divine.

The Faith of a Child

When President Boyd K. Packer was called to be a General Authority, he was living in Utah Valley with his wife and ten children. They had a farm that included "a cow and a horse and chickens and lots of children."[186] He told the story about one particular weekend when he was supposed to catch a plane to fly out to the Gridley Stake in California.

Before leaving, however, he went out to check on a cow that was about ready to calf. As he went out to her pen, he saw that she was in trouble. He called the veterinarian, who came and ran some tests. After the tests, the vet bore the grave news that the cow had swallowed a wire, which had actually punctured her heart. He told President Packer that the cow would be dead before the day was over. Continuing the story, President Packer said,

The next day the calf was to come, and the cow was important to our economy. Also, she kind of "belongs"—you know how that gets to be. I asked him if he could do anything, and he said he could but it would likely be useless, money down the drain. I said, "Well, what will it cost me?" He told me—and it did. I told him to go ahead. The next morning the calf was there but the cow was lying down gasping. I called the vet again, thinking the calf might need some attention. He looked the cow over and said she would be dead within an hour or so. I went in to the telephone directory, copied down the number of the animal by-products company, put it on the nail by the phone, and told my wife to call them to come and get the cow later in the day.[187]

Before leaving on his trip, President Packer gathered his family together for family prayer. He invited one of his little sons to be voice in their family prayer that day. President Packer recounted how their son began his prayer with his usual requests, "asking Heavenly Father to 'bless Daddy that he won't get hurt in his travels,' 'bless us at school,' and so on." As he went through the process of *"saying his prayers,"* President Packer said that he paused for a moment, and then really started to pray. In other words, what was about to come next was not a trite, repetitious request but rather was the deepest desire of a small child. He said, "Heavenly Father, please bless Bossy so that she will get to be all right."[188] President Packer noted that this calf was given to this little boy, so he felt doubly connected to it.

As President Packer flew out and arrived at his assigned chapel, where he would provide leadership training, he used this story to teach those in attendance. He was talking to them about prayer and, after recounting the story, he said, "I am glad he prayed that way, because he will learn something. He will mature and he will learn that you do not get everything you pray for just that easy. There is a lesson to be learned."[189]

Well, "there was a lesson to be learned, but it was I who learned it, not my son. When I returned Sunday night, Bossy had 'got to be all right.' . . . The gift of the Holy Ghost operates equally with men, women, and even little children. It is within this wondrous gift and power that the spiritual remedy to any problem can be found."[190] This cute story can actually be seen as a powerful example of what can happen when the faithful prayer of a humble child is offered in

accordance with the will of God. The Lord has made clear that any of us who choose to pay the price to faithfully learn how to draw on His power can access His divine influence to experience miracles in our own lives. One of the most dramatic examples of this principle comes from the life of Mahonri Moriancumer, more commonly known as the brother of Jared.

The Leadership of the Brother of Jared

Most of what we learn about the brother of Jared comes to us from Moroni's abridgement of the twenty-four plates that contained the history of the Jaredite people. These plates had been "discovered by a small Nephite exploring party and given to Mosiah, a prophet-king, who translated them into the Nephite language through the use of seer stones (Mosiah 8:8–9; 28:11–16)."[191] From this record, we learn that the brother of Jared was "a large and mighty man, and a man highly favored of the Lord" (Ether 1:34). We know that he and his family lived around the time of the Tower of Babel. The Lord was merciful unto them and did not confound their language. Elder Cecil O. Samuelson pointed out that "his specific name, his physical stature, and even his unique relationship with his brother Jared are not nearly as important to us, however, as are the characteristics that he demonstrated and the lessons from the Savior that he learned—tutorials from which we can also benefit if we, as he, choose to ponder, search, liken unto ourselves, and incorporate them into our own lives."[192] Indeed, there is much to learn from this righteous—yet mortal—man as we seek to experience the Savior's influence in our own lives.

The narrative begins with the Lord scattering the people and confounding their language as a consequence of their wickedness in building the Tower of Babel. From the start, we get a sense of the leadership and faith of Moriancumer, as Jared approaches him specifically and asks him to pray to the Lord that He will show mercy to their people. I can understand this move because whenever I am in special need of a blessing, particularly when I go to teach a class or speak at a fireside, I ask my little boys to pray for me. It may not be a good thing to confess, but I trust their sweet, pure faith even more than I trust my own. It seems clear that Jared had a similar kind of trust and confidence in his brother. The Lord heard the faithful prayer of the brother of Jared and, having compassion on him, promised that He would go before them and lead them "into a land which is choice above all the lands of the earth" (Ether 1:42).

In preparing to depart, they gathered together food and provisions, and then "the Lord came down and talked with the brother of Jared; and he was in a cloud, and the brother of Jared saw him not" (Ether 2:4). We learn that the Lord continued to guide the Jaredites "and did talk with them as he stood in a cloud, and gave directions whither they should travel" (Ether 2:5). They did go forth into the wilderness and, according to the commands of the Lord, they built barges that could be used to cross the waters that they encountered. The Lord led them to the seashore with the intention to lead them forth "even unto the land of promise, which was choice above all other lands, which the Lord God had preserved for a righteous people" (Ether 2:7). The Jaredites, however, pitched their tents and dwelt upon the seashore for four years.

We learn that at the end of the four years, the Lord came to the brother of Jared and, once again, stood in a cloud. "And for the space of three hours did the Lord talk with the brother of Jared, and chastened him because he remembered not to call upon the name of the Lord" (Ether 2:14). After reading about and learning how faithful and righteous the brother of Jared was, doesn't it seem strange that he just *forgot* to pray every day for four years? More likely is the idea that the prayers were said too casually, without sincere supplication and consecrated communion. Elder Samuelson added, "Because of the brevity of the abridged record, all of the details of the peaceful and apparently comfortable four years Jared's party spent on the seashore are not available. One might wonder whether the brother of Jared and those with him really did not pray at all during the four-year period or whether their efforts at prayer had become routine and perfunctory, as they were quite comfortable with their satisfactory circumstances and the apparent lack of impending doom or crisis. Had they merely not remembered to really 'call upon the name of the Lord' (Ether 2:14) with the intent, feeling, power, and concentration necessary to make their petitions meaningful?"[193] Regardless of the reason for the rebuke, the record is clear that this led the

brother of Jared to repent, which allowed the Lord to forgive him with the divine injunction to "not sin any more" and remember that His "spirit will not always strive with man" (Ether 2:15). "It is difficult to imagine what a three-hour rebuke from the Lord might be like, but the brother of Jared endured it. With immediate repentance and prayer, this prophet again sought guidance for the journey they had been assigned and those who were to pursue it. God accepted his repentance and lovingly gave further direction for their crucial mission."[194]

The Lord Expects Us to Act for Ourselves

With greater motivation and an increased urgency, "the brother of Jared did go to work, and also his brethren, and built barges after the manner which they had built, according to the instructions of the Lord" (Ether 2:16). I should pause to mention the continued guidance of the Lord and the brother of Jared's continued reliance on His merciful hand. Both before and after his divine chastening, Moriancumer received continual direction from the Lord. This same reliance on the Lord is absolutely necessary for each of us if we are to allow the Lord to truly direct us through our mortal journey.

You will recall that when these barges were completed, there was a glaring absence: "As miraculously designed and meticulously constructed as they were, these ships had one major, seemingly insoluble limitation. Such a tight, seaworthy design provided no way to admit light for the seafarers."[195] As the brother of Jared returned to report to the Lord, he first reported that he had done what he had been asked. Then humbly, perhaps even hesitatingly, he pointed out, "Behold there is no light in them. Behold, O Lord, wilt thou suffer that we shall cross this great water in darkness?" (Ether 2:22). The Lord's response surely came as a surprise to Moriancumer as He asked, "What will ye that I should do that ye may have light in your vessels?" (Ether 2:23). Commenting on this situation, Elder Bruce R. McConkie explained:

> The Lord talked to him about it a little, and then He said this: 'What will ye that I should do that ye may have light in your vessels?' (Ether 2:23). In effect, 'What are you asking me for? This is something you should have solved.' And he talked a little more, and he repeated in

essence the question: 'What will ye that I should prepare for you that ye may have light when ye are swallowed up in the depths of the sea?' (Ether 2:25). In other words, 'Moriancumer, this is your problem. Why are you troubling me? I've given you your agency; you are endowed with capacity and ability. Get out and solve the problem.'"[196]

As divine children of our Father in Heaven, we have been endowed with the gift of agency; we have the ability to act for ourselves and not just to be acted upon. In this situation, the Lord provided the brother of Jared with an opportunity to stretch himself, to grow and progress on his personal path of discipleship. Helping us find application here, President Harold B. Lee added the following interpretation of the situation as the Lord asked of Moriancumer: "'Well, have you any good ideas? What would you suggest that we should do in order to have light?' . . . Then the Lord went away and left him alone. It was as though the Lord were saying to him, 'Look, I gave you a mind to think with, and I gave you agency to use it. Now you do all you can to help yourself with this problem; and then, after you've done all you can, I'll step in to help you.' This is the principle in action. If you want the blessing, don't just kneel down and pray about it. Prepare yourselves in every conceivable way you can in order to make yourselves worthy to receive the blessing you seek."[197] To his everlasting credit, the brother of Jared immediately got to work, climbed a mountain, and began to "molten out of a rock sixteen small stones; and they were white and clear, even as transparent glass" (Ether 3:1).

Upon returning to the Lord, the brother of Jared is clearly humble and hesitant about the solution he came across. He said, "Now behold, O Lord, and do not be angry with thy servant because of his weakness before thee. . . . O Lord, look upon me in pity, and turn away thine anger from this thy people, and suffer not that they shall go forth across this raging deep in darkness; but behold these *things* which I have molten out of the rock" (Ether 3:2–3; emphasis added). With his familiar wit, Elder Holland commented on this exchange:

> *Things.* The brother of Jared hardly knew what to call them. *Rocks* undoubtedly did not sound very inspiring. Here, standing next to the Lord's magnificent handiwork, the impeccably designed and marvelously unique seagoing barges, the brother of Jared offered for his

contribution rocks. As he eyed the sleek ships the Lord had provided, it was a moment of genuine humility.

He hurried on: "And I know, O Lord, that thou hast all power, and can do whatsoever thou wilt for the benefit of man; therefore touch these stones, O Lord, with thy finger, and prepare them that they may shine forth in darkness; and they shall shine forth unto us in the vessels which we have prepared, that we may have light while we shall cross the sea. Behold, O Lord, thou canst do this. We know that thou art able to show forth great power, which looks small unto the understanding of men" (Ether 3:4–5). . . .

Obviously Jehovah found something striking in the childlike innocence and fervor of this man's faith. *"Behold, O Lord, thou canst do this."* In a sense there may be no more powerful expression of faith spoken in scripture. It is almost as if the brother of Jared was encouraging God, emboldening him, reassuring him. Not "Behold, O Lord, I am sure thou canst do this." Not "Behold, O Lord, thou hast done many greater things than this." However uncertain the prophet was about his own ability, he had *no* uncertainty about God's power. This was nothing but a single, assertive declaration with no hint of vacillation. It was encouragement to him who needs no encouragement but who surely must have been touched by it. "Behold, O Lord, thou canst do this."[198]

Preparatory Faith and Piercing the Veil

As was already mentioned, the brother of Jared had become familiar with the voice of the Lord and gained greater confidence in his ability to be directed by Him. All of these experiences, however, were but a preamble to one of the most dramatic and inspiring divine encounters in the Book of Mormon. You will recall that the brother of Jared invited the Lord to stretch forth His hand and touch the stones that he had fashioned, that they might be used to illuminate the barges. In so doing, we read, "And the veil was taken from off the eyes of the brother of Jared, and he saw the finger of the Lord" (Ether 3:6). He is then told that because of his faith, he was granted the opportunity to pierce the veil and see what he saw.

When asked if he saw more than the finger of the Lord, the brother of Jared asked the Lord to show Himself unto him. In what is a profound preliminary, faith-testing question, the Lord asked,

"Believest thou the words which I *shall* speak?" (Ether 3:11; emphasis added). Note that the Lord was not asking if the brother of Jared believed what has been spoken in the past, or even if he believed what was then being taught; rather, He was asking if he had faith, confidence, and trust in something God would yet reveal. Elder Holland again provided invaluable insight into this intriguing question. He said,

> Preparatory faith is formed by experiences in the past—by the known, which provides a basis for belief. But redemptive faith must often be exercised toward experiences in the future—the unknown, which provides an opportunity for the miraculous. Exacting faith, mountain-moving faith, faith like that of the brother of Jared, *precedes* the miracle and the knowledge. He had to believe *before* God spoke. He had to act *before* the ability to complete that action was apparent. He had to commit to the complete experience in advance of even the first segment of its realization. Faith is to agree unconditionally—and in advance—to whatever conditions God may require in both the near and distant future.[199]

When Moriancumer confirmed that he did believe the words that the Lord *would yet* speak, he was saying that he had such a deep and abiding trust in the Lord that he knew He would not say anything that was not true and would not bless him and his people.

What followed is one of the greatest theophanies in all of scripture. In fact, as Jehovah revealed His antemortal person to this faith-filled disciple, He told him, "Never have I showed myself unto man whom I have created, for never has man believed in me as thou hast" (Ether 3:15). "The Lord could not withhold anything from him, for he knew that the Lord could show him all things" (Ether 3:26). Understanding that the Lord had manifested Himself prior to this experience, Elder Holland gave this helpful insight:

> A final explanation—and in terms of the brother of Jared's faith the most persuasive one—is that Christ was saying to the brother of Jared, 'Never have I showed myself unto man *in this manner, without my volition, driven solely by the faith of the beholder.*' As a rule, prophets are invited into the presence of the Lord, are bidden to enter his presence by him and only with his sanction. The brother of Jared, on the other hand, seems to have thrust himself through the veil, not as an unwelcome guest but perhaps technically as an uninvited one. Said Jehovah,

'Never has man come before me with such exceeding faith as thou hast; for were it not so ye could not have seen my finger. . . . Never has man believed in me as thou hast.' Obviously the Lord himself was linking unprecedented faith with this unprecedented vision. If the vision itself was not unique, then it had to be the faith and how the vision was obtained that was so unparalleled. The only way that faith could be so remarkable was its ability to take the prophet, uninvited, where others had been able to go only with God's bidding.[200]

And so it was. The faith of Moriancumer brought him back into the presence of the Creator. Later in Ether, the prophet Moroni underscored the faith of Moriancumer, as he said, "There were many whose faith was so exceedingly strong, even before Christ came, who could not be kept from within the veil, *but truly saw with their eyes the things which they had beheld with an eye of faith*, and they were glad" (Ether 12:19; emphasis added). What a powerful way of describing this deep and abiding faith! When we see things with our eyes, it is but a repeat of what we have already beheld with our spiritual eye of faith. This idea seems to echo the reality that before anything was physically created, it was first created spiritually. And so we see that because of his faith and his unyielding faithfulness, the brother of Jared came to know the Redeemer and commune with Him in a most sacred manner.

Attributes of Discipleship

As we reflect on this experience, it is important to see that while the brother of Jared was described as a strong and mighty man, his faith in Christ and in His words is his most significant attribute. Elder Samuelson provided us with an application from this divine experience. He said: "As we consider the brother of Jared and the clearly responsive attention that he received from the Lord, we might profitably consider some of his characteristics or traits that seem to have facilitative functions in the Lord's interactions with him. While there are others that might be mentioned, several seem worthy of our consideration and emulation as we attempt to better understand the Messiah and His expectations for us."[201] To help us connect ourselves to this faithful disciple, consider the following actionable attributes identified by Elder Samuelson. He explained how Mahonri Moriancumer:

- Consistently acted in faith (see Ether 3:9)
- Carefully analyzed and thoughtfully examined the dilemmas that faced him (see Ether 3:4)
- Accepted counsel and advice (see Ether 1:38–39)
- Clearly and most often regularly prayed to the Lord to express praise and gratitude for blessings (see Ether 6:9)
- Expected answers to his prayers (see Ether 3:12)
- Repented (see Ether 2:15)
- Regularly followed the Lord's commandments and followed through[202]

From this list, we can see that while the experience of the brother of Jared was extraordinary in many ways, those attributes that led him to said experience are relatively ordinary. By *ordinary*, I am suggesting that these attributes are achievable to those who make them a priority, like he did, and are willing to pay the price to develop them.

One final consideration in terms of actionable principles comes again from Elder Samuelson, as he taught, "The absolute recognition that both seemingly small and courageously mighty prayers are answered by the Lord, if asked in true and deep faith, is clearly demonstrated by the experiences of the brother of Jared. The encounters of this prophet with Jesus Christ give evidence that the Lord reveals what is needed but usually not much more. Once blessings or specific acts of assistance are rendered by the Lord, more should not be expected until that portion which is received is appropriately and adequately used and applied."[203] This takeaway point underscores the principle that as we seek spiritual experiences and strive to connect with heaven, we need to remember that God the Father; His Son, Jesus Christ; and the Holy Spirit all operate under the timeless idea of "line upon line, precept upon precept, here a little and there a little" (2 Nephi 28:30). Perhaps a few examples would be helpful.

Line upon Line, Precept upon Precept

First, consider the timeline of the Restoration and Joseph Smith's experiences. As Elder Bednar observed, "The fundamental doctrines and principles of the restored gospel were not delivered to the Prophet Joseph Smith in the Sacred Grove in a neatly organized binder. Rather, these priceless treasures were revealed line upon line as circumstances

warranted and as the timing was right."[204] We could also appropriately add that further light and knowledge were not provided until Joseph and others demonstrated their obedience to the prior revelation. Such was certainly the case with the First Vision, the initial and subsequent visits from Moroni, the Book of Mormon translation process, the restoration of the Church itself, the restoration of the Aaronic and the Melchizedek priesthoods, and so many more events. There may not be a better example of this truth than the entire Restoration (continuing even now in our day).

Elder Richard G. Scott provided another inspiring and instructive example of the need to act on prior revelation before receiving more from the Lord. You may recall that he told of an experience, where he was in a priesthood meeting in Mexico City. He recalled how a humble priesthood leader meekly struggled to communicate the truths of his lesson. He explained that this priesthood leader was full of the pure love of Jesus Christ and clearly had great desires to help others feel as he felt. Elder Scott recalled how, "His sincerity, purity of intent, and love permitted a spiritual strength to envelop the room. I was deeply touched. Then I began to receive personal impressions as an extension of the principles taught by that humble instructor. They were personal and related to my assignments in the area. They came in answer to my prolonged, prayerful efforts to learn." As the impressions came, he would write them down to ensure that they were appropriately captured and kept sacred.

Elder Scott then shared another experience in which he attended a Sunday School class in his home ward. He said that a well-educated individual was teaching and seemed to be using this teaching setting to impress the class with his knowledge and experience. As Elder Scott sat in class that day, he began to feel strong spiritual impressions and once again began to write them down. As he wrote, more and more impressions flooded into his heart and mind. As he reread his notes, he pondered over them and prayed, asking the Lord if he had appropriately captured inspiration that had come. In his own words, he received an answer:

> When a feeling of peace came, I thanked Him for the guidance given. I was then impressed to ask, "Was there yet more to be given?" I received further impressions, and the process of writing down the impressions,

pondering, and praying for confirmation was repeated. Again I was prompted to ask, "Is there more I should know?" And there was. When that last, most sacred experience was concluded, I had received some of the most precious, specific, personal direction one could hope to obtain in this life. Had I not responded to the first impressions and recorded them, I would not have received the last, most precious guidance.

What I have described is not an isolated experience. It embodies several true principles regarding communication from the Lord to His children here on earth. I believe that you can leave the most precious, personal direction of the Spirit unheard because you do not respond to, record, and apply the first promptings that come to you.[205]

What an important principle, one that we can apply as we seek to experience divine guidance in our own lives. Perhaps in our efforts to experience the closeness of heaven, we can act on these divine principles and revelations, analyze our behaviors in an effort to confirm that they match up with the guidance already received, and then seek to learn if there is yet more to do in order to be true to that guidance. In so doing, we show the Lord that He can trust us with more, perhaps even greater experiences. Such was certainly the case with the brother of Jared.

Tight like unto a Dish

When the brother of Jared went to work to build barges, we are told that the barges "were exceedingly tight, even that they would hold water like unto a dish" (Ether 2:17). While that verse gives us the clear idea that these barges were tight, the point is then belabored as the record says, "and the bottom thereof was *tight like unto a dish*; and the sides thereof were *tight like unto a dish*; and the ends thereof were peaked; and the top thereof was *tight like unto a dish*; and the length thereof was the length of a tree; and the door thereof, when it was shut, was *tight like unto a dish*" (Ether 2:17; emphasis added). So, what *do* we know from these descriptions of the barges? We know that they were tight . . . like unto a dish.

The significance of this phrase comes as the Jaredites actually board their vessels to begin their journey. We are told that "when they were buried in the deep there was no water that could hurt them, their vessels being tight like unto a dish, and also they were tight like

unto the ark of Noah" (Ether 6:7). Not only were these vessels tight like a dish, they were also similar to Noah's ark in at least this one way. So, what was it that made Noah's ark tight? In preparing the ark, Noah was told, "Make thee an ark of gopher wood; rooms shalt thou make in the ark, and shalt *pitch* it within and without with *pitch*" (Genesis 6:14; emphasis added). Physical pitch is something like black tar that would have been used to seal the ship tightly. The most common Hebrew word for this kind of pitch is *zetteth*. However, when looking at the text surrounding Noah's ark, the Hebrew word that is translated as pitch actually comes from the word *kapher*, which means "to cover" or "to make atonement." Thus, when Noah built the ark, he not only used physical pitch to ensure its tightness but he also relied completely on the mercies of the Lord to protect him and his family from the elements and dangers around him. We see this same idea manifest with the Jaredite voyage. They too had sealed their barges by the command of the Lord and went forward, "commending themselves unto the Lord their God" (Ether 6:4).

Indeed, we read that "the Lord God caused that there should be a furious wind blow upon the face of the waters, towards the promised land," and that as "they were encompassed about by many waters they did cry unto the Lord, and he did bring them forth again upon the top of the waters. And it came to pass that the wind did never cease to blow towards the promised land" (Ether 6:5,7–8). The brother of Jared and his people were completely reliant on the protective power of Christ as they commended themselves unto Him and His will.

And Thus We See

Throughout this chapter, we have seen that the Lord smiled upon the simple and pure faith of Mahonri Moriancumer. We know that he was an unwavering man, who trusted in the Lord and overcame the weakness of the flesh. In his humility, he acknowledged his reliance on the merciful, protecting, and transformative power of the Lord Jesus Christ. From him, we learn something of the price to be paid to receive revelation from the Lord and connect ourselves with Him. The Lord expects us to do our part in coming unto Him, and as we approach Him in humility, He can make weak things become strong through His grace. We likewise learn that as we act on divine direction, the Lord will give us further direction and understanding. Perhaps most powerfully, from the brother of Jared we see evidence of simple, true, redemptive faith. His trust in the Lord ran so deeply that he could confidently say he even believed in the words that the Lord had not yet spoken. This pure faith granted this resolute man miraculous experiences with the Messiah.

Elder Holland once said that "the Book of Mormon is predicated on the willingness of men and women to 'rend that veil of unbelief' in order to behold the revelations—and the Revelation—of God (Ether 4:15). . . . The brother of Jared may not have had great belief in himself, but his belief in God was unprecedented. In that there is hope for us all. His faith was without doubt or limit."[206] Note that it was not Moriancumer's natural prowess or his academic training that provided him with these precious experiences with the divine. Rather, it was his willingness to be tutored by the Lord and commend his life, dreams, and future unto His hands. He had learned that eternally significant truth that "men and women who turn their lives over to God will find out that he can make a lot more out of their lives than they can. He will deepen their joys, expand their vision, quicken their minds, strengthen their muscles, lift their spirits, multiply their blessings, increase their opportunities, comfort their souls, raise up friends, and pour out peace."[207] Perhaps we can likewise more fully commend ourselves unto the Lord.

Think back with me to that pivotal prayer of faith from the brother of Jared. In humility, he said, "I know, O Lord, that thou hast all power, and can do whatsoever thou wilt for the benefit of man; therefore touch these stones, O Lord, with thy finger" (Ether 3:4). As we read this inspiring account, it becomes apparent that "from the moment of that utterance, the brother of Jared and the reader of the Book of Mormon would never again be the same."[208] Elder Holland taught that "once and for all it was declared that ordinary people with ordinary challenges could rend the veil of unbelief and enter the realms of eternity. And Christ, who was prepared from the foundation of the world to redeem His people, would stand in all His glory at the edge of that veil, ready to receive the believers and show them 'how great things the

Father had laid up' for them at the end of faith's journey."[209] Through this account, we can plainly see that the Savior desires us to seek Him, to be close to Him, and to rely on Him.

To conclude this chapter, I would like to share an experience that underscores the truth that miracles happen as we rely completely on the rescuing and redeeming power of Christ. My wife and I were awakened shortly after midnight by a loud scream, followed by weeping (not a unique experience with five small children). I ran into my son's bedroom to find him gasping for air between shrieks. For some reason, whenever he would get sick, it seemed to always turn to croup. This croup cough would make it difficult for him to catch his breath. My wife ran in, gathered him in her arms, and took him outside, hoping the cool air would help clear him up. As she sang to him on the front porch, she eventually got him back to sleep. However, within about ten minutes, he was awake again, and the deep wheezing (coupled with screaming) resumed.

We went back inside, and as my wife ran to find his medicine, I held him in my arms, trying to comfort him. He was terrified, I was nervous, and my wife was frantically running throughout the house, trying to find the medicine. As I previously noted, my son seemed terrified because the croup had never been this severe before. He would cough, and that would make him gasp for air. He would gasp for air, and that would scare him, which would make him cry. The crying would lead to more gasping, which would then scare him again. It was an awful cycle. At one point, my little boy looked up at me with tear-swollen eyes and, between the screaming, gasping, and wheezing, he cried out, "Daddy, I need Jesus to help me!" As I choked back my own tears, I thought to myself, *Never before have I seen faith in its most simple and pure form* (see 3 Nephi 19:35). To a humbled father, the tutoring and merciful Lord brought to mind the pleading phrase of Alma, "O Jesus, thou Son of God, have mercy on me" (Alma 36:18), and coupled it with the innocent utterance, "I need Jesus to help me." That night, not only did I learn what true faith was, but I truly felt what it means to need, trust in, and rely on Jesus. As we study the account of the brother of Jared, we can see that same innocent yet powerful faith demonstrated by this devoted disciple.

Chapter 13: Mormon and Moroni

Having lived and ministered during grossly iniquitous times, these great leaders help us to see that we can find direction and power in the strength of the Lord. Further, we learn that when it appears that all other safe havens are gone, and we are seemingly wandering in isolation, we can confidently and continually rest peacefully in the protective grace of the Good Shepherd.

A Day of Confusion and Uncertainty

When I was young boy, my parents allowed me to have a paper route. I loved my job and I really enjoyed the opportunity to make a little money. I remember dreading delivering the paper on Thanksgiving though, because it was about eight times the size of a normal paper, being full of advertisements for Black Friday. I grew up in Pendleton, Oregon, and remember feeling like the city was like a massive bowl that seemed to have hills on every side.

One particular route I had was up on a big hill, and so every single house had a massive set of stairs that I would have to go up to deliver their newspaper. While this created all sorts of challenges for me, my youthful and innovative imagination helped me make it an enjoyable experience. After a while, I would be riding my bike or rollerblading and would look up at all of those stairs and think to myself, *There has got to be a better way to do this.* My immature and overly competitive mind conjured up a brilliant idea (and concluded that it would be fun to see if I could) of throwing the newspaper the fifty plus feet over the front yard and railing and making it land on the porch.

I would be lying if I said I made it every time. I would also be lying if I said that I never threw my customer's newspaper hard into their screen door, under-threw it into their sprinklers, or overthrew it on top of their house. I may have done all of those things multiple times. Fortunately, a lot of people were patient with my unwise decision, and I learned a lot of invaluable lessons.

This job gave me a great chance to meet people, get chased by angry dogs, and get yelled at by angry people (looking back, it was great preparation for my mission). Perhaps the thing I enjoyed most (besides getting paid) was the opportunity to briefly skim through the headlines, looking for anything interesting. While skimming, I would often enjoy reading the strange headlines, like these:

- County to Pay $25,000 to Advertise Lack of Funds
- Poison Control Center Reminds Everyone Not to Take Poison
- Federal Agents Raid Gunshop, Find Weapons
- Tips to Avoid Alligator Attacks: Don't Swim in Waters Inhabited by Large Alligators
- Wisconsin Couple Says Pet Chicken Alerted Them to Blaze
- New Jersey Capital City Running Out of Toilet Paper
- Teacher Quits School to Be a Rapper
- Massachusetts Cops Caught Egging Superior Officer's Home
- Cat Caught Sneaking Saw, Phone into Brazil Prison
- Unruly Passenger Taped to Seat on Icelandair Flight

While I found significant entertainment in many of these headlines, others often troubled me. While I do not have the exact headlines I read in those days, here are samples of what one might read today. All of these headlines were taken from the newspaper on the exact same day:

- Prominent Rights Judge Is Convicted in Spain
- Syria Said to Continue Onslaught
- Libya Struggles to Curb Militias as Chaos Grows

- The Piracy Problem: How Broad?
- Utah Supreme Court Hears Lunch-Lady Sex Case
- Fugitive Sibling Pleads Guilty in Colorado Deal
- Shooting Victim Found in Road
- Gender-Bending Model Pushes Limits of the Runway
- Powell's Sister Angry, Says She Never Thought Josh Could Kill His Sons
- Stolen Car Suspect Tries to Hide on LA Rooftops
- Greenland Mourns Victims of Triple Homicide

The reality is that we live in a world of confusion, anger, and uncertainty. As we look around, we see individual struggles, the collapse of families, and ultimately the collapse of nations. However, with all of that said, our beloved prophet, who is a continual optimist, has given us reassurance, declaring that the future can be as bright as our faith, and that as we trust in the Lord, we can find peace in these troubled times.[210]

Throughout the Book of Mormon, we find many examples of individuals who endured similar trials and remained faithful to the covenants they made. Perhaps the most extreme examples of men who were surrounded by war, apostasy, and despair are Mormon and his son, Moroni. In this chapter, we will study the lives of these two mighty men of valor and look at how they came to know, trust in, and continually rely on Jesus Christ.

Becoming Mormon

Suppose you were asked to name the person described in the following list:[211]

- A prophet came to him when he was young and told him of records engraved on metal plates that he had hidden in a hill. The prophet told him that he was to go to the hill when he was older and obtain the plates (see Mormon 1:1–3; Joseph Smith—History 1:33–35, 42).
- In his mid-teens, he was visited of the Lord (see Mormon 1:15; Joseph Smith—History 1:17).
- He tried to share part of what he had learned, but the people hardened their hearts (see Mormon 1:16; Joseph Smith—History 1:21–22).

- He was in his early twenties when he received the plates (see Mormon 1:3; 2:16–17; Joseph Smith—History 1:59).
- He was large in stature (see Mormon 2:1; *Church History in the Fulness of Times: Religion 341–43* [student manual, 1993], 49).
- He had the same name as his father (see Mormon 1:5; Joseph Smith—History 1:4).
- The people in his time lived in a state of apostasy (see Mormon 1:13; Joseph Smith—History 1:18–19).
- He led his people as a military leader, prophet, and record keeper (see Mormon 2:1; D&C 43:1–5; *Church History in the Fulness of Times*, 223).
- He was forced by his enemies to leave his home and move with his people from city to city (see Mormon 2:4–6; 4:19–20; 5:6–7; D&C 124 heading; Joseph Smith—History 1:61).
- His enemies finally succeeded in killing him (see Mormon 8:3; D&C 135:4).

When reading through that list, it becomes clear that these points provide a perfect description of the Prophet Joseph Smith, the mighty prophet of the Restoration. However, as you probably noted while looking at the scriptural references, each descriptive item from the list could also describe the prophet Mormon.

This reality underscores the significance of the life and ministry of Mormon. Elder Spencer J. Condie wrote, "If there ever lived a person who resisted and withstood the evil influence of a depraved world to become a worthy servant of the Lord, this person was Mormon."[212] From the time Mormon was eleven years old, he lived in a place where "wickedness did prevail upon the face of the whole land, insomuch that the Lord did take away his beloved disciples, and the work of miracles and of healing did cease because of the iniquity of the people" (Mormon 1:13). We read of the carnage of war, of human sacrifice "unto their idol gods" (Mormon 4:14), rape, robbery, cannibalism, sorcery, and witchcrafts.

In short, "the power of the evil one was wrought upon all the face of the land" (Mormon 1:19). This surely must have been an onerous and difficult time in which to grow up.

When Mormon was at the tender age of ten, Ammaron approached him, telling him that he was "a sober child, and [was] quick to observe" (Mormon 1:2). He commissioned Mormon to observe the dealings of his people, and then, when he was twenty-four, he was to write what he had seen. We learn that when he was eleven years old, his father, Mormon, moved the family to the land of Zarahemla (see Mormon 1:6). In describing the culture he was being raised in, he explained that "there were no gifts from the Lord, and the Holy Ghost did not come upon any, because of their wickedness and unbelief" (Mormon 1:14).

However, in the next verse, Mormon helps us to see how the wickedness that surrounded him did not weaken his own ability to connect with the Lord. It reads, "And I, being fifteen years of age and being somewhat of a sober mind, therefore *I was visited of the Lord, and tasted and knew of the goodness of Jesus*" (Mormon 1:15, emphasis added).

What an effective way to describe his sacred encounter with the Living Christ! Mormon's description is reminiscent of the great Psalm that reads, "O taste and see that the Lord is good: blessed is the man that trusteth in him" (Psalms 34:8). Beginning with his description of knowing the goodness of Jesus, Mormon went to painstaking lengths to ensure that the reader would understand that he personally knew the Lord. Furthermore, he seemed to want readers to see that this firsthand experience with the grace of Jesus Christ was the beginning of a deeply personal and meaningful divine relationship. While we will not take the time here to detail his entire narrative, consider the following examples that illustrate Mormon's constant focus on Christ, even amid "the horrible scene of the blood and carnage which was among the people" (Mormon 4:11):

- "They did not come unto Jesus with broken hearts" (Mormon 2:14)
- "My heart has been filled with sorrow because of their wickedness, all my days; nevertheless, I know that I shall be lifted up at the last day" (Mormon 2:19)
- "The strength of the Lord was not with us; yea, we were left to ourselves" (Mormon 2:26)

- "I did cry unto this people, but it was in vain; and they did not realize that it was the Lord that had spared them" (Mormon 3:3)
- "I had led them many times to battle, and had loved them, according to the love of God which was in me, with all my heart" (Mormon 3:12)
- "And for this cause I write unto you, that ye may know that ye must all stand before the judgment-seat of Christ . . . and also that ye may believe the gospel of Jesus Christ" (Mormon 3:20–21)
- "I would that I could persuade all ye ends of the earth to repent and prepare to stand before the judgment-seat of Christ" (Mormon 3:22).
- "They looked upon me as though I could deliver them from their afflictions. But behold, I was without hope . . . for they repented not of their iniquities, but did struggle for their lives without calling upon that being who created them" (Mormon 5:1–2)
- "They will sorrow that this people had not repented that they might have been clasped in the arms of Jesus" (Mormon 5:11)
- "That they may be persuaded that Jesus is the Christ, the Son of the living God; that the Father may bring about, through his most Beloved, his great and eternal purpose" (Mormon 5:14)
- "They are without Christ and God in the world; and they are driven about as chaff before the wind. They were once a delightsome people, and they had Christ for their shepherd; yea, they were led even by God the Father" (Mormon 5:16–17)
- "Know ye not that ye are in the hands of God? . . . Therefore, repent ye, and humble yourselves before him" (Mormon 5:23–24)
- "O ye fair ones, how could ye have departed from the ways of the Lord! O ye fair ones, how could ye have rejected that Jesus, who stood with open arms to receive you!" (Mormon 6:17)
- "Know ye that ye must . . . repent of all your sins and iniquities, and believe in Jesus Christ, that he is the Son of God . . . and he hath brought to pass the redemption of the world" (Mormon 7:5, 7)

A Reliance on Christ

One of Mormon's final points of emphasis is that because of the Savior, we can be redeemed and found guiltless at the last day. He testified that because of Christ, we can dwell "in the presence of God in his kingdom, to sing ceaseless praises with the choirs above, unto the Father, and unto the Son, and unto the Holy Ghost, which are one God, in a state of happiness which hath no end" (Mormon 7:7). As readers, we can feel the deep longing of Mormon's heart to be with the Master whom he has so diligently served throughout his life. Is it any wonder that Mormon, in his letters to his son, talked at length about "the grace of God the Father, and our Lord Jesus Christ" (Moroni 7:2), becoming "the peaceable followers of Christ" (Moroni 7:3), "the Spirit of Christ" (Moroni 7:16), "the light of Christ" (Moroni 7:18, 19), being "a child of Christ" (Moroni 7:19), having "faith in Christ" (Moroni 7:25, 32, 39), having "hope through the atonement of Christ" (Moroni 7:41), being filled with "the pure love of Christ" (Moroni 7:47), being made "alive in Christ" (Moroni 8:12, 22), and remaining "faithful in Christ" (Moroni 9:25) so that we may one day be lifted up by Christ (see Moroni 9:25)?

Through his writings, we see that Mormon's divine experience as a fifteen-year-old began a revelatory lifestyle that would shape him into a mighty prophet, military leader, historian, author, and man of Christ.

We also see that because of his faith and trust in Christ, Mormon was able to remain faithful in the midst of heinous and horrific scenes of wickedness. What an important lesson for those of us living in the last days! Mormon exemplifies how to live in the light of Christ as the world around us grows ever darker.

Mormon as an Impactful Father

In addition to Mormon's exemplary life as prophet, leader, editor, and author, he was also a great example of a father. As the editor and abridger of the Book of Mormon, Mormon "was well aware of the prophecies about his people, [and] knew that his newly born son would experience a lifetime of bloodshed, turmoil, and strife. Prophecies in the scriptures were clear that the once-mighty Nephite civilization would deteriorate, divide, and finally end in tragic destruction during Moroni's lifetime" (see 1 Nephi 12:11–15; Alma 45:9–14; Helaman 13:5–10).[213]

Mormon lived in a time of extreme wickedness, selfishness, and cowardice. One gets a sense that as Mormon found himself surrounded by all this filth, he likely looked for inspiration on how to fight against it and overcome such conditions. From the record, it would seem that he "looked for inspiration to another young general, who lived over 400 years earlier and was able to inspire his people to victory through righteousness.

Captain Moroni, chief captain of the Nephite armies, was a man Mormon greatly admired. He devotes a large part of his abridgment to the wars fought by Captain Moroni."[214] Perhaps as Mormon thought of his baby boy and about the environment he would be raised in, he wanted to ensure that this little boy knew he was going to have to be strong and deeply devoted to the cause of Christ.

Indeed, "knowing the difficulties his son would encounter, Mormon, no doubt, named his infant son after the legendary prophet and military leader Captain Moroni, whose history he had abridged (see Alma 43:16–62:43)."[215] Listen to the words that Mormon had previously written about Captain Moroni, and consider his desire for his son to emulate this example:

> And Moroni was a strong and a mighty man; he was a man of a perfect understanding; yea, a man that did not delight in bloodshed; a man whose soul did joy in the liberty and the freedom of his country, and his brethren from bondage and slavery;
>
> Yea, a man whose heart did swell with thanksgiving to his God, for the many privileges and blessings which he bestowed upon his people; a man who did labor exceedingly for the welfare and safety of his people.
>
> Yea, and he was a man who was firm in the faith of Christ, and he had sworn with an oath to defend his people, his rights, and his country, and his religion, even to the loss of his blood. . . .
>
> Yea, verily, verily I say unto you, if all men had been, and were, and ever would be, like unto Moroni, behold, the very powers of hell would have been shaken forever; yea, the devil would never have power over the hearts of the children of men. (Alma 48:11–13, 17)

Through his letters to his son, we can feel the love that Mormon had for Moroni and the deep connection they shared as they remained among the few faithful followers of Christ still living in their society. It is significant that among the final recorded words of his counsel we have are, "My son, be faithful in Christ; and may not the things which I have written grieve thee, to weigh thee down unto death; but may Christ lift thee up" (Moroni 9:25). Because of the faithful mentoring of his father, Moroni was indeed able to establish a divine connection with the Father and Jesus Christ, and thus fulfilled his destiny as the final steward of the plates and the possessor of the "keys of the record of the stick of Ephraim" (D&C 27:5).

President Gordon B. Hinckley wrote, "Of all the characters who walk the pages of the Book of Mormon, none stands a greater hero, save Jesus only, than does Moroni, son of Mormon."[216] After having read about all of the powerful leaders in this remarkable record, consider how bold that statement is.

This statement from President Hinckley begs the question: What is it that would set Moroni apart from these other great leaders? This section will attempt to underscore that bold statement by President Hinckley.

A Symbol of the Restoration

I have long been interested in organizational behavior and how organizations function as they struggle or succeed. In most cases, successful organizations have developed a symbol or a logo that communicates a strong message that they want to convey to their target market. The objective with this is that when an individual sees that symbol, they think of the message and mission of the organization as a whole.

As members of The Church of Jesus Christ of Latter-day Saints, we have been invited to "establish the temple of the Lord as the great symbol of [our] membership."[217] As you ponder this invitation from President Howard W. Hunter, consider the following account from President Hinckley, his prophetic successor:

> From my window I frequently look at the figure of Moroni on the tallest tower of the Salt Lake Temple. He has been there since April 6, 1892, the date on which the capstone was laid before the largest

crowd ever assembled in Salt Lake City up to that time. When the capstone was placed, thousands of voices joined in singing, 'Hosanna to God and the Lamb.' Later that day, the statue was placed on top of the capstone. . . . [Moroni] is a symbol of the restoration of the gospel in this the dispensation of the fulness of times.[218]

While the temple, the Lord's house on earth, is the great symbol of our membership, perhaps the statue of Moroni represents the message we hope the world will consider when they see that majestic figure. Consider, for example, that the Church chose the symbol of the angel Moroni to be placed on such digital applications as "LDS Gospel Library," "the Mormon Channel," and even on the top of the temple on "LDS Tools."

Thus, when members and nonmembers alike drive by our temples or download our applications, they are reminded of our latter-day message and mission to take the restored gospel to all of the world. Interestingly, the sculptor who created the design for the figure that most statues are patterned after today was actually not even a member. In 1893, shortly after the completion of the Salt Lake Temple, a man by the name of Cyrus Dallin was asked to create this new design. Speaking of his experience with this project, he said that it "brought me nearer to God than anything I ever did. It seemed to me that I came to know what it means to commune with angels from heaven."[219] How fitting it is that the Lord would take the symbols' message deep into the heart of the man who helped to design it.

While the primary message of the symbol of the angel Moroni is the declaration to all of the world that the fulness of the gospel has been restored and will be preached "to every nation, and kindred, and tongue, and people" (Revelation 14:6), consider also how the life and ministry of Moroni could send a powerful message to all who gaze upon that magnificent statue.

Moroni's Insecurities

Unfortunately, the record is relatively quiet with regards to Moroni's family life and his formative years. Outside of learning about his father and his continual mentoring and influence on Moroni, we

know basically nothing about his family (his mother, siblings, and so on). One scholar succinctly summarized Moroni's life in the following way:

> The Lord chose Moroni to complete the Nephite dispensation of the gospel of Jesus Christ. He finished his father's inspired abridgment of the Nephite millennial-long history; he commanded 10,000 soldiers at Cumorah in their final battles with the Lamanites; he abridged the writings of Ether, the record of the Jaredites, a once mighty civilization that preceded his own on this western hemisphere; and he recorded the lengthy writings of the brother of Jared on the gold plates and sealed them up. He wandered alone about the land for many years, not only concerned about his personal safety, but also fully aware of his responsibility to preserve the plates until he was commanded to hide them in the earth. Finally, after traveling extensively and fulfilling priesthood responsibilities, he deposited the plates in a hillside in what is now western New York State. What Moroni accomplished has blessed many people and will yet bless many more.[220]

Unfortunately, because of the dearth of information from Moroni's formative years, we do not have a clear record of the divine experiences that molded him into the stalwart, exemplary man we read about in the Book of Mormon. One wonders if Moroni's own insecurities kept him from writing about such experiences. You will recall his humble confession, in which he declared, "Thou hast made us that we could write but little, because of the awkwardness of our hands. Behold, thou hast not made us mighty in writing like unto the brother of Jared, for thou madest him that the things which he wrote were mighty even as thou art, unto the overpowering of man to read them" (Ether 12:23–24).

Consider what Moroni may have been trying to communicate. He had been immersed in the brother of Jared's singular experience, in which he seems to have thrust himself through the veil and into the presence of the antemortal Jehovah.

While this experience is certainly miraculous and inspiring in many ways, Moroni seems be focusing here on the brother of Jared's ability to articulate and communicate the experience. He seems to be implying that when he read of the experience from Moriancumer, it was a powerful and overwhelming experience. Perhaps Moroni felt inadequate, because of his self-proclaimed weakness in writing, to actually articulate the experience of being visited by the Lord and His divine grace. As one scholar noted, "The weakness that troubles Moroni is his inability to express in writing what he feels inside, what he can express in speech through the power of the Spirit. He is obviously moved by the literary power and skill of the brother of Jared. His own writing pales by comparison, and he feels below the task of translating and abridging the work of this great writer and prophet. We can understand Moroni's feelings of inadequacy. A comparable task for us might be to paraphrase and abridge all 38 of Shakespeare's plays, preserving some of the continuity and brilliance of the originals."[121]

Perhaps Moroni felt that his direct experiences with the Lord were so personal and divine that, in his weakness, he could not possibly communicate the solemnity of the encounter. This is not unlike Ammon's humble conclusion: "I cannot say the smallest part which I feel" (Alma 26:16).

The Lonely Path of Discipleship

With all of that said, one cannot read the words engraved by Moroni, nor follow his narrative, without immediately realizing that, like his father, *he* had been visited by the Lord and had likewise tasted and knew firsthand of the goodness of Jesus. In a letter written by his father, we read these words, "I rejoice exceedingly that your Lord Jesus Christ hath been mindful of you, and hath called you to his ministry . . . [and] that he, through his infinite goodness and grace, will keep you through the endurance of faith on his name" (Moroni 8:2).

Throughout Moroni's ministry in this life, we see the Lord sustain, comfort, protect, and direct him. While this does not claim to be an exhaustive list, consider how the following scriptural passages demonstrate the feelings of Moroni toward the Savior, and of the Savior's involvement in his life:

- "Behold, look ye unto the revelations of God" (Mormon 8:33)
- "Jesus Christ hath shown you unto me" (Mormon 8:35)
- "Why are ye ashamed to take upon you the name of Christ?" (Mormon 8:38)

- "Cry mightily unto the Father in the name of Jesus" (Mormon 9:6)
- "Who can comprehend the marvelous works of God?" (Mormon 9:16)
- "[They] know not the God in whom they should trust" (Mormon 9:20)
- "Come unto the Lord with all your heart" (Mormon 9:27)
- "Ask with a firmness unshaken, that ye will yield to no temptation, but that ye will serve the true and living God" (Mormon 9:28)
- "The Lord knoweth the things which we have written" (Mormon 9:34)
- "In the gift of his Son hath God prepared a more excellent way" (Ether 12:11)
- "Therefore the Lord hath commanded me, yea, even Jesus Christ" (Ether 12:22)
- "And I [the Lord] show unto them that faith, hope and charity bringeth unto me—the fountain of all righteousness. And I, Moroni, having heard these words, was comforted" (Ether 12:28–29)
- "And it came to pass that the Lord said unto me: If they have not charity it mattereth not unto thee, thou hast been faithful; wherefore, thy garments shall be made clean. And because thou hast seen thy weakness thou shalt be made strong, even unto the sitting down in the place which I have prepared in the mansions of my Father" (Ether 12:37)
- "Then shall ye know that I have seen Jesus, and that he hath talked with me face to face" (Ether 12:39)
- "And now, I would commend you to seek this Jesus of whom the prophets and apostles have written, that the grace of God the Father, and also the Lord Jesus Christ, and the Holy Ghost, which beareth record of them, may be and abide in you forever" (Ether 12:41)
- "And then cometh the New Jerusalem; and blessed are they who dwell therein, for it is they whose garments are white through the blood of the Lamb" (Ether 13:10).
- "I, Moroni, will not deny the Christ" (Moroni 1:3)

- "Keep them continually watchful unto prayer, relying alone upon the merits of Christ, who was the author and the finisher of their faith" (Moroni 6:4)
- "Remember how merciful the Lord hath been" (Moroni 10:3)
- "I speak it according to the words of Christ" (Moroni 10:26)
- "Come unto Christ, and lay hold upon every good gift" (Moroni 10:30)
- "Come unto Christ, and be perfected in him" (Moroni 10:32)
- "By the grace of God ye are perfect in Christ" (Moroni 10:32)
- "Sanctified in Christ by the grace of God" (Moroni 10:33)

In a most sobering and somber passage, Moroni mused,

And now it came to pass that after the great and tremendous battle at Cumorah, behold, the Nephites who had escaped into the country southward were hunted by the Lamanites, until they were all destroyed. And my father also was killed by them, and I even remain alone to write the sad tale of the destruction of my people. But behold, they are gone, and I fulfil the commandment of my father. And whether they will slay me, I know not. Therefore I will write and hide up the records in the earth; and whither I go it mattereth not. Behold, my . . . father hath been slain in battle, and all my kinsfolk, and I have not friends nor whither to go; and how long the Lord will suffer that I may live I know not. (Mormon 8:2–5)

Imagine the challenges, discouragement, and overwhelming sense of loneliness and isolation that Moroni surely must have felt at this time. His dad, who incidentally was also the prophet, his mentor, and seemingly his closest confidante, had died. Furthermore, he was witnessing the destruction he always knew was inevitable. Surely this historic moment was difficult, as Moroni remained alone to witness the entire annihilation of his people.

It is amid this isolation that we get a glimpse into Moroni the man. With his back against the proverbial wall, we are given a view into the heart of a determined, stalwart, and consecrated Christian. Indeed, it is in the midst of this narrative that we see the enabling power of Jesus Christ manifested in divine companionship to one who felt so alone and isolated. Commenting on this truly vulnerable moment in Moroni's life, President Hinckley wrote,

Who can sense the depth of his pain, the poignant loneliness that constantly overshadowed him as he moved about, a fugitive relentlessly hunted by his enemies? For how long he actually was alone we do not know, but the record would indicate that it was a considerable period. His conversation was prayer to the Lord. His companion was the Holy Spirit. There were occasions when the Three Nephites ministered to him. But with all of this, there is an element of terrible tragedy in the life of this man who became a lonely wanderer.[222]

True to His Witness of Christ

In what he then thought would be his final counsel to both the Gentiles and his own people, Moroni bid farewell by speaking of the time when all will "meet before the judgment-seat of Christ. . . . And then shall ye know that I have seen Jesus, and that he hath talked with me face to face, and that he told me in plain humility, even as a man telleth another in mine own language, concerning these things" (Ether 12:38–39).

Surely these divine conversations with the Lord provided him with the strength to continue his long, lonely journey of discipleship. In the midst of these conversations, the Lord demonstrated great mercy and compassion on His sorrowful servant. As Moroni pondered upon the ultimate destruction and annihilation of his people, the Lord granted him a vision of what was to come and the work that would come forth. Moroni recounted, "Behold, I speak unto you as if ye were present, and yet ye are not. But behold, Jesus Christ hath shown you unto me, and I know your doing" (Mormon 8:35). While this vision was certainly an act of mercy from the Lord, it also seemed to drive Moroni to write with a sense of urgency to those of us who would eventually receive "these things" in the last day (Moroni 10:3).

Even as Moroni witnessed the work that would eventually come forth, the Lord also seems to have shown him the disbelief and secularization of the last days. In Mormon 9, Moroni speaks to those who do not believe in Christ. As we read his stinging rebuke and warning to those of us in this final dispensation, we again get a glimpse at how deeply he loved the Lord and how committed he was to this divine work. He said, "Behold, will ye believe in the day of your visitation—behold, when the Lord shall come . . . then will ye longer deny the Christ, or can ye behold the Lamb of God? Do ye suppose that ye shall dwell with him under a consciousness of your guilt? Do ye suppose that ye could be happy to dwell with that holy being, when your souls are racked with a consciousness of guilt that ye have ever abused his laws?" (Mormon 9:2–3).

As any great gospel teacher would, immediately following his stern rebuke, Moroni invited them to repent and come unto Christ: "O then ye unbelieving, turn ye unto the Lord; cry mightily unto the Father in the name of Jesus, that perhaps ye may be found spotless, pure, fair, and white, having been cleansed by the blood of the Lamb, at that great and last day" (Mormon 9:6).

After witnessing, conversing with, and taking direct counsel from the Lord, Moroni clearly became one of the great defenders of the reality of the resurrected Savior.

In a moment of pure integrity and inspiring faithfulness, Moroni demonstrated his final resolve to stay true to the God who stayed so close to him, even when he was utterly alone. He wrote, "Now I, Moroni, after having made an end of abridging the account of the people of Jared, I had supposed not to have written more, but I have not as yet perished; and I make not myself known to the Lamanites lest they should destroy me. For behold, their wars are exceedingly fierce among themselves; and because of their hatred they put to death every Nephite that will not deny the Christ. *And I, Moroni, will not deny the Christ*" (Moroni 1:1–3; emphasis added). Indeed, Moroni had learned firsthand of the fellowship of Christ's sufferings. He understood the hope of salvation in Christ and would remain true to this cause, regardless of what came!

Moroni's Final Invitation

After wandering for over twenty years, Moroni was entrusted with the significant responsibility of writing the concluding words of both his book and the entire Book of Mormon. In his concluding words, he demonstrated his complete devotion and reliance on the Savior, whom he had come to love and trust in so deeply. Knowing full well the destiny of the plates on which he wrote, Moroni concluded

the record with a poignant invitation and promise to those of us who would "receive these things" (Moroni 10:3).

In some ways, this final invitation seems to be a way in which Moroni ensured that the reader does not miss the overall purpose and objective of the Book of Mormon. On the title page of the Book of Mormon, Moroni took the time to help us see that one of the overarching messages and purposes of the book is to convince the reader "that Jesus is the Christ, the Eternal God, manifesting himself unto all nations."[223] He then underscored this purpose with the following final invitation: "Yea, come unto Christ, and be perfected in him, and deny yourselves of all ungodliness" (Moroni 10:32). What a powerfully concise summary of the entire message of the Book of Mormon!

As this book has attempted to highlight, the Book of Mormon is a record of individuals who heeded this invitation and thus experienced a life-altering divine encounter with the living Son of the Living God. Moroni's invitation is also linked with a promise. He would go on to say, "And if ye shall deny yourselves of all ungodliness, and love God with all your might, mind and strength, then is his grace sufficient for you, that by his grace ye may be perfect in Christ . . . that ye become holy, without spot" (Moroni 10:32–33).

Once again, Moroni seemed to be trying to ensure that the reader does not miss the purpose of this inspiring record, as he poured out his soul in petitioning us to come unto Christ and to rely wholly upon His grace for our salvation and consolation. Indeed, Moroni himself is a great example of one who relied on the Savior for comfort and strength during times of trial, and who has also obtained what his father once called "hope through the Atonement of Christ" (Moroni 7:41).

As was previously mentioned, *Preach My Gospel* provides extremely valuable insight regarding this hope of which Mormon spoke of. It states, "Hope is an abiding trust that the Lord will fulfill His promises to you. It is manifest in confidence, optimism, enthusiasm, and patient perseverance. It is believing and expecting that something will occur."[224]

Because of Moroni's experiences with the Lord, he had a "perfect brightness of hope" (2 Nephi 31:20) that was demonstrated in this final testimony and farewell: "And now I bid unto all, farewell. I soon go to rest in the paradise of God, until my spirit and body shall again reunite, and I am brought forth triumphant through the air, to meet you before the pleasing bar of the great Jehovah, the Eternal Judge of both quick and dead. Amen" (Moroni 10:34). Truly, Moroni's confidence had waxed strong in the presence of God, and this hope provided him the assurance that he would be made worthy to dwell with the Lord in the eternities.

Moroni was a man of Christ who put the kingdom of God first in his life. He fearlessly and courageously stayed true to his witness of Christ. His love for the Savior and his gratitude for the continual involvement of the Lord in his life must have strengthened him during the many lonely days and throughout so much heartache. No matter what challenges he faced, he overcame them "by the blood of the Lamb, and by the word of [his] testimony," and because he loved not his life unto death (Revelation 12:11). Indeed, his father could have written these now immortal words about his own son: "If all men had been, and were, and ever would be, like unto Moroni, behold, the very powers of hell would have been shaken forever; yea, the devil would never have power over the hearts of the children of men" (Alma 48:17).

Truly, Moroni was prepared for his marvelous mission. His life exemplified a life *in* Christ and how to trust in the Savior during times of sorrow, trial, and loneliness.

And a Thus We See

Both Mormon and Moroni stand as pillars when it comes to maintaining faith, hope, and charity during the challenges of mortality. As we move closer to the Second Coming of the Lord, we will need to draw from their examples and live as they lived, trust as they trusted, and minister as they ministered.

Elder Neal A. Maxwell provided invaluable insight into trusting the Savior during challenging times. He said, "Since this is a gospel of growth and life is a school of experience, God, as a loving father, will stretch our souls at times. The soul is like a violin string: it makes music only when it is stretched. God will tutor us by trying us because he loves us, not because of indifference."[225]

Similarly, John Taylor taught, "I heard the Prophet Joseph say, in speaking to the Twelve on one occasion: 'You will have all kinds of trials to pass through. And it is quite as necessary for you to be tried as it was for Abraham and other men of God, and (said he) God will feel after you, and He will take hold of you and wrench your very heart strings, and if you cannot stand it you will not be fit for an inheritance in the Celestial Kingdom of God.'"[226]

Certainly both Mormon and Moroni experienced such wrenching and were found to be faithful, even in the midst of such difficulty. Their writings are a testament that "no pain that we suffer, no trial that we experience is wasted. . . . All that we suffer and all that we endure, especially when we endure it patiently, builds up our characters, purifies our hearts, expands our souls, and makes us more tender and charitable. . . . It is through sorrow and suffering, toil and tribulation, that we gain the education that we come here to acquire."[227] As so many of us have experienced on so many different occasions, I have felt the Lord feeling after my heartstrings and have had to completely rely on Him during my own personal tutorials.

I will never forget an experience my wife and I had a few years ago, wherein we felt alone and afraid. One of our little boys was a couple weeks away from starting kindergarten, and we were all excited for him to be taking this step. We were sitting on the couch one afternoon, when my wife and I noticed that he began making a little squeaking noise.

At first, we just brushed it off and didn't think much of it. However, the squeaking continued, so I asked him why he was making that noise. He wasn't even sure what I was talking about at first, but he then said he wasn't sure why he was doing it.

As the days went on, the squeaks became more frequent. As they became more frequent, he also started to shrug his shoulders at the same time as he squeaked. We weren't quite sure what to make of it, and so we started doing a bit of research. It quickly became apparent that our son's "ticks" were one of the most common signs of Tourette's syndrome.

As the ticks became even more frequent over the next week—he would squeak every four or five seconds—we determined that we should take him in to his doctor to find out what was going on. Unfortunately, the only time to meet with him was while I was at work, so my wife took our son in to the pediatrician.

After meeting with them for a bit, the doctor told my wife that this was the worst case of Tourette's syndrome that he had seen in his twenty-plus years of pediatric practice. My wife's heart sank, and she asked if there was any hopeful news or anything else he could tell her. He said if we wanted, we could take him to a specialist and get a second opinion, just to be sure. Because of how severe this case of the disorder was, we were able to get an appointment with a pediatric neurologist that week at Primary Children's Hospital in Salt Lake City, Utah.

Those were some of the most difficult days of our lives as we grappled with the bleak report from that doctor. Unfortunately, my mind began to negatively predict the future as I thought of what this would mean for our son.

My biggest concern was that, because I am around teenagers all of the time at junior high and high schools, I knew exactly what happens within those walls. I know of the bullying, laughing, and mocking that takes place. I've seen the overwhelming insecurities that seem to ooze out of teenagers, and that these insecurities are often manifest through backbiting, teasing, and gossiping. I also knew that my little boy was an incredibly confident, funny, sweet, and happy five-year-old, and I became terrified that the children in his class would make fun of him and damage his powerful, innocent spirit.

I was heartbroken. I prayed, wept, and prayed and wept some more. I confided my feelings to my wife, and she to me, and we both wept together. There were sleepless nights and discouraging days as we worried about our son and about the implications of this diagnosis. I poured out my heart to the Lord. I told him of my concerns for my son and how I did not want him to have to go through the social ostracism that seemed imminent.

While my wife and I tried to confide in and comfort one another, it seemed clear that, at least in some ways, we were each going to have to process our feelings and emotions in our own ways. It was a trying time for me personally as I pounded on the doors of heaven, questioning why the Lord would ask our little boy to have to carry such an onerous burden.

In the midst of our despair and anguish, the Lord showed forth His mercy and goodness in His own way and in His own time. To my wife, he sent mortal angels to comfort and sustain her. One sweet woman in particular always came at just the right time and with the just the right words. She will forever be remembered as a minister of grace during this difficult time for us.

As for me, I had a powerful experience as I woke up early one morning after a restless night and was on my way to the seminary building. I was tired, confused, emotionally exhausted, and seeking any help from heaven. As I started my car, I looked for a general conference talk to listen to on my commute. I happened to select a talk from President Henry B. Eyring.

To this day, I still do not remember exactly the specific session of conference, nor do I remember the specific talk. But as I heard the sweet and tender voice of a living prophet and Apostle of the Lord, I was completely overwhelmed with the Spirit. My heart did "brim with joy" (Alma 26:11) and my soul was filled with light! Indeed, my soul had been "illuminated by the light of the everlasting word" (Alma 5:7), and I began to weep. I became so emotional that I had to pull my car to the shoulder of the road until I could gain control of myself.

During that moment, I felt encircled in the immortal arms of the Savior, the closeness of heaven, and the mercy and goodness of God. Rather than sending words, he sent a feeling, and that feeling penetrated my heart and gave me the comfort I had so desperately been pleading for.

In His own way, the Lord was reminding me to trust Him and rely on His goodness, both for myself and for my son. He was telling me that he would be with me and my family. In the midst of our anxieties, He spoke in a way that was as unmistakable as it was eternal. I did not know what would happen with my sweet little boy, but what I *did* know was that no matter what happened to him, the Lord was going to be with him to strengthen him.

After visiting with the specialist, we were told that this actually was not Tourette's syndrome, but rather it was something that the doctor called "simple motor ticks." We were told that he would likely always have them, and that these motor ticks would likely come and go throughout his life, probably more severe at some points than others. We were also told that the best thing we could do was ignore that they were even happening, as they were most likely linked to anxiety.

Now, three years later, our sweet little kindergartener is now a sweet little third grader. Yes, his ticks have continued, and they come and go. What has remained constant, however, is the goodness of God in reaching out and comforting the hearts of a mother and a father who are ever more dependent on His help.

The stories of Mormon and Moroni underscore the truth that because of who God wants us to become, our lives "cannot be both faith-filled and stress-free," as Elder Maxwell so eloquently put it. "Therefore, how can you and I really expect to glide naively through life, as if to say, 'Lord, give me experience, but not grief, not sorrow, not pain, not opposition, not betrayal, and certainly not to be forsaken. Keep from me, Lord, all those experiences which made Thee what Thou art! Then let me come and dwell with Thee and fully share Thy joy!' "228

Indeed, it is in the midst of such experiences that the Lord shapes us into the men and women He desires us to be, even men and women of Christ.

The consecrated lives of Mormon and Moroni can be symbols for and a reminder of a covenant life in Christ. As we see the name of Mormon on that precious volume of scripture, we should think of his devotion toward God and his charity toward others, even in the midst of persecution, rebellion, and unthinkable wickedness.

As we look at the symbol of the angel Moroni, let us always think of the gospel going forth and being declared to all the world. But let us also remember the faith, commitment, and devotion of Moroni in staying true to the God who stayed true to him. When we see that angelic symbol, let us remember that the Lord has been, is now, and always will be closest to us when we feel alone and in despair.

Indeed, let us remember that no matter what the world is like around us, and no matter what trials we are facing in our lives, the Lord is our great constant. As we come to rely upon His merits, mercy, and grace, we can, as Moroni promised, find "hope for a better world, yea, even a place at the right hand of God" (Ether 12:4).

Conclusion

The Book of Mormon Will Change Your Life

In 1990, President Henry B. Eyring gave an address to seminary and institute teachers in the Church Educational System. He shared an experience he had when his boys were still in high school. He explained that his son, Matthew, had been called to serve on the seminary council and had just returned from a meeting where they were determining their theme for that particular school year. As Matthew walked in, he told his dad that he was hoping he would be willing to carve something for the seminary. He then handed President Eyring a piece of paper that had the phrase that was to be the theme for the year. The theme they had selected was a quote from President Ezra Taft Benson, which said, "The Book of Mormon will change your life."

President Eyring carved that phrase onto a beautiful plaque for the seminary. He shared how that plaque had been hanging in that particular seminary building for several years and how he had hoped the students who saw it would come to believe it.

Because his audience was a group religious educators, he explained how the Book of Mormon itself is the greatest curriculum ever developed because it is designed to lead to a divine change in the hearts of its readers. He said, "You know and I know that if a person will read the Book of Mormon, it will describe that change and how to have it and will draw you to it more than any other book on earth."[229]

One of the summation messages of this book is that the Book of Mormon not only *describes* this change, but that it also illustrates how to *experience* it. As we read the accounts of the characters in the Book of Mormon, we are drawn into their stories. We come to see what they saw, feel what they felt, and are inspired to experience what they have experienced.

President Eyring passionately pled, "I beg of you, for yourselves and for the students, to have faith that they will want to read it, not that you must drive them to it, but that it will draw them to it as it will draw you. I urge you that when you feel you are too tired and do not want to read, that you would have confidence that Nephi knew how to help. The Lord wrote the book. He showed Nephi how to do it in such a way that it would draw you. And, it will draw your students."[230] Surely this is why our beloved President Monson recently invited those who have not read the Book of Mormon to do so. As readers are drawn into the Book of Mormon, they come to meet, know, and love the many inspiring characters, whose lives were touched and changed by the Lord Jesus Christ.

The Book of Mormon's Primary Character

Elder Jeffrey R. Holland once posed an important question for us to consider. The question he asked was, "Who is the primary character of the Book of Mormon?"

> If one were to ask a casual reader of the Book of Mormon to name the principal character in that book, the responses would undoubtedly vary. For one thing, any record covering more than a thousand years of history—with all the persons such a history would include—is unlikely to have any single, central figure emerge over such an extended period as the principal character. Nonetheless, after acknowledging that limitation, perhaps some might list any one of several favorite, or at least memorable, persons. Such names as Mormon, the abridger for whom the book is named; or Nephi, the book's early and very recognizable young prophet; or Alma, to whom so many pages are devoted; or Moroni, the fearless captain who flew the title of liberty; or his namesake, who concluded the book and

delivered it some fourteen hundred years later to the young Joseph Smith—these would undoubtedly be among some of those figures mentioned.

All of these responses would be provocative, but they would also be decidedly incorrect. The principal and commanding figure in the Book of Mormon, from first chapter to last, is the Lord Jesus Christ, of whom the book is truly "another testament." From the first page—indeed, from the book's title page—to the last declaration in the text, this testament reveals, demonstrates, examines, and underscores the divine mission of Jesus Christ.[231]

A focused and prayerful study of the Book of Mormon can draw its readers in. As we are drawn in, we develop a relationship, of sorts, with Lehi, Nephi, Alma, Moroni, and so many others. Because Jesus Christ is the central character in the Book of Mormon, one of its primary purposes is to help us come to know *Him*. As Elder Maxwell so eloquently put it, "The more we know of Jesus, the more we will love Him. The more we know of Jesus, the more we will trust Him. The more we know of Jesus, the more we will want to be like Him and to be with Him by becoming the manner of men and women that He wishes us to be."[232]

As we are drawn into the Book of Mormon, we truly come to know Christ. While studying its pages, we see example after example of individuals who came to know firsthand His majesty. These examples illustratively show us *how* we can "come unto Christ, and be perfected in Him" (Moroni 10:32).

Flooding the Earth with the Book of Mormon

We live in a day when the Lord is hastening the work of salvation. As the work moves forward, we are expected to do our part in bringing others to experience the divine grace of Jesus Christ. It is not just happenstance that the Prophet Joseph's first order of business in the early days of the Restoration was to bring forth the Book of Mormon. As Elder Holland said, "With its declared title-page purpose of testifying that Jesus is the Christ, little wonder that the Book of Mormon was the first—and is still the greatest—missionary tract of this dispensation. As Lehi says to me and to you, 'How great the importance to make these things [of the Atonement] known unto the inhabitants of the earth.' I testify to you that we will change lives, including our own, if we will [study and] teach the Atonement through the Book of Mormon."[233] The stick of Ephraim is the primary tool the Lord has provided to "sweep the earth as with a flood" to gather His elect (Moses 7:62). It is designed to impact the entire world, one changed heart at a time.

To accomplish this great change, it will not be enough for us to simply talk more about the Book of Mormon, though that of course is a necessary step in "flooding the earth with the Book of Mormon."[234] President Eyring once told a story about a conversation he and his wife were having. She was invited to teach a lesson in her ward, and they had spoken "about the fact that although the lesson had one subject and several different aims, the only way you could get at it was to teach the Atonement." They concluded that "if you are teaching anything that matters, you are teaching about the Atonement."[235]

As they continued this conversation, they remembered that their eighteen-year-old son was listening. Their son then courageously said, "You could bear testimony to young people. You could teach that the Atonement is something they need. You could teach them that they need to have faith in the Lord Jesus Christ, to repent, and to be baptized. They need to feel the Holy Ghost. You can do all that, and they will hear you. But they may not believe you. They need to experience it before they will believe they need it."[236]

It truly is all about the personal experiences we have with the Lord. In Lehi's dream, he had partaken of the fruit of the tree and desired his loved ones to also come and partake. Likewise, after Alma had partaken of the love of God, he immediately wanted others to taste even as he had tasted. As President Benson has testified, after our hearts have experienced this mighty change, one of our main objectives is to use the Book of Mormon to "arouse mankind's interest in studying it, and [then] to show how it answers the great questions of the soul."[237]

We can then trust that they will study, understand, and experience this divine change. They will taste, even as we have tasted, and will come to know, even as we know. In so doing, they will come to live their lives in a way that is "consistent with that character which ought to be maintained by one who was called of God" (Joseph

Smith—History 1:28). The book has been preserved, set apart, and blessed to lead to this sanctifying transformation.

Designed and Blessed to Lead Souls to Christ's Grace

The Book of Mormon is, in essence, a story of devoted men and women who cried out for the merciful and redeeming grace of the Lord Jesus Christ. It is a story about men and women who are clearly imperfect, fallen, and mortal. In moments of desire, determination, and divine discontent, they call upon the name of God and are blessed with sacred, firsthand, and personal experiences with the Son of God. We then see evidence, time and again, that after these encounters "with the living Son of the living God, *nothing* [was] ever again to be as it was before."[238] Their lives were transformed as they learned how to rely on the merciful hand of the great Rescuer.

Elder David A. Bednar recently taught that one of the enduring lessons we learn from these stories "is the importance of experiencing in our personal lives the blessings of the Atonement of Jesus Christ as a prerequisite to heartfelt and authentic service that stretches far beyond merely 'going through the motions.' "[239] Perhaps a few concluding stories will help bring us full circle in considering the Book of Mormon's role in our personally experiencing the grace of Jesus Christ.

The first story comes from the life of the Prophet Joseph Smith. In October of 1839, he and a few others made a visit to Washington, DC. After visiting with government officials regarding the Missouri persecutions, Joseph and others stopped in Philadelphia to speak to a large congregation of around three thousand people.

Parley P. Pratt was in attendance and gave the following report of what took place that day:

> While visiting with brother Joseph in Philadelphia, a very large church was opened for him to preach in, and about three thousand people assembled to hear him. Brother Rigdon spoke first, and dwelt on the Gospel, illustrating his doctrine by the Bible. When he was through, brother Joseph arose like a lion about to roar; and being full of the Holy Ghost, spoke in great power, bearing testimony of the visions he had seen, the ministering of angels which he had enjoyed; and how he had found the plates of the Book of Mormon, and translated them by

the gift and power of God. He commenced by saying: "If nobody else had the courage to testify of so glorious a message from Heaven, and of the finding of so glorious a record, he felt to do it in justice to the people, and leave the event with God."

The entire congregation was astounded; electrified as it were, and overwhelmed with the sense of the truth and power by which he spoke, and the wonders which he related. A lasting impression was made; many souls were gathered into the fold. And I bear witness, that he, by his faithful and powerful testimony, cleared his garments of their blood. Multitudes were baptized in Philadelphia and in the regions around.[240]

The Prophet Joseph clearly knew of the important mission of the Book of Mormon and of its divine latter-day purpose. Indeed, the Lord had already stingingly rebuked these early leaders because they had "treated lightly the things [they had] received—which vanity and unbelief [had] brought the whole church under condemnation" (D&C 84:54–55). The Lord told them that this condemnation would continue "until they repent and remember the new covenant, even the Book of Mormon" (D&C 84:57).

Why such a severe rebuke? Because God's work and glory is "to bring to pass the immortality and eternal life of man" (Moses 1:39). He had commissioned prophets for over a thousand years to painstakingly inscribe His experiences with them on metal plates. They went to such great lengths to preserve this record because it was to be the primary instrument in helping the Lord fulfill His work and glory in the latter-days. It promises that if the reader will lay hold upon it, he or she will be led to sit down at the right hand of God in the kingdom of heaven (see Helaman 3:29–30). Now, some 1,400 years later, the people whom He had chosen to take this record to all the nations of the world were neglecting it in their ministry. Joseph clearly knew this, and his testimony of the Book of Mormon caused many to come into the fold.

The Book of Mormon was made to bring faith, happiness, and hope to those of us living in these last days. As we study the Book of Mormon, we see the Lord constantly pouring out these same blessings upon those individuals who sought divine help in the travails of their own day. The significant spiritual impact we all experience as we study this record is, at least in part, because of the profound spiritual impact

of the experiences of those characters in it who had come to know the Lord. If we seek this same witness, we must, as Elder Neal A. Maxwell once put it, stop behaving "like hurried tourists, scarcely venturing beyond the entry hall to the mansion." He went on to say,

> For my part, I am glad the book will be with us "as long as the earth shall stand." I need and want additional time. For me, towers, court-yards, and wings await inspection. My tour of it has never been completed. Some rooms I have yet to enter, and there are more flaming fireplaces waiting to warm me. Even the rooms I have glimpsed contain further furnishings and rich detail yet to be savored. There are panels inlaid with incredible insights and designs and decor dating from Eden. There are also sumptuous banquet tables painstakingly prepared by predecessors which await all of us. . . . May we come to feel as a whole people beckoned beyond the entry hall. May we go inside far enough to hear clearly the whispered truths from those who have "slumbered," which whisperings will awaken in us individually the life of discipleship as never before.[241]

Studying More Sacramentally

If we seek our own spiritual witness, we need to ensure that our studies of this miraculous record are calculated and consecrated. Perhaps we could even study more *sacramentally*. Elder Holland once taught that "a sacrament could be any one of a number of gestures or acts or ordinances that unite us with God and his limitless powers."[242] Joseph Fielding Smith demonstrated how this could be applied to studying the scriptures. He taught, "Our attitude . . . toward the scriptures should be in harmony with the purposes for which they were written. They are intended to *enlarge man's spiritual endowments and to reveal and intensify the bond of relationship between him and his God.*"[243] Indeed, the divine purpose of the Book of Mormon is to reveal and intensify the bond between *us* and *our God*.

Elder D. Todd Christofferson once described this "sacramental" approach to scripture study. He said,

> I see you sometimes reading a few verses, stopping to ponder them, carefully reading the verses again, and as you think about what they mean, praying for understanding, asking questions in your mind, waiting for spiritual impressions, and writing down the impressions and insights that come so you can remember and learn more.

Studying in this way, you may not read a lot of chapters or verses in a half hour, but you will be giving place in your heart for the word of God, and He will be speaking to you.[244]

As we approach our study of the Book of Mormon more sacramentally, we will come to both see and feel God at work. We will see Him at work in the lives of these ancient Nephites—but even more important, we will see Him at work in our own lives.

As you read this true account, consider how the Book of Mormon has been blessed to bring about this change in the lives of honest seekers of truth:

I was living alone in Provo, Utah, in a small apartment close to the center of town. I was working as a salesman in a small furniture store in Provo, and it was during the long weekend surrounding the New Year's holiday that this incident occurred.

We had a long weekend holiday. It was Thursday, December 31, New Year's Eve. We had been given from Thursday through Sunday off from work, and I was in my apartment without any plans of celebration. I was preparing my dinner, waiting for it to bake and wanted something to read. Not having anything in the apartment I went next door to ask some young men who were living there (students at BYU) if they had something—hoping for a copy of *Field & Stream* or something of that order. They said they did not have any magazines, but they did have a book I might like to read. They handed me a copy of the Book of Mormon.

While I had heard of the Mormon Church (who in Utah hasn't?), I was not familiar with the book. I thanked them and took it to my apartment. During dinner, I thumbed through it and started to read. I admit that I scanned through several parts, trying to find out the plot. There were names and places I had never heard before, and I just couldn't get into it. So after dinner, I took the book back and returned it with a "no thank you."

"Did you pray about it?" one young man asked. "Pray about it?" I responded. "I just wanted something to read, not something I had to pray about." This started a very interesting conversation about the content of the Book of Mormon. They told me that it was a book of scripture, a book that if I would first pray about and then read with a real desire to know if it was true or not, that Jesus Christ would reveal the truth of it to me by the power of the Holy Ghost.

I had been brought up a Catholic, and though I was not active at the time, I held onto my membership in the Catholic church with a stranglehold because it was all that I had ever known. The only praying I had ever done was the Lord's Prayer, the Hail Mary, and reading in my missal, something I had not done in a long, long time. And now, some young men were asking me to pray to a God I did not really know and to ask Him to tell me if the book was true or not.

Well, what the heck, I did not have anything else to do, and it was going to be a long, long weekend. I took the book home, opened up a bottle of beer, lit up a cigarette, and got down on my knees and asked God to tell me if this book was true. Then I started to read: "I, Nephi, having been born of goodly parents."

The names and places were the same as those I had read about just a couple of hours before. The only difference this time was a "suspension of disbelief" that had magically come over me. I was literally in the book! I could see Nephi; I could see his brothers, and it ticked me off when they mistreated him. I liked Nephi! I cheered the good guys on and I felt sorry for the bad guys. I read for hours, and I couldn't put the book down. When I finally looked at my watch, it was almost five o'clock in the morning. I wished myself Happy New Year and went to sleep.

I woke up about 8:30 and instinctively reached for this book. And that is the way the rest of the weekend went. Like Brother Parley Pratt, the thought of food was a nuisance; I did not want anything to disturb me. I took my phone off the hook and read all day with only occasional interruptions for quick snacks. Like the first night, I would finally realize it was early in the morning, sleep a few hours, pick up the book, and continue with my self-imposed marathon. Finally, about five o'clock on Monday morning, I finished the book and I fell asleep, exhausted.

Just before Christmas that year, I had sold a large carpet job in the American Fork area. It was a specialized type of carpet, and my boss wanted me to supervise the carpet layers. My boss was a former bishop in the Provo area and had talked to me about the Church on several occasions, but I would have none of it. He was a good boss, but you did not want to get him angry because he had a temper. It was on this Monday morning, at eight o'clock that I was supposed to supervise the carpet installation. The appointed time came, and I did not appear; nine o'clock, then ten.

Finally around 10:30, my boss, mad as a wet hen, came to my apartment, walked in the door (ready to tear my head off), saw me lying on the couch with the Book of Mormon lying on my chest, and changed his mind. He quietly closed the door and went back to the shop, confident that he could get the layers started.

Just after 11:30, I awoke (not knowing of my boss's visit), looked at the clock, and. for the second time in a relatively short time, said another prayer. I quickly dressed, knowing when I got there that I probably would not have a job left, got into my car, and sped to the job site.

I saw my boss there and went up to him to apologize. He turned around, a grin came onto his face, and he asked, "How did you like the book?" Realizing what must have happened, my mind went back to the previous weekend and, through tear-filled eyes, I said the only thing I could have said, "The book is true. The Book of Mormon is the word of God."

I then started to cry, and he came and put his arms about me and held me. I was baptized a member of the Church on the 22nd of January, 1965.[245]

This account underscores the change that can come as we allow ourselves to be drawn into the experiences of these people in the Book of Mormon. The Book of Mormon was divinely designed to draw the reader in and to help them feel—at least a portion of—the same Spirit felt by those in the book. But for this change to happen, we need to slow down and have a little less distraction and a lot more prayer. In so doing, we begin our own spiritual journey as we seek to commune with the living God and draw upon His divine power and guidance.

A Personal Witness of the Transformative Power of the Book of Mormon

In this gospel, we believe and teach that this is not only the *true* Church, but it is also a *living* Church (see D&C 1:30). The primary reason we reference the Church as a living Church is because the living Christ leads it. It is the resurrected Lord who stands at its head. Furthermore, we teach and testify of living prophets and Apostles, who are called to be special witnesses "of the name of Jesus Christ in

all the world, particularly of his divinity and of his bodily resurrection from the dead" (Bible Dictionary, under "Apostle").

With this knowledge comes the reality that the Savior's ministry is a living and active ministry and will be as long as "there shall be one man upon the face [of the earth] to be saved" (Moroni 7:36). Against that backdrop, I wish to close with an autobiographical example of the transforming power of these divine encounters. I suppose the experiences outlined in this book have resonated so deeply with me because I feel like they give words to my own personal experiences, where I have been unable to "say the smallest part which I feel" (Alma 26:16).

These experiences were initiated as I began to drink deeply from the pages of the Book of Mormon, and I was thus drawn into these inspiring stories. As I felt the penetrating power of the Holy Ghost, I realized that I was not yet the person the Lord expected me to be. I began to view myself in *my own* "carnal state, even less than the dust of the earth" (Mosiah 4:2). Indeed, *I* felt "racked with torment" and "harrowed up by the memory of my many sins" (Alma 36:12, 17).

It was in the midst of this pain and suffering that *I* cried within *my* heart my own version of, "O Jesus, thou Son of God, have mercy on me, who am in the gall of bitterness, and am encircled about by the everlasting chains of death" (Alma 36:18). For a small moment, I wondered if relief would come. I continued my prayer with my own version of, "if there is a God, and if thou art God, wilt thou make thyself known unto me, and I will give away all my sins to know thee" (Alma 22:18).

As I continued this "wrestle which *I* had before God, before I received a remission of *my* sins" (Enos 1:2; emphasis added), I began to feel peace and "my soul was filled with joy as exceeding as was my pain!" (Alma 36:20). Indeed, "there can be *nothing* so exquisite and sweet as was *my* joy" (Alma 36:21; emphasis added), as I felt "encircled about eternally in the arms of his love" (2 Nephi 1:15). I remember feeling relief and hope as I was touched by the Savior's amazing grace. I remember thinking, like Enos, "Lord, how is it done?" (Enos 1:7). I wondered how my guilt could be swept away, taking with it all the pain, sorrow, and feelings of being unclean. The familiar answer came softly and gently, "Because of thy faith in Christ" (Enos 1:8).

I now had my witness. This experience led me on a mission and caused me to choose as my missionary plaque scripture: Mosiah 28:3, which reads, "Now they were desirous that salvation should be declared to every creature, for they could not bear that any human soul should perish; yea, even the very thoughts that any soul should endure endless torment did cause them to quake and tremble." I chose that verse because I felt that those were the deepest thoughts and feelings of *my* heart. I felt like *I* was "the very vilest of sinners" and was deeply humbled that "the Lord saw fit in his infinite mercy to spare [*me*]" (Mosiah 28:4).

I thought that if others were feeling the pains of transgression, they too should have the opportunity to be sanctified and cleansed. Having learned for myself, I—like Alma—have tried to "manifest unto the people that I had been born of God," as I have "from that time even until now, . . . labored without ceasing, that I might bring [others] unto repentance; that I might bring them to taste of the exceeding joy of which I did taste" (Alma 36:24).

I had learned firsthand that after an encounter with the Living Son of the Living God, nothing is ever again the same. My desires changed. My focus changed. My dreams changed. My music, my language, my interpersonal relationships, my commitment to my covenants, my love for the word of God, my professional ambitions—it *all* changed.

As I felt the grace of Christ sanctify my soul, I felt that which was spiritual dross melt from my heart. In saying all of that, I continue to have those moments where I am less than I should be, and I cry out, "O wretched man that I am!" (2 Nephi 4:17). I continue to be "encompassed about, because of the temptations and the sins which do so easily beset me . . . nevertheless, *I* know in whom *I* have trusted" (2 Nephi 4:18; emphasis added).

In this mortal journey, I am still not the person I ought to be and am certainly not who I want to be or hope to be in some future day. But still, I am not what I once used to be and, as the Apostle Paul said, "*by the grace of God I am what I am*" (1 Corinthians 15:10; emphasis added). And that, to me, is one of the most important messages from the Book of Mormon.

Ryan H. Sharp

God be thanked for His mercy in providing us these powerful examples and patterns to follow as we strive to experience this change through our own continual encounters with the divine.

Endnotes

1. Ezra Taft Benson, "The Book of Mormon—Keystone of Our Religion," *Ensign*, November 1986, 4; emphasis added.

2. Jeffrey R. Holland, "The First Great Commandment," *Ensign*, November 2012; emphasis added.

3. Ezra Taft Benson, "Born of God," *Ensign*, July 1989.

4. Introduction to the Book of Mormon.

5. Russell M. Nelson, "Be Thou an Example of the Believers," *Ensign*, November 2010.

6. Thomas S. Monson, "Precious Promises of the Book of Mormon," *Liahona*, October 2011.

7. "Making and Keeping Covenants," Missionary Satellite Broadcast, April 1997.

8. Neal A. Maxwell, *The Book of Mormon: A Great Answer to "The Great Question"* (Provo, Utah: Religious Studies Center, Brigham Young University, 1888).

Endnotes

9. Ezra Taft Benson, "The Book of Mormon Is the Word of God," *Ensign*, January 1988.

10. Boyd K. Packer, "Little Children," *Ensign*, November 1986, 17.

11. *Teachings of the Prophet Joseph Smith*, sel. Joseph Fielding Smith (Salt Lake City: Deseret Book, 1938), 121; emphasis added.

12. See Susan Easton Black, *Finding Christ Through the Book of Mormon* (Salt Lake City: Deseret Book, 1987), 15.

13. Jeffrey R. Holland, *Christ and the New Covenant: The Messianic Message of the Book of Mormon* (Salt Lake City: Deseret Book, 2006), 95.

14. Bruce R. McConkie, *The Promised Messiah* (Salt Lake City: Deseret Book, 1978), 516–17.

15. Richard Lyman Bushman, *Joseph Smith: Rough Stone Rolling* (New York: Alfred A. Knopf Publishing, 2005), 87.

16. Jeffrey R. Holland, "The First Great Commandment."

17. Neal A. Maxwell, "'O Divine Redeemer,'" *Ensign*, November 1981, 8.

18. Dallin H. Oaks, "Timing," BYU Devotional, January 29, 2002.

19. David A. Bednar, "Pray Always," *Ensign*, November 2008.

20. Neil L. Anderson, "Come unto Him," *Ensign*, May 2009.

21. Orson F. Whitney, in Conference Report, April 1929, 110.

22. Neal A. Maxwell, "Lessons from Laman and Lemuel," *Ensign*, November 1999, 8; emphasis added.

23. David A. Bednar, "Come and See," *Ensign*, November 2014.

24. Author correspondence.

25. Neal A. Maxwell, "Teaching by the Spirit—'The Language of Inspiration,'" CES symposium on the Old Testament, Brigham Young University, Provo, Utah, August 15, 1991, 4.

26. See also Jeffrey R. Holland, in Conference Report, April 2006, 72.

27. Dunglison's account is in *The Autobiographical Ana of Robley Dunglison, M.D.* (Philadelphia, 1963); see also Randall, *Life* 3:547–49.

28. *Discourses of Brigham Young*, comp. John A. Widtsoe (Salt Lake City: Deseret Book, 1954), 458–59.

29. *Journal of Discourses*, 26 vols. (London: Latter-day Saints' Book Depot, 1854), 12:269–70.

30. *Discourses of Brigham Young*, 458–59.

31. Leonard J. Arrington, *Brigham Young: American Moses* (New York: Alfred A. Knopf, 1985), 399.

32. "Nephi's Courage," *Children's Songbook*, 120–21.

33. Dallin H. Oaks, "As He Thinketh in His Heart," CES Evening with a General Authority Devotional, February 8, 2013.

34. Neal A. Maxwell, "Notwithstanding My Weakness," *Ensign*, November 1976, 12.

35. Neal A. Maxwell, "Consecrate Thy Performance," *Ensign*, May 2002.

36. John Newton, *Olney Hymns*, February 1779.

37. John Newton, as quoted in *The Christian Pioneer*, ed. Joseph Foulkes Winks (1856), 84; also found in *The Christian Spectator*, vol. 3 (1821), 186.

38. See LDS Bible Dictionary, under "Isaiah."

39. Monte Nyman, *Great Are the Words of Isaiah* (Salt Lake City: Book-craft, 1980), 48.

40. Neal A. Maxwell, "Settle This in Your Hearts," *Ensign*, November 1992.

41. Neal A. Maxwell, as quoted in Bruce C. Hafen's *Spiritually Anchored in Unsettled Times* (Salt Lake City: Deseret Book, 2009), 23.

42. *History of The Church of Jesus Christ of Latter-day Saints*, comp. B. H. Roberts (Salt Lake City: The Church of Jesus Christ of Latter-day Saints, 1980), 4:227.

43. "More Holiness Give Me," *Hymns*, no. 131.

44. James E. Faust, "I Believe I Can, I Knew I Could," *Ensign*, November 2002.

45. See LDS Bible Dictionary, under "Prayer."

46. Thomas Paine, "The Day of Freedom," *A Library of American Literature: An Anthology in Eleven Volumes* (New York: Charles L. Webster & Company, 1891).

47. Joseph Fielding McConkie and Robert L. Millet, *Doctrinal Commentary on the Book of Mormon: Volume II—Jacob through Mosiah* (Salt Lake City: Deseret Book, 1988), 95.

48. Spencer W. Kimball, *Faith Precedes the Miracle* (Salt Lake City: Deseret Book, 1975), 211.

49. David R. Seely, "Enos and the Words Concerning Eternal Life," in *The Book of Mormon: Jacob through Words of Mormon, To Learn with Joy*, eds. Monte S. Nyman and Charles D. Tate Jr. (Provo, Utah: Religious Studies Center, Brigham Young University, 1990), 221–33.

50. Spencer W. Kimball, *Faith Precedes the Miracle*, 210.

51. See http://www.merriam-webster.com/dictionary/wrestle.

52. Spencer W. Kimball, *Faith Precedes the Miracle*, 211.

53. Bruce C. Hafen, "The Atonement: All for All," *Ensign*, May 2004.

54. Spencer W. Kimball, *Faith Precedes the Miracle*, 211.

55. Ibid.

56. Ibid.

57. *Preach My Gospel: A Guide to Missionary Service* (Salt Lake City: The Church of Jesus Christ of Latter-Day Saints, 2004), 117.

58. Jeffrey R. Holland, "The Inconvenient Messiah," BYU Devotional, February 27, 1982.

59. Edward L. and Andrew E. Kimball, *Spencer W. Kimball: Twelfth President of the Church of Jesus Christ of Latter-day Saints* (Salt Lake City: Bookcraft, 1977), 192–95.

60. 60 *Ibid.,* 188–95.

61. Neal A. Maxwell, "Those Seedling Saints Who Sit before You," CES symposium on the Old Testament, August 19, 1983.

62. C. Richard Chidester, "Christ-Centered Teaching," *Ensign*, October 1989, 7.

63. Neal A. Maxwell, "Teaching by the Spirit: 'The Language of Inspiration,'" CES symposium, August 1991.

64. Robert L. Millet, "The Vision of the Redemption of the Dead (D&C 138)," in *Sperry Symposium Classics: The Doctrine and Covenants*, ed. Craig K. Manscill (Provo, Utah: Religious Studies Center, Brigham Young University, 2004), 314–31.

65. Susan Easton Black, "King Benjamin: In the Service of Your God," in *The Book of Mormon: Mosiah, Salvation Only Through Christ*, ed. Monte S. Nyman and Charles D. Tate Jr. (Provo, Utah: Religious Studies Center, Brigham Young University, 1991), 37–48.

66. *Teachings of the Prophet Joseph Smith*, 216.

67. Dieter F. Uchtdorf, "You Matter to Him," *Ensign*, November 2011.

68. Ezra Taft Benson, "The Book of Mormon and the Doctrine and Covenants," *Ensign*, May 1987.

69. Ibid.

70. Boyd K. Packer, "Little Children," *Ensign*, November 1986, 17.

71. *Teachings of the Prophet Joseph Smith*, 121.

72. Neal A. Maxwell, *Meek and Lowly* (Salt Lake City: Deseret Book, 1987), 94.

73. J. Rueben Clark Jr. "Charted Course for the Church in Education," an address to seminary and institute leaders, August 8, 1938.

74. Howard W. Hunter, "The Great Symbol of Our Membership," *Ensign*, November 1994, 3.

75. David A. Bednar, "In the Strength of the Lord (Words of Mormon 1:14; Mosiah 9:17; Mosiah 10:10; Alma 20:4)," BYU Devotional, October 23, 2001.

76. David A. Bednar, "Clean Hands and a Pure Heart," *Ensign*, November 2007.

77. Jeffrey R. Holland, "The First Great Commandment."

78. David A. Bednar, "Panel Discussion," *Worldwide Leadership Training Meeting*, 2010.

79. Ezra Taft Benson, "Born of God," *Ensign*, July 1989.

80. David O. McKay, in Conference Report, April 1962, 7.

81. Marlin K. Jensen, "Stand in the Sacred Grove," CES Devotional, May 6, 2012.

82. Ibid.

83. Ralph Waldo Emerson, "The Preacher," from *The Complete Works* (1904).

84. Alma's experience is another example of the idea of the stewardship of reputation. He spoke the same words as Abinadi but was able to have significantly more success.

85. *Preach My Gospel*, 1.

86. Jeffrey R. Holland, "The First Great Commandment."

87. Joseph B. Wirthlin, *Heroes from the Book of Mormon* (Salt Lake City: Bookcraft, 1995), 89.

88. Ibid.

89. Neal A. Maxwell, "The Holy Ghost: Glorifying Christ," *Ensign*, July 2002, 56–61.

90. Jeffrey R. Holland, "Laborers in the Vineyard," *Ensign*, May 2012.

91. Ibid.

92. Ibid.

93. Spencer W. Kimball, *The Teachings of Spencer W. Kimball* (Salt Lake City: Bookcraft, 1982), 99.

94. Dallin H. Oaks, "Sin and Suffering," *Ensign*, July 1992, 71–72.

95. Ezra Taft Benson, "The Book of Mormon and the Doctrine and Covenants."

96. Robert L. Millet, *The Vision of Mormonism: Pressing the Boundaries of Christianity* (St. Paul, Minnesota: Paragon House, 2007), 39.

97. Jeffrey R. Holland, *However Long and Hard the Road* (Salt Lake City: Deseret Book, 1985), 85; emphasis added.

98. Neal A. Maxwell, "Becoming a Disciple," *Ensign*, June 1996, 12.

99. Boyd K. Packer, "The Brilliant Morning of Forgiveness," *Ensign*, November 1995, 18.

100. Ibid.

101. Alma 36:24 says that from the time of his conversion "even until now," he had labored in the vineyard. Alma 36 was written in 73 BC, and Alma was "buried by the hand of the Lord" in the same year (see Alma 45:18–20).

102. Jeffrey R. Holland, "Alma, Son of Alma," *Ensign*, March 1977, 79.

103. Jeffrey R. Holland, "Prophets in the Land Again," *Ensign*, November 2006, 107.

104. "More Holiness Give Me," *Hymns*, no. 131.

105. Ezra Taft Benson, "Jesus Christ—Gifts and Expectations," in *Speeches of the Year, 1974* (Provo: Brigham Young University Press, 1975), 313.

106. Jeffrey R. Holland, "Alma, Son of Alma."

107. Quentin L. Cook, "The Restoration of Morality and Religious Freedom," BYU–I Devotional, September 2012.

108. Spencer W. Kimball, "When the World Will Be Converted," *Ensign*, October 1974, 4.

109. M. Russell Ballard, "Put Your Trust in the Lord," *Ensign*, November 2013.

110. Jeffrey R. Holland, "Are You True?" BYU Devotional, September 2, 1980.

111. Fred B. Craddock, *Overhearing the Gospel* (Nashville, Tennessee: Parthenon Press, 1978).

112. *History of the Church*, 4:227.

113. John Newton, "Amazing Grace," *Olney Hymns*.

114. Henry B. Eyring, "We Must Raise Our Sights," CES conference on the Book of Mormon, August 14, 2001.

115. *Teachings of the Prophet Joseph Smith*, 241.

116. Dieter F. Uchtdorf, "A Word for the Hesitant Missionary," *Ensign*, February 2013.

117. Author correspondence.

118. "Praise to the Man," *Hymns*, no. 27.

119. *Teachings of the Prophet Joseph Smith*, 304.

120. *History of the Church*, 2:428.

121. Dieter F. Uchtdorf, "The Hope of God's Light," *Ensign*, April 2013.

122. Ibid.

123. Dallin H. Oaks, *The Lord's Way* (Salt Lake City: Deseret Book, 1991), 3–4.

124. Bruce C. Hafen, "The Atonement: All for All," *Ensign*, May 2004.

125. Spencer W. Kimball, *The Miracle of Forgiveness* (Salt Lake City: Bookcraft, 1969), 203.

126. S. Michael Wilcox, "Heart of a Lion: Lessons about Christ from Lewis' Aslan," *Deseret News*, December 9, 2010.

127. C. S. Lewis, *The Voyage of the Dawn Treader* (London: Geoffrey Bles, 1952).

128. Ibid.

129. S. Michael Wilcox, "Heart of a Lion: Lessons about Christ from Lewis' Aslan."

130. Lawrence E. Corbridge, "The Way," *Ensign*, November 2008.

131. C. S. Lewis, *Mere Christianity* (New York: HarperCollins, 2001), 196.

132. Steven Robinson, *Believing Christ* (Salt Lake City: Deseret Book, 1992), 91–92.

133. M. Russell Ballard, "Building Bridges of Understanding," *Ensign*, June 1998, 65.

134. Robert L. Millet, *Claiming Christ* (Grand Rapids, Michigan: Brazos Press, 2007), 188.

135. Spencer W. Kimball, *The Miracle of Forgiveness*, 203.

136. David A. Bednar, "Converted unto the Lord," *Ensign*, November 2012.

137. Howard W. Hunter in Harold B. Lee, *Stand Ye in Holy Places* (Salt Lake City: Deseret Book, 1974), 330.

138. *Journal of Discourses*, 11:14.

139. M. Russell Ballard, "The Greatest Generation of Missionaries," *Ensign*, November 2002.

140. Joe J. Christianson, "Captain Moroni: An Authentic Hero," *Heroes from the Book of Mormon*, (Salt Lake City: Bookcraft, 1995), 128.

141. Ibid.

142. Jeffrey R. Holland, "Therefore, What?" CES conference on the New Testament, August 8, 2000.

143. Jeffrey R. Holland, "Teaching and Learning in the Church," *Worldwide Leadership Training Meeting*, 2010.

144. Ezra Taft Benson, "The Power of the Word," *Ensign*, May 1986, 80.

145. "I Need Thee Every Hour," *Hymns*, no. 98.

146. Richard G. Scott, "The Power of Scripture," *Ensign*, November 2011.

147. Author correspondence.

148. "As I Search the Holy Scriptures" *Hymns*, no. 277.

149. David A. Bednar, "In the Strength of the Lord."

150. *Preach My Gospel*, 117.

151. Alonzo Gaskill, *Odds Are, You're Going to Be Exalted* (Salt Lake City: Deseret Book, 2008), 19.

152. As cited in Robert L. Millet, *Within Reach* (Salt Lake City: Deseret Book, 1995), 10.

153. Joseph Fielding McConkie, *The Bruce R. McConkie Story* (Salt Lake City: Deseret Book, 2003), 400.

154. Ibid., 401.

155. Ibid., 409.

156. Ibid., 410.

157. Bruce R. McConkie, "The Purifying Power of Gethsemane," *Ensign*, May 1985.

158. Lawrence E. Corbridge, "The Best of Times," BYU–I Devotional, June 18, 2013.

159. Neal A. Maxwell, *We Will Prove Them Herewith* (Salt Lake City: Deseret Book, 1982) 19.

160. Patricia Auxier, "Save Her!" *New Era*, September 2007.

161. Ibid.

162. Jay E. Jensen, "Arms of Safety," *Ensign*, November 2008.

163. Ralph Waldo Emerson, *Nature* (Boston: James Munroe and Company, 1836), section 1.

164. Jeffrey R. Holland, "The Will of the Father in All Things," BYU Devotional, January 17, 1989.

165. Ibid.

166. Introduction to the Doctrine and Covenants.

167. See http://ldsmag.com/11430/article/1/page-1.

168. Ezra Taft Benson, *A Witness and a Warning* (Salt Lake City: Deseret Book, 1988), 40.

169. Jeffrey R. Holland, *Christ and the New Covenant: The Messianic Message of the Book of Mormon* (Salt Lake City: Deseret Book, 1997), 127; emphasis added.

170. Merrill J. Bateman, "One by One," BYU Devotional, September 9, 1997.

171. Ibid.

172. Neal A. Maxwell, "O Divine Redeemer," *Ensign*, November 1981, 8.

173. David A. Bednar, a 2011 address to seminary and institute instructors.

174. Jeffrey R. Holland, *Christ and the New Covenant*, 268.

175. Merrill J. Bateman, "A Pattern for All," *Ensign*, November 2005.

176. Howard W. Hunter, "Reading the Scriptures," *Ensign*, November 1979.

177. Dieter F. Uchtdorf, "The Hope of God's Light," *Ensign*, April 2013; emphasis added.

178. Jay E. Jensen, "Arms of Safety," *Ensign*, November 2008.

179. Ibid.

180. Merrill J. Bateman, "One by One."

181. Jeffrey R. Holland, " 'Look to God and Live,' " *Ensign*, November 1993.

182. Neal A. Maxwell, *All These Things Shall Give Thee Experience* (Salt Lake City: Deseret Book, 1980), 6.

183. Neal A. Maxwell, " 'O Divine Redeemer,' " *Ensign*, November 1981, 8.

184. Neil L. Anderson, "Come unto Him," *Ensign*, May 2009.

185. Jeffrey R. Holland, *Christ and the New Covenant*, 29.

186. Boyd K. Packer, "Prayer and Promptings," *Ensign*, November 2009.

187. Boyd K. Packer, "The Ideal Teacher," an address to seminary and institute faculty, June 28, 1962.

188. Ibid.

189. Ibid.

190. Boyd K. Packer, "Prayer and Promptings."

191. Grant R. Hardy and Robert E. Parsons, "Plates and Records in the Book of Mormon," *To All the World* (2000).

192. Cecil O. Samuelson, "The Brother of Jared," *Heroes from the Book of Mormon* (Salt Lake City: Bookcraft, 1995), 180–81.

193. Ibid., 182.

194. Jeffrey R. Holland, *Christ and the New Covenant*, 15.

195. Ibid.

196. Bruce R. McConkie, "Agency or Inspiration?" *New Era*, January 1975.

197. Harold B. Lee, *Stand Ye in Holy Places*, 243–44.

198. Jeffrey R. Holland, "Rending the Veil of Unbelief" in *The Voice of My Servants: Apostolic Messages on Teaching, Learning, and Scripture*, ed. Scott C. Esplin and Richard Neitzel Holzapfel (Provo, Utah: Religious Studies Center, 2010), 143–64.

199. Jeffrey R. Holland, *Christ and the New Covenant*, 18–19.

200. Ibid., 23.

201. Cecil O. Samuelson, "The Brother of Jared," 183.

202. Ibid.,183–84.

203. Ibid., 185.

204. David A. Bednar, " 'Line upon Line, Precept upon Precept,' " *Ensign*, September 2010.

205. Richard G. Scott, "To Acquire Spiritual Guidance," *Ensign*, November 2009.

206. Jeffrey R. Holland, *Christ and the New Covenant*, 29.

207. Ezra Taft Benson, "Jesus Christ—Gifts and Expectations."

208. Jeffrey R. Holland, *Christ and the New Covenant*, 29.

209. Ibid.

210. Thomas S. Monson, "Be of Good Cheer," *Ensign*, May 2009, 92.

211. *The Book of Mormon Student Manual, Religion 121–122* (Salt Lake City: The Church of Jesus Christ of Latter-day Saints, 1996).

212. Spencer J. Condie, "Mormon: Historian, General, Man of God," *Heroes from the Book of Mormon* (Salt Lake City: Bookcraft, 1995), 168.

213. H. Donl Peterson, "Moroni, the Last of the Nephite Prophets" in *Fourth Nephi, From Zion to Destruction*, ed. Monte S. Nyman and Charles D. Tate Jr. (Provo, Utah: Religious Studies Center, 1995), 235–49.

214. Gary Layne Hatch, "Mormon and Moroni: Father and Son," in *Fourth Nephi, From Zion to Destruction*, ed. Monte S. Nyman and Charles D. Tate Jr. (Provo, Utah: Religious Studies Center, 1995), 105–15.

215. H. Donl Peterson, "Moroni, the Last of the Nephite Prophets," 235–49.

216. Gordon B. Hinckley, "Moroni," *Heroes from the Book of Mormon* (Salt Lake City: Bookcraft, 1995), 195.

217. Howard W. Hunter, "The Great Symbol of Our Membership," *Ensign*, November 1994.

218. Gordon B. Hinckley, "Moroni," *Heroes from the Book of Mormon*.

219. See http://www.mormonnewsroom.org/article/angel-moroni-statues-atop-mormon-temples-are-more-than-decoration.

220. H. Donl Peterson, "Moroni, the Last of the Nephite Prophets," 235–49.

221. Gary Layne Hatch, "Mormon and Moroni: Father and Son," 105–15.

222. Gordon B. Hinckley, "Moroni," *Heroes from the Book of Mormon*, 197.

223. *History of the Church*, 1:71.

224. *Preach My Gospel*, 117.

225. Neal A. Maxwell, *All These Things Shall Give Thee Experience*, 28.

226. *Journal of Discourses*, 24:197.

227. Orson F. Whitney, as quoted in Spencer W. Kimball, *Faith Precedes the Miracle*, 98.

228. Neal A. Maxwell, "Lets Ye Be Wearied and Faint in Your Minds," *Ensign*, May 1991.

229. Henry B. Eyring, "The Book of Mormon Will Change Your Life," CES symposium on the Book of Mormon, August 17, 1990.

230. Ibid.

231. "Rending the Veil of Unbelief" in *A Book of Mormon Treasury: Gospel Insights from General Authorities and Religious Educators* (Provo, Utah: Religious Studies Center, 2003).

232. Neal A. Maxwell, "Plow in Hope," *Ensign*, May 2001.

233. Jeffrey R. Holland, "Missionary Work and the Atonement," *Ensign*, March 2003.

234. Ezra Taft Benson, "Flooding the Earth with the Book of Mormon," *Ensign*, November 1988.

235. Henry B. Eyring, "The Book of Mormon Will Change Your Life."

236. Ibid.; emphasis added.

237. Ezra Taft Benson, "Flooding the Earth with the Book of Mormon."

238. Jeffrey R. Holland, "The First Great Commandment"; emphasis added.

239. David A. Bednar, "Come and See," *Ensign*, November 2014.

240. Parley P. Pratt, *Autobiography of Parley P. Pratt* (Deseret Book: Salt Lake City, 2000), 298–99.

241. Neal A. Maxwell, *The Book of Mormon: A Great Answer to "The Great Question."*

242. Jeffrey R. Holland, "Of Souls, Symbols, and Sacraments," BYU Devotional, January 12, 1988.

243. Joseph Fielding Smith, *Juvenile Instructor*, April 1912, 204; emphasis added.

244. D. Todd Christofferson, "When Thou Art Converted," *Ensign*, May 2004.

245. Lynn G. Robbins, "Tasting the Light," CES fireside, May 3, 2015.

Notes

Notes

Notes

Notes

Notes

Notes

Notes

Notes

Notes

Notes

Notes

Notes

Notes

About the Author

Ryan Sharp is a full-time religious educator, a speaker at Especially for Youth, Best of EFY, and at Brigham Young University's Campus Education Week. He served as a full-time missionary in the Auckland New Zealand Mission. He earned a bachelor's degree in American studies from Brigham Young University. He completed a master's degree in educational leadership and is just finishing his PhD in health promotion and education, both from the University of Utah. He married Jessica Farish in 2005, and they are the parents of five incredible and energetic little boys. He loves sports, writing, spending time with his family, wrestling his boys, and studying and teaching the restored gospel.